*Twayne's English Authors Series*

Sylvia E. Bowman, *Editor*

INDIANA UNIVERSITY

*Walter Pater*

TEAS 207

Walter Pater
*(after a photograph by Elliott and Fry, c. 1889)*

# WALTER PATER

By GERALD MONSMAN
*Duke University*

**TWAYNE PUBLISHERS**
A Division of G. K. Hall & Co.
Boston, Massachusetts, U. S. A.

**Library of Congress Cataloging in Publication Data**

Monsman, Gerald Cornelius.
    Walter Pater.

    (Twayne's English author's series  ;   TEAS 207)
    Bibliography:   p. 197 - 201.
    Includes index.
    1.    Pater, Walter Horatio, 1839 - 1894.
2.      Authors, English—19th century—Biography.
PR5136.M6  c      824'.8      [B]          76-58511
ISBN 0-8057-6676-6  P295

MANUFACTURED IN THE UNITED STATES OF AMERICA

To
Nancy

*. . . poichè la bellezza è un dono della fortuna;
e l'amore, il figlio di un mistero gaudioso.*

# *Contents*

# About the Author

Gerald Monsman is associate professor of English at Duke University. He teaches creative writing to the undergraduates and Victorian literature to the M.A. and Ph.D. degree candidates. Professor Monsman received his undergraduate training from Calvin College, Grand Rapids, Michigan (1957 - 59) and The Johns Hopkins University, Baltimore, Maryland (1959 - 61). In 1961 he was elected to Phi Beta Kappa. He holds the B.A. (1961), M.A. (1963), and Ph.D. (1965) degrees from The Johns Hopkins University.

Dr. Monsman is the author of *Pater's Portraits* (Hopkins, 1967), a study of mythic patterns in Walter Pater's fiction; and he has also written on Walter Pater, Gerard Manley Hopkins, and J. R. R. Tolkien in *The South Atlantic Quarterly, Studies in Philology,* and *The University of Toronto Quarterly.* Two of his short stories have been awarded the Blackwood Prize by *Blackwood's Magazine,* Edinburgh, Scotland—"Nicholai" for 1967 and "An Inheritance" for 1969.

# Preface

When Walter Pater exhorted the young men of Oxford to burn with a "hard, gemlike flame," he was challenging them in the concluding paragraphs of *Studies in the History of the Renaissance* to devote their lives to a new ideal, to the search for beauty and to "the love of art for art's sake." Unfortunately, his description of the aesthetic life seems to have seduced many of his younger contemporaries into the pursuit of naked beauty up the stairs of the ivory tower. That was not the life Pater had meant to describe, but the confusion persisted, and until recently his reputation suffered. T. S. Eliot's essay on Pater is representative of the disrepute in which his writings were held during the decades after World War I. Eliot found *Marius the Epicurean* a "hodge-podge" because Pater's mind was "incapable of sustained reasoning"—which meant for Eliot and his readers that Pater was primarily neither a philosopher, nor a literary critic, nor a classicist, nor a master of any other systematic discipline. Furthermore, because Pater's mind was "morbid" and because he had confused art and life in his studies in *The Renaissance*, Eliot charged him with the blame for a number of "untidy lives" among his self-proclaimed disciples in the 1890s.[1] So, tarred with decadence and covered with the feathers of too many disciplines, the Paterian corpus was borne from academia in derision.

But, since the mid-1960s, something like a rehabilitation has been underway, accompanied by a shift in the focus of criticism. The publication of Pater's letters and the appearance of several book-length studies and an increased number of journal articles have begun not only to soften the conventional view of Pater as the high priest of precious prose and tainted beauty but also to rescue the coherence of his writings from the limbo of multiple fields of specialization. However, recent scholarship has not yet resolved the problem of the Aesthetic hero, the star-bright man of perfect culture, which all of Pater's writings portray. Put simply, Pater's heroes seem mere spectators, dreamers separated from all the general purposes of life. If withdrawing into a private life of exquisite sensations is a requisite for burning with a hard, gem-like flame, then Pater's ideal is at best a dubious counsel of perfection. Although critics have conceded that in *Marius* Pater turns toward a more social, collective ideal of sympathy, the tendency ever since the first reviews of the novel has been to criticize the hero's passivity. Marius, said Oscar Wilde, "is little more than a spectator: an ideal spectator indeed, and one to whom it is given 'to contemplate the spectacle of life with appropriate emotions,' which Wordsworth defines as the poet's true aim; yet a spectator merely, and perhaps a little too much occupied with the comeliness of the benches of the sanctuary to notice that it is the sanctuary of sorrow that he is gazing at."[2] This study aims to reverse that negative judgment by defining the "common mental atmosphere" in which the spectator's mind actively engages the mind-in-art of humanity.

The origins of Pater's Aesthetic hero lay in the new science being proclaimed by men such as Charles Darwin, Thomas Henry Huxley, John Tyndall, John Stuart Mill, and Herbert Spencer; namely, the new spirit of relativism, of flux. In the opening paragraphs of the "Conclusion" to *The Renaissance*, Pater challenged man's sense of fixed identity by describing his fundamental oneness with the perpetual flux—the human body as the confluence of random physical forces soon parting and the psyche as a web of impressions continually weaving and unweaving. The individual seems merely a centripetal converging of elements scattered by the centrifugal thrust of the flux; his circle of self has no definite boundary that endures through time; moment by moment he changes. Identity, temporalized in this fashion, consists in a succession of selves, each of which merely contains a "relic" of the self that preceded it. But, unlike David Hume, Pater finds among the relics of selfhood certain luminous memories of aesthetic experience that bind perceptions together. These heightened moments become the substrata of identity, the constituents of stability, the avenues of escape from the solipsistic prison of fleeting impressions. In much the same fashion as his contemporary, the German historian Wilhelm Dilthey, Pater escapes through memory into autobiography and then outward to biography and to history. These stages in the expansion of selfhood, as Dilthey discovers, are made possible by a "whole web of connections which stretches from individuals concerned with their own existence to the cultural systems and communities and, finally, to the whole of mankind, which makes up the character of society and history."[3]

By de-emphasizing metaphysical and theological interpretations of history in favor of a critical study of the principal modes of experience, Pater approximates Dilthey's modern historical method. "Dogmas," the young Pater boldly asserts, "are precious as memorials of a class of sincere and beautiful spirits, who in a past age of humanity struggled with many tears, if not for true knowledge, yet for a noble and elevated happiness. That struggle is the substance, the dogma only its shadowy expression."[4] No explanation of reality can have meaning for Pater unless it arises from the temporal and historical structure of human life; "history itself," as Dilthey says, becomes "the productive force for the creation of valuations, ideals and purposes by which the significance of people and events is measured."[5] Yet the individual's awareness of relations points Pater (and Dilthey too, on his own terms) toward a conception of ultimate reality not as a mere including system, but as a relater of parts, a unifier of selves. The Aesthetic hero, as Pater defined him, is a creature of two worlds, dwelling in the isolating "now" of fleeting impressions but also participating in language, laws, customs, ideas, art—in what Pater terms "a general consciousness." Far from being "merely" a spectator of life, the hero's perception of a common cultural sphere of meaning in the products, contents, or *disjecta membra* of lives in the past ties him directly to the substance of history, the "struggle" of "sincere and beautiful spirits." By identifying himself with them, the hero epitomizes in the hard, gem-like flame of his being the greater Heraclitean fire of history itself.

Just why T. S. Eliot's generation could so lightheartedly dismiss Pater's Goethe-and-Gautier Aestheticism, as they called it, may in part be explained by the fact that younger writers no longer wished to admit, nor really understood, their debt to the Victorians. The recent publication of Pater's letters has not greatly clarified the outlines of a life and philosophy still tangled in the misconceptions of rumor and distortion, for Pater was, as he himself confessed, a poor letter writer. He emerges from his correspondence—or rather half-emerges, like some Victorian equivalent to Michelangelo's unfinished sculptures—as a shy Oxford don, a creature of routine, painstaking in the publication of his writings, and certainly not given to epistolary revelations of character. He remains "faintly-grey" as Henry James noted, adding, "I think he has had—will have had—the most exquisite literary fortune: i.e. to have taken it out all, wholly, exclusively, with the pen (the style, the genius,) and absolutely not at all with the person. He is the mask without the face, and there isn't in his total superficies a tiny point of vantage for the newspaper to flap his wings on."[6] Pater deliberately chose to live his true life in his art; and, with the exception of the outcry caused by the "Conclusion" to *The Renaissance*, he seems almost to have succeeded in passing through his times with hardly a trace.

There have been no biographies of Pater in English (except for a rather slight, commemorative outline by Arthur Symons) since the brief or inaccurate tributes and studies before World War I, and the time has come for a full-length study to combine such facts of Pater's life as can be established with a careful analysis of his art. Centering on the Aesthetic hero, this study attempts to present Pater's fiction and biography as lucidly as possible, so that the general reader, the undergraduate, and the fledgling graduate student will benefit from its critical reading as much as the Victorian specialist. Since the scope of a few hundred pages limits consideration to the more significant writings, this study has been weighted in the direction of Pater's completed imaginative work, utilizing his reviews, lectures, critical appreciations, and unfinished fiction and other fragments only when the occasion warrants. And finally, inasmuch as any new line of critical inquiry that also aspires to be a broad-based reassessment of Pater's theory of culture must build upon a core of established insights, I have not hesitated when appropriate both to incorporate my previously published readings or to draw on the excellent recent work of Lawrence Evans, Harold Bloom, J. Hillis Miller, Ian Fletcher, and a number of others who have enriched my understanding of the subject.

As a point of mechanics, it should be noted here that parenthetical citations made within the text to Pater's work are by abbreviated titles and pagination taken from the ten volumes of the *New Library Edition of the Works of Walter Pater* (London, 1910); these citations are shortened to only the page number if they follow a previous parenthetical reference to the identical volume. Citations within the text to *The Letters of Walter Pater* (Oxford, 1970) are by dates, which supply factual information and render pagination superfluous. For the remainder of the quotations, the usual apparatus of footnotes has been used.

GERALD MONSMAN

*Duke University*

# Acknowledgments

For help during the preparation of this book, grateful acknowledgment is made to Professors Clyde L. de Ryals, R. G. Frean, Ian Fletcher, and Elgin Mellown; to Dr. Casey Jason, Mr. Samuel Wright, and Mr. Chris Willerton; to my students, too numerous to mention, who were the anvils on which I hammered out my ideas; and to the Duke University Research Council for financial aid. Acknowledgment also is made to the Duke University Press for permission to use portions of "Pater, Hopkins, and Fichte's Ideal Student," *South Atlantic Quarterly*, LXX (Summer, 1971), 365 - 76, as well as portions of "Walter Pater: Style and Text," *South Atlantic Quarterly*, LXXI (Winter, 1972), 106 - 23 (for which I also thank S. Wright), and finally to the University of Toronto Press for permission to use parts of "Pater's Aesthetic Hero." *University of Toronto Quarterly*, XL (Winter, 1971), 136 - 51. Quotations from the *Letters of Walter Pater*, ed. Lawrence Evans (Oxford, 1970), are by permission of The Clarendon Press, Oxford.

# Chronology

1839　Walter Horatio Pater is born August 4 in Shadwell, East London, the second son of Dr. Richard Glode Pater and Maria, née Hill.

1844　Dr. Pater dies January 28; his widow moves with her four children to a small house in the northern London suburb of Enfield.

1853　The family moves to the village of Harbledown, near Canterbury, so that Pater may enroll (February 3) at the King's School as a day student.

1854　Pater's mother dies February 25; Hester E. M. Pater ("Aunt Bessie") becomes the guardian of the children.

1858　Pater matriculates (June 11) at Queen's College, Oxford, with a King's School scholarship of sixty pounds a year for three years; his studies begin in October; Aunt Bessie takes his two sisters to Heidelberg to complete their education.

1861　Between January and March, Pater receives private tutorials in Greek from Benjamin Jowett.

1862　Pater receives B.A. with second-class honors in *Literae Humaniores* and takes rooms on Oxford's High Street to coach private pupils, among them C. L. Shadwell, a future friend; Aunt Bessie dies (December 28) in Dresden, leaving the sisters to fend for themselves in Germany for several years until they return to take a house with Pater in Oxford.

1863　Early in the year Pater and Ingram Bywater are elected members of the radical Old Mortality Society.

1864　Pater is elected on probation (February 5) to a classical fellowship at Brasenose College, going into residence there as its first non-clerical fellow; his February 20 essay on J. G. Fichte's Ideal Student, read before the Old Mortality, causes a stir in Oxford; he writes "Diaphanéité" in July as an Old Mortality essay.

1865　Pater is granted continuous academic tenure; he proceeds routinely to the Master of Arts degree; that summer in the company of Shadwell he travels for the first time in Italy, particularly to Ravenna, Pisa, and Florence.

1866   Pater breaks into print with "Coleridge's Writings," the first of three iconoclastic articles in the *Westminster Review*.

1873   *Studies in the History of the Renaissance* is published March 1; an immediate hostile reaction to its supposedly hedonistic Aestheticism occurs.

1877   The second edition of *The Renaissance* is published with the "Conclusion" omitted as a consequence of the machinations of Jowett and of others and such public ridicule as W. H. Mallock's satiric attack in *The New Republic*.

1883   Pater returns in January from Rome where he had worked for two months on the background to *Marius the Epicurean;* he resigns his Brasenose tutorship (but remains a fellow of the college) to devote himself completely to its composition.

1885   *Marius the Epicurean* is published March 4; Pater gives up his Oxford house and, during vacation time, lives in London with his sisters at 12 Earl's Terrace, Kensington.

1887   William Pater, Walter's older brother, dies on April 24; *Imaginary Portraits* is published May 24.

1888   *Gaston de Latour* runs serially in *Macmillan's Magazine*, but Pater's pace falters and he abandons it after the October issue; third edition of *The Renaissance* is published with the "Conclusion" restored and slightly toned down.

1889   *Appreciations* is published November 15 and contains one of Pater's most important essays, "Aesthetic Poetry" (the retitled 1868 review-essay of William Morris' poetry); it is suppressed in all subsequent editions.

1891   Pater reviews Oscar Wilde's *The Picture of Dorian Gray* and condemns the loss of "the moral sense" in Wilde's heroes.

1893   *Plato and Platonism* is published February 10; in the summer Pater and his sisters give up their London house and return to Oxford, 64 St. Giles' Street.

1894   Pater is made an honorary LL.D. of Glasgow on April 13; he dies July 30 in Oxford of a heart attack following rheumatic fever and pluerisy; buried in Holywell Cemetery.

# CHAPTER 1

## *Emergence in the 1860s*

ARTHUR Symons once asked Walter Pater if he were really descended from Jean-Baptiste Pater, the eighteenth-century Flemish painter fictionally portrayed in Pater's sketch of Jean Antoine Watteau. Pater whimsically replied, "I think so; I believe so; I always say so."[1] But such a relationship could have been at most only collateral, for Pater's ancestors were already living in England in the eighteenth century. Perhaps they may have arrived from the Lowlands earlier, in the time of William of Orange as some members of the family thought, when a Dutch admiral by the name of Pater supposedly crossed the North Sea to settle in England; certainly the family name, Latinized in typical Dutch fashion, is common in the Netherlands. There is evidence that early in the eighteenth century one of Pater's forebears, who was engaged in the lace trade, migrated from a Dutch enclave on the Norfolk seaboard to the lace-making town of Weston-Underwood, near Olney in Buckinghamshire (where later in the century the poet William Cowper was fellow-townsman and an intimate friend of several Paters). The Dutch connection seems to have been given its last expression by Pater's grandfather, who emigrated to America to practice as a physician among the Dutch colony in New York.

After the birth of Walter's father, Richard Pater, the family returned to England (in indignation over the War of 1812) to settle in London in the poor quarter of Shadwell. Richard Pater, a medical practitioner like his father, continued in partnership with his brother after his father's death, working with dedication among the poor people in the East End and refusing to move to a more fashionable part of town. He married Maria Hill and had two sons and two daughters. The elder son, William, who continued in the family profession, became head medical superintendent of a mental hospital. Next in line was Hester; then Walter, born on August 4,

1839; and, finally, Clara. In later years Hester and Clara, who like
Walter never married, created a home for their brother and continued to be his faithful companions all his life. Richard Pater died
prematurely (the males in the family all died early) and afterwards
Walter Pater could scarcely remember his father. At his death, the
family went to live with Elizabeth Pater—Aunt Bessie, as she was
familiarly called by the children—in the London suburb of Enfield.

## I  *Childhood and School Days*

Barely a decade earlier, Charles and Mary Lamb had left Enfield;
and at the end of his essay on Lamb, Pater pays tribute to its trees
and fields where he

remembers, on a brooding summer's day, to have heard the cuckoo for the
first time. Here, the surface of things is certainly humdrum, the streets
dingy, the green places, where the child goes a-maying, tame enough. But
nowhere are things more apt to respond to the brighter weather, nowhere is
there so much difference between rain and sunshine, nowhere do the
clouds roll together more grandly; those quaint suburban pastorals gathering a certain quality of grandeur from the background of the great city,
with its weighty atmosphere, and portent of storm in the rapid light on
dome and bleached stone steeples. (*Appreciations*, 122 - 23)

In his fictionalized autobiographical sketch, "The Child in the
House" (1878), Pater gives an idealized impression of the large, old-
fashioned garden at Enfield and of the ancient, rambling mansion
of his great-aunt in Kent. The dreamlike world of Florian Deleal,
Pater's fictional alter ego, is one of natural beauty in all forms, and
it creates in him the aesthetic capacity which in later life allowed
him to appreciate artistic beauty. Such events as the early death of
his father and the great cry announcing the decease of his grandmother are combined in this sketch into the single haunting cry
lamenting the death of Florian's father in a distant land. With the
beauty and sadness of childhood there also comes for Pater-Florian
a spontaneous religiousness, "a kind of mystical appetite for sacred
things" (*Miscellaneous Studies*, 193). For some generations, the
sons in the Pater family had been brought up as Roman Catholics
and the daughters as Anglicans. Pater's father, however, had left the
Roman church before his marriage; and, although he adopted no
particular faith himself, his children were reared as Anglicans. One
of the favorite amusements of Pater's quiet and dreamy childhood

was to play at being a priest, complete with costumed processions and sermons preached to his indulgently admiring aunt. Something of this early sense of ritual and of the sacredness of common incidents which shaped the early psychology of Pater remained with him throughout life and was even embodied in the boy-priest hero of his later novel, *Marius the Epicurean*.

When he was thirteen, Pater left the private tutorials given by the headmaster of the Enfield grammar school and went to the King's School, Canterbury. As a day boy, Pater walked to Canterbury from the village of Harbledown where, for his benefit, the family moved. His *Plato and Platonism* (1893), *Gaston de Latour* (1888), and "Emerald Uthwart" (1892), written many years after, all catch something of the shock of rigid discipline and of contact with active, domineering boys that the King's School had on him after the feminine placidity of life at Enfield. In *Plato,* Pater describes the effect of such an environment upon the Spartan nature: "A young Lacedaemonian, then, of the privileged class, left his home, his tender nurses in those large, quiet old suburban houses early, for a public school. . . . If a certain love of reserve, of seclusion, characterised the Spartan citizen as such, it was perhaps the cicatrice of that wrench from a soft home into the imperative, inevitable gaze of his fellows, broad, searching, minute, his regret for, his desire to regain, moral and mental even more than physical ease" (*Plato,* 220 - 21). Pater's description of Gaston's arrival at Chartres, a city dominated like Canterbury by its great cathedral, is clearly another autobiographical touch. Gaston "saw the beautiful city for the first time as if sheathed in repellent armour. In his most genial subsequent impressions of the place there was always a lingering trace of that famous frost through which he made his way, wary of petrifying contact against things without, to the great western portal, on Candlemas morning" (*Gaston,* 27 - 28). Pater, too, had entered Canterbury in 1853 on Candlemas morning, and the memory of "that famous frost" is certainly his own, for *The Annual Register, 1853* records the weather during his first month of school as exceedingly severe and snowy.

Most transparently autobiographical of all is the portrayal of Emerald Uthwart's transition from a soft home to a rigorous school. The "old ecclesiastical city" to which he comes is an exact description of Canterbury with its "austere beautifully proportioned" cathedral that contains the shrine of Thomas à Becket and with its seventh-century cathedral school where the boys learned "their pagan Latin and Greek under the shadow of medieval church-towers, amid the haunts, the traditions, and with something of the discipline, of monasticism" (*Miscellaneous Studies*, 205). The features of this cathedral and its school remained with Pater as his earliest experience of aesthetic pleasure. Certainly his early taste for religious ceremony was given its fitting expression in this larger setting, and he spent much of his free time that first year in solitary exploration of the cathedral precincts. Pater was never popular at school, largely because he had absolutely no interest in the outdoor games of the other boys; and, when his mother died, hardly a year after he had first entered, he must have reached the low-point of his school days. In these first years, he was idle and backward; and he did not hit his stride until he reached the sixth form. That he had any pleasant school memories at all was largely owing to two close companions: John Rainier McQueen and Henry Dombrain. The boys, called "the Triumvirate," spent their time talking incessantly and playing boisterously in the ancient forest between Canterbury and Faversham.

Serious and meditative in manner, unless drawn out by McQueen or Dombrain, Pater was slightly humpbacked, and had a prematurely whiskered, impassive, frog-like face. McQueen describes him as having "an overhanging forehead, brown hair, deep-set mild eyes near together, a nose very low at the bridge, a heavy jaw, a square chin, and a curious malformation of the mouth."[2] Later, at the suggestion of his friends at Oxford, Pater grew a heavy Bismarckian moustache to cover his mouth, and to the end of his life he kept this grotesque disguise, looking, as Paul Bourget said, like "un amant de Circe transformé en dogue."[3] His innate grace of manner and his charming conversational style probably compensated more than he supposed for his aesthetic shortcomings; yet throughout his life he admired and envied the handsome physique he supposed common to the Greek athletes of antiquity. After the fashion of a Renaissance artist, he gloried in the perfection of physical form: " 'Hercules, Discobolus, Samson, these'—exclaimed one of Pater's admirers—'these be thy gods, O Pater.' "[4] An injury which occurred to him midway through his school years at Canterbury aggravated his physical shortcomings. It is reported that in August, 1856, a number of boys viciously attacked him at school "and in the midst of the scuffle a ruffianly boy . . . gave Pater a dreadful kick, with the result that he had at once to be conveyed home, where he lay ill for many weeks. . . . From the results of this lamentable occurrence, however, he never, it has been assumed, really recovered, and the peculiarity of his gait which marked him all the rest of his life is attributable to it."[5] He may have sustained an acute slip of the femoral growth plate and consequent bone degeneration, but Richard Aldington has stressed the psychological damage as paramount.[6]

Pater's aspiration to become a clergyman was stimulated during his school days by a visit he paid to the house of friends where he met John Keble, author of *The Christian Year* (1827). Keble, who had been one of the motive forces behind the High Church movement of the 1830s, which is also known as the Oxford or Tracterian Movement, made a lasting impression on Pater; and their meeting may have stimulated his writing of poetry. Two of his early poems, "The Fan of Fire" and "The Chant of the Celestial Sailors," are colored by Keble's *Christian Year* and *Hymns for Emigrants;* and many of his other poems composed during these years are infused with religious fervor. Pater wrote his poems in a manuscript book and made copies for friends; a few also seem to have been printed, possibly in some country newspaper. "The Chant of the Celestial Sailors," one of two poems presently accessible to students of Pater, is a visionary account of spiritual voyagers who are crossing the sea of life to heaven's haven. Another poem, "St. Elizabeth of Hungary," is interesting primarily because its virginal heroine (although married and having three children as history records) anticipates the virgin mother Cecilia in Pater's novel, *Marius the Epicurean.*

When William Sharp, then an aspiring young poet, asked Pater in 1881 if he had ever written verse, Pater told him

that before his twenty-fifth year he had written a good deal in verse, and had made many metrical translations from the Greek anthology, from Goethe, and from Alfred de Musset and other French poets. "At twenty-five I destroyed all, or nearly all—everything in verse which had survived. In none of my original efforts was there any distinction. Not one had that atmosphere of its own which there is no mistaking. But I learned much through the writing of verse, and still more through metrical translation. I have great faith in scrupulous and sympathetic translation as a training in English composition. At one time I was in the habit of translating a page from some ancient or modern prose writer every day: Tacitus or Livy, Plato or Aristotle, Goethe or Lessing or Winckelmann, and once, month after month, Flaubert and Sainte-Beuve."[7]

This testimony is the most explicit we have as to the creative habits of the young Pater. Perhaps the destruction of his poetry—which coincided with his election to a Brasenose fellowship—occurred because he felt that its schoolboy religiosity and aesthetic amateurishness might prove embarrassing to him as an Oxford don. The destruction is reported to have been effected by burning, in imitation of Goethe's action.

If Keble stimulated Pater's ambition toward a religious vocation and, perhaps incidentally, reinforced both a tendency toward ritualism and a taste for religious verse, the lofty prose of John Ruskin opened to Pater the world of art. When shortly before he left Canterbury Pater read the first four volumes of *Modern Painters* (the fifth and final volume was published in 1860), he discovered in Ruskin's melodious and decorative style a stimulus that turned his imagination to the criticism of beauty, allowing his impressions to be shaped not by Classical rules but by the suggestiveness of the aesthetic object; that is, by the subjective effect which beauty has upon the perceiver. Later, this impressionistic approach was to become the ruling principle of Pater's aesthetic criticism and the foundation of the Aesthetic Movement. At this time, Pater certainly must have been impressed also by the connection that Ruskin's moral aesthetic postulated between art and religion. Ruskin shifted the criteria of aesthetic judgment from well-established traditions of "taste" to the perception by the artist of a moral order in the universe. Later, finding himself out of sympathy with Ruskin's puritanical renunciation of the senses, Pater, in his first published collection of essays, challenged the validity of such an unbalanced aesthetic.

In 1858, at the end of the school year, Pater won prizes for scholarship in both Latin and ecclesiastical history as well as the three-year Oxford scholarship which the King's School offered annually to the student who wrote the best examination. It was a crucial award, for Pater's means were severely limited; and, when he settled into his eyrie high above the back quadrangle at Queen's College, his rooms were called "the Spartan Chambers" because he could not afford to decorate them. That Pater by this time had developed into a student of merit is evident, and he began his studies in the "home of lost causes and impossible loyalties"—as Matthew Arnold, the recently installed Professor of Modern Poetry, once described that ancient university—with high academic hopes.

## II  *Queen's College Student*

When Pater went up to Oxford in 1858, the city still had a
medieval flavor—"a vision of grey-roofed houses and a long street,
and the sound of many bells"[8] had been William Morris' impression
a few years earlier. Some years later, Gerard Manley Hopkins
described the "towery city," unchanged since Duns Scotus' time, as
"cuckoo-echoing, bell-swarmèd, lark-charmèd, rook-racked, river-
rounded."[9] Religiously, however, Oxford was anything but
medieval; even the High Church movement had now largely
become a ghost of the past. Inaugurated in the 1830s by John Keble, John Henry Newman, and Edward Pusey, Tractarianism had
attempted to bring the Anglican Church closer to the Catholic
tradition by stressing authority, dogma, and the creeds of the early
Christian church rather than the Protestant sense of the responsibility of the individual conscience in spiritual matters. The spirit
of rationalism, following the condemnation of Tract XC (1841) and
J. H. Newman's conversion to Roman Catholicism in 1845, set the
tone at Oxford. The geological and biological investigations of
Charles Lyell, Robert Chambers, and Charles Darwin, together
with the philosophical writings of J. S. Mill, Herbert Spencer,
Auguste Comte, and G. W. F. Hegel, served to weaken faith in absolute standards of moral conduct and in the literal truth of the Bi-
ble. The Broad Church party of Arthur Stanley and Benjamin
Jowett, deprecating ancient rituals and complicated doctrines, looked to German higher criticism for its methods of scriptural exegesis
and to modern scientific opinion for its program of social amelioration. But this liberal theology, instead of strengthening Pater's faith
by putting it in tune with the time, seems to have precipitated a
break with Christianity during his first years at the university.

Pater's Voltaire-like attacks upon religion pained McQueen, his
faithful friend until then, beyond the point of endurance. In his second year, Pater had observed to his serious-minded companion,
"What fun it would be to be ordained and not to believe a single
word of what you are saying."[10] This cynical remark may, however,
have been uttered partly for the sake of shock effect since, as late as
1860, Pater's sentiment in his private poetry is strongly pietistic.
Although a brief reconciliation between the friends lasted until
1860, the rupture was made irreconcilable when in December,
1862, after Pater's graduation, McQueen wrote to the bishop of
London on the advice of Henry Parry Liddon, Oxford's famous

pulpit orator, to prevent Pater's ordination in the Church of
England. Pater nevertheless persisted in contemplating holy orders
as late as 1863 when he twice competed unsuccessfully for a clerical
fellowship. The religious sentiment held him as surely now as when
he pretended as a child to be a priest. In his first published essay,
"Coleridge's Writings" (1866), he exhibited a curious clinging to
High Church ritual without the substance of belief. What had
replaced faith was a religion of art:

There are aspects of the religious character which have an artistic worth distinct from their religious import. Longing, a chastened temper, spiritual
joy, are precious states of mind, not because they are part of man's duty or
because God has commanded them, still less because they are means of ob-
taining a reward, but because like culture itself they are remote, refined, intense, existing only by the triumph of a few over a dead world of routine in
which there is no lifting of the soul at all. If there is no other world, art in
its own interest must cherish such characteristics as beautiful spectacles. . . . Religious belief, the craving for objects of belief, may be refined out of our hearts, but they must leave their sacred perfume, their
spiritual sweetness, behind.[11]

After he was obliged to relinquish the idea of entering the Church
of England, Pater for a time apparently toyed with the idea of
becoming a Unitarian minister; however, by 1866 he had also abandoned that possibility (if it was one).

Pater's substitution of art for religion was a gradual process, and
many subtle influences during his quiet years at Queen's prepared
the way for his first published statements of the full-blown
Aesthetic creed. His formal training was in Greek and Latin
literature, and his college tutor was W. W. Capes, a scholar whose
study of the Roman Empire of the second century may have given
Pater some necessary background for his later novel, *Marius the
Epicurean*. During the 1861 Lent term, he prepared a weekly essay
for Benjamin Jowett, then professor of Greek and later the re-
nowned master of Balliol and translator of Plato. It is recorded that
Jowett, pleased with a remark of Pater, observed to him, "You have
a mind that will attain eminence." Thomas Wright speculates that
it may have been Jowett's influence that caused Pater to give up
writing poetry.[12] Pater later described this most famous of the Oxford dons as an "encouraging but really critical judge" of undergraduate work. "He seemed to have taken the measure not
merely of all opinions, but of all possible ones, and to have put the

last refinements on literary expression. . . . When he lectured on Plato, it was a fascinating thing to see those qualities, as if in the act of creation, his lectures being informal, unwritten, and seemingly unpremeditated, but with many a long-remembered gem of expression, or delightfully novel idea."[13] When Pater turned to the study of Plato in 1891, something of Jowett's inspiration may have come to fruition. And, although Jowett took offense at the Aesthetic philosophy when Pater's study of the Renaissance appeared in 1873, their lengthy estrangement was ended in 1893 when the famous translator of Plato congratulated his former pupil on his *Plato and Platonism*.

Ingram Bywater, a close friend in Pater's early years (whose edition of Heraclitus would be used later for *Marius* and *Plato*), described Pater's character and preoccupations during this period. "He was," says Bywater, "a queer, strange creature. His reading was extraordinarily wide—I think he would have done better in the examinations if it had been less so—and he was full of ability. At first his interests were theological, but in this respect his mind soon underwent a change, and he became more literary and philosophical. The period of which I am speaking was one of great unrest at Oxford. The famous Oxford movement had spent itself, and the *Essays and Reviews* [written in 1860 by seven broad churchmen including Jowett] were influencing the minds of the young men, who were immersed in Herbert Spencer and Mill and Hegel."[14] It appears, then, that Pater's chief interest, apart from his prescribed work, was British and German philosophy. His vacations were spent in Heidelberg, where his sisters had moved with Aunt Bessie, and he acquired there a sound knowledge of German, reading enthusiastically J. J. Winckelmann, G. E. Lessing, J. C. F. Schiller, J. G. Fichte, G. W. F. Hegel, F. W. J. Schelling, and J. W. Goethe. Goethe in particular seems to have had a pervasive influence on Pater, and it is curious that he never later devoted any single work to his esteemed mentor, possibly because Thomas Carlyle seemed to have cornered the market on Goethe-worship.

In 1862, Pater was awarded second-class honors in his final examination, a keen disappointment to him, but one not surprising considering his extracurricular reading habits. Another misfortune occurred in the last week of 1862 when Aunt Bessie, who had taken the Pater children under her wing after the death of their parents and grandmother, herself died suddenly in Dresden. Biographical facts for the following years are scant, but one can conjecture that the sisters may have supported themselves for a time in Germany as governesses. Because Pater had his way into the church blocked, he perforce devoted himself to literature, taking rooms on High Street and reading with private pupils. Among them was Charles Lancelot Shadwell, the future provost of Oriel, who was to remain Pater's close friend in later years.

### III   Aesthetic Rebel

Early in 1863 (or perhaps toward the end of 1862), Pater and Bywater both joined the Old Mortality Society, and to this group Pater read his first statements on the Aesthetic life. The Old Mortality was a literary society founded by John Nichol, afterwards professor of English literature at Glasgow, which numbered some thirty-five undergraduates and fellows during the decade that it flourished (1856 - 66). Its membership included such future notable figures as Algernon Charles Swinburne, John Addington Symonds, Thomas Hill Green, Edward Caird, James Bryce, and, of course, Walter Pater. Knowledge of Pater's contributions to this society is scanty, but it is said that his first essay for the Old Mortality was "philosophical; Caird described it as a 'hymn of praise to the Absolute,' " and another member later wrote that "I remember it was said of Pater that his speculative imagination seemed to make the lights burn blue."[15] Within this group, Bywater and Shadwell were Pater's closest friends; and Bywater recalled many years later that at this time Pater's "mind was much more mature than mine and he completely subjugated me by his verve, and originality of view."[16] Shadwell, who had joined the society in 1861, is said to have served as the model for the ideal personality sketched in Pater's Old Mortality essay, "Diaphanéité." Although others from the Old Mortality circle—such as J. W. Hoole and O. J. Reichel, for example, both Queen's College men—were doubtless important in Pater's life, the general tone of the society was probably of greatest significance for Pater. In literature, art, politics, and religion the society was avowedly "radical." These future poets, critics, historians, philosophers, professors, clergymen, and public servants who met weekly in each other's rooms were fiercely dedicated to social amelioration, liberty of thought, and the ultimate validity of human reason in matters secular and sacred.

All the available evidence of Pater's participation in Old Mortality indicates that the portrayal of the Aesthetic hero, which was to occupy him in both his criticism and fiction, dates from about

February, 1864, the month in which he was elected to the fellowship at Brasenose College. His election seems to have coincided with a remarkable awakening of literary endeavor, for the essays written in the five years from 1864 to 1868 established the foundation for all his future thought. Although Pater was intensely concerned with Aesthetic theory during this first period, there is no indication of the topic of his 1873 *Studies in the History of the Renaissance* in the essays that he produced during this time. This is not to say that some of this material did not eventually find its way into his first volume, largely by virtue of an unusually inclusive definition of the Renaissance, but to note instead that he does not yet seem to have hit upon the Renaissance "focus" for his studies in aesthetics. The young Pater is wholly absorbed in exploring the Aesthetic temperament and challenging the ossified moralities of Victorianism. Not moral earnestness but aesthetic passion was to be the chief end of man. From 1864 onwards Pater steadily gained a reputation for going against the grain, displaying in his casual speech that Wildeian strategy of treating the serious things of life with a sincere and studied triviality. The story is told that he once was asked whether his college duties were a burden to him, to which he gravely replied, "Well, not so much as you might think. The fact is that most of our men are fairly well-to-do, and it is not necessary that they should learn very much. At some Colleges I am told that certain of the young men have a genuine love for learning; if that were so here, it would be quite too dreadful."[17] Often the perverse paradoxes and irreverent wit that he displayed before the distinguished guests at the rector's lodgings of Mark Pattison at Lincoln College were directed against Christian doctrines, especially Anglican orthodoxy. Indeed, by 1869 there is even the hint of the dandy's costume; for, when Pater appeared at the private view of the Royal Academy, he was not in typical donnish dress but startlingly arrayed in a new top hat and brilliant apple-green silk tie.

Humphry Ward, one of Pater's earliest pupils at Brasenose and later his colleague there, recalled that by 1864 Pater was already "vaguely celebrated," rumored "to have a new and daring philosophy of his own."[18] Pater especially owed this celebrity to the essays that he read before the Old Mortality. Not only did he read several unpublished pieces to the society, but he also apparently previewed parts of three review-essays later published in the *Westminster Review*. A. C. Benson states that Pater's earliest published studies—"Coleridge's Writing" (1866), "Winckelmann" (1867), and "Poems by William Morris" (1868)—originally "seem to have been essays for Societies."[19] These studies were, however, unsigned when published, and although they did raise the enthusiasm of the cultivated public, only those within the walls of Oxford knew the source of the ideas. Since the essays during the years 1864 - 68 were either unpublished or unsigned, it seems justifiable to regard them as exploratory and candid in nature. Certainly Pater's early style, with its comparatively shorter sentences and highly colored vocabulary, suited the iconoclastic nature of his ideas. The storm that broke in 1873 when the philosophy of the anonymous articles appeared under Pater's own name suggests there was a distinction between the image the Oxford don was expected to uphold in public and his freedom to be quite another person within his private circle. The end of Pater's for-the-record anonymity came with the appearance after 1868 of the Renaissance portraits in the *Fortnightly Review* where he found freedom from the formal review-essay requirements to select topics of his own.

Pater's earliest published studies espouse the predominantly Positivist philosophy of the *Westminster Review* in which they were published, and their empirical-scientific spirit owes much to his reading of J. S. Mill, Sir William Hamilton, and G. H. Lewes on Comte, as well as T. H. Huxley, Herbert Spencer, John Tyndall, St. G. Mivart, W. K. Clifford, and any number of other scientific contributors to the more intellectual and progressive periodicals. To identify articles such as Spencer's "The Ultimate Laws of Physiology" (1857) or Huxley's "On the Basis of Physical Life" (1869) as definite sources of Pater's imagery is often difficult, although clearly his early writings draw imaginatively on biological, chemical, physical, and geological terminology ("cell," "fibre," "genera," "element," "force") to bolster with scientific authority his views of historical development.[20] In the sum of his writings only Francis Bacon and, less frequently, Darwin are among scientists directly quoted or named (with a single mention of Isaac Newton). Yet typically a reference to the applicability of the Baconian method for defining the motion of heat (*Plato*, 160) covertly alludes to John Tyndall's popular *Heat: A Mode of Motion* (1863), indicating that Pater did not hesitate to supplement Bacon's *Novum Organum* (1620) with modern technical concepts. Certainly Darwin's influence on Pater's interpretation of historical development is paramount but diffused, and it must often be deduced from indirect echoes as when Pater quotes the familiar phrase "*Natura nihil per saltum*" (*Plato*, 5) to which the *Origin of Species* (1859) makes several references.

Seemingly an established rhetoric of science, typified perhaps in the "tangled bank" passage at the end of the *Origin* or in the closing sentences of Tyndall's *Heat*, which Pater echoes in his "Conclusion" to *The Renaissance*, allowed a transference of information from professional to educated layman. What marks Pater out from other men of letters of the late 1860s and early 1870s is not so much his grasp of scientific theory (which was very much that of a layman) but his excited acceptance of what he took to be aspects of the scientific spirit, his enthusiasm for daring new ideas (the intellectually risqué) whose covert or direct materialism was a challenge to Oxford orthodoxy. But even then this youthful enthusiasm for scientific theory was tempered by a certain ambiguity which may be seen, for instance, at the conclusion to the essay on "Winckelmann": "Natural laws we shall never modify, embarrass us as they may; but there is still something in the nobler or less noble attitude with which we watch their fatal combinations" (*Renaissance*, 231). Ultimately, Pater qualifies somewhat Positivism's mechanistic and necessitarian conception of natural law not by positing some teleological explanation of reality, but by utilizing the empirical authority of Darwinian evolution to confirm as the central historical fact the continuity of a conscious, purposeful process of cultural change and growth.

## IV  *The February 20 Essay*

The essay which Pater read to the Old Mortality on the bitterly cold Saturday evening of February 20, 1864—hardly two weeks after he had been elected a fellow of Brasenose College—seems to have opened another phase in the old battle of the tracts between liberal and conservative factions. During this drawn-out theological struggle, many had come to view the Tractarian position as necessarily Roman and had thrown in their lot with the liberals. "If you crush Tractarianism," countered its defenders, "you must fight Germanism." Since it was Pater's extracurricular knowledge of German philosophy fully as much as Greek philosophy that gained for him a classical fellowship at Brasenose, he might well be expected to throw his weight on the side of the new "Germanism" in the combat with High and Low Church advocates. But Pater's brand of

"Germanism" was so extreme that it was considered to be more akin to atheism than to theology. S. R. Brooke, a conservative who was at odds with the liberal temperament of the society, described Pater's essay as one of "the most thoroughly infidel productions" to which it had ever been his "pain" to listen. In short, Pater "advocated 'self-culture' upon eminently selfish principles, and for what to us appeared, a most unsatisfactory end. To sit in one's study all [day] and contemplate the beautiful is not a useful even if it is an agreeable occupation, but if it were both useful and agreeable, it could hardly be worth while to spend so much trouble upon what may at any time be wrested from you. If a future existence is to be disbelieved the motto 'Let us eat and drink for to-morrow we die,' is infinitely preferable."[21] Clearly an attempt such as that of Ruskin and the Pre-Raphaelites to recapture the medieval spirit by imitating its external adornments has here resulted in the complete divorce of art from religion. Naturally a certain allowance has to be made for the inflexibility of Brooke's religious conservatism, yet it is evident that for Pater in 1864 the criterion of right conduct is not an external standard of morality but the comeliness of the individual life.

Brooke, whose turn to read came the following Saturday, "endeavoured to the best of our power to shew the absurdity of that belief put prominently forward by W. H. Pater on Feb. 20th, 'that a future state is impracticable.' " Describing the Old Mortality with a certain unconscious humor, Brooke related:

The arguments we used were close at hand, and we cannot but think to the point, but the sight of the Old Mortality is not the sight of ordinary beings and consequently its members failed to appreciate what should have been thoroughly convincing. Pater is said to [be the] best philosopher in Oxford, yet if what Pater affirms is to be understood intelligibly we can only say that Oxford is a very unfortunate place, and that philosophers must be very deluded people. If a man cannot make an original remark, if he cannot cut out a new figure he will hack and carve the old ones. Pater seldom makes what may be considered a really original remark, but he is fond of criticising original remarks, and drawing fine distinctions between identical conceptions.

Brooke indicates that Pater had attempted to draw a distinction in his essay between "Subjective Immortality" (the memory one leaves behind in the minds of others) and annihilation without any afterlife. Since friends die, Brooke rightly reasoned, subjective immortality is hardly distinguishable from annihilation:

In the case of Subjective Immortality the dead man is indeed without corporeal existence, but lives as it were in the memory of his friends. In the case of Annihilation the man lives in no way. This apparently subtle distinction means no more than that all men undergo Annihilation, but that in some cases they leave friends behind them, in other cases they do not. Therefore to talk of "Subjective Immortality" is simply to talk nonsense. But the term is also thoroughly inconsistent for "friends" must die, and therefore the term *"Immortality"* is about the worst term that could be applied to such a case.[22]

Brooke apparently spread the word. William Bright, afterwards Regius Professor of Ecclesiastical History and canon of Christ Church, records in a journal entry for March, 1864, that "Pater, now of B.N.C., at his essay society in Brooke's hearing *averred his unbelief in a future state* and that Conington got up to rebuke him."[23] Events followed swiftly after the February 20 reading. In the diary of H. P. Liddon for Monday, March 7, 1864, we find the following entry: "Walk with Hopkins of Balliol. He told me about Pater's paper on Fichte's Ideal Student at the Old Mortality Club, in which he denied the immortality of the Soul." And at the end of the week, on Friday, March 11, 1864, his second entry informs us that "Hopkins mentioned to [me] the project of an essay club, of a church character, as a set-off against the Old Mortality."[24] Since G. M. Hopkins had met Brooke on May 3, 1863, in Frederick Gurney's rooms where Brooke was playing the piano "gorgeously," it seems evident that Brooke gave the information to Hopkins and that Hopkins relayed it to Liddon, who was, incidentally, Hopkins' first confessor.

The outcome of this event was the formation of the Hexameron, a club designed, as Hopkins' friend W. Addis explained in a letter to Madan of March 16, "to preserve men who come up with good church feeling and a disposition to lead from the snare of such societies as the 'Old Mortality' which almost avowedly formed themselves on the denial of much which is dear to all of us."[25] The following day, Liddon wrote to the Bishop of Salisbury: "During the last fortnight I have been trying to organise an Essay Club among the abler undergraduates (some of them Jowett's own pupils) whom I happen to know. There are already two such clubs in existence, which are a great means of propagating sheer unbelief, *e.g.* one Paper which obtained great notoriety at the beginning of this Term was directed against the immortality of the soul. It was written by a junior Fellow of a College." The contents of this letter were echoed somewhat later in Liddon's letter to John Keble (who perhaps never guessed this was what became of the pensive boy who moved him so deeply) on Whitsunday, 1864: "I told you of the Essay Club at which last Term the immortality of the soul was denied outright as a vulgar notion (by one of our younger imitators of Fichte). And I fear that 'nice pleasant fellows who believe nothing at all' is a true definition of not a few of the cleverer men who are turned out hence into the London world."[26] Hopkins himself had seemingly not yet met Walter Pater; for the earliest recorded meeting of the two is in Hopkins' *Journals* for May 2, 1866: "Coaching with W. H. Pater this term. Walked with him on Monday evening last, April 30. 'Bleak-faced Neology in cap and gown.' No cap and gown but very bleak." Hopkins evidently came to hear more of Pater's clever cuts at God, for he wrote at the end of the month (May 31): "A little rain and at evening and night hard rain—Pater talking two hours against Xtianity."[27]

Precisely what Pater said in his explosive initial essay of February 20 must be pieced together from the scattered comments of his hearers, but his anti-Christian remarks apparently impressed Brooke more strongly than certain of his more imaginative cultural assertions. The references to Fichte in Liddon's diary and letter illuminate Pater's position on the relationship of self-culture to subjective immortality and allow us to correct Brooke's distortions and to surmise what Pater may have said. In his series of lectures on "The Nature of the Scholar," Fichte states that the Divine Idea "lies concealed behind all natural appearances" and that "a certain part of the meaning of this Divine Idea of the world is accessible to, and conceivable by, the cultivated mind . . . . In every age, that kind of education and spiritual culture by means of which the age hopes to lead mankind to the knowledge of the ascertained part of the Divine Idea, is the Learned Culture of the age; and every man who partakes in this culture is a Scholar of the age." Furthermore, "the true-minded Scholar will not admit of any life and activity within him except the immediate life and activity of the Divine Idea; . . . he suffers no emotion within him that is not the direct emotion and life of the Divine Idea which has taken possession of him . . . . His person, and all personality in the world, have long since vanished from before him, and entirely disappeared in his effort after the realization of the Idea."[28]

The Divine Idea, then, is accessible through the culture of an age, and he who is most truly cultivated is most perfectly possessed of the divine. This explains the significance of "self-culture" in Pater's essay. And in answer to the question, "Do I survive after death?" Pater possibly combined the Positivists' idea of remaining incarnate in the memory of friends with Fichte's argument that the individual is ultimately submerged in an impersonal Absolute. That Pater may have been trying to compel Positivist and Idealist views to tentative levels of correspondence by an insistence upon the continuity of the self-cultured mind within the empirical context of history doubtless escaped Brooke. Indeed, it is questionable if any of the Old Mortals recognized the full significance of the Aesthetic hero when Pater read his essay, yet it was Oxford's first glimpse of a new personality; and as an imaginative creation, Pater's Aesthetic hero ranks with Carlyle's tyrant and Nietzsche's superman in significance. Unfortunately, Brooke's suggestion that hedonism might be the logical implication of self-culture set the stage for Mallock's later notorious caricature of Pater in *The New Republic* as an impotent aesthete deflowering voluptuous words. But Pater's culture hero could not be further removed from a decadent toying with beauty, and in the final analysis, Pater's belief in the aesthetic moment had a sounder ethical basis than the moralistic theories that Ruskin was then providing for his enthusiasms and prejudices in his highly acclaimed Oxford lectures as Slade Professor of Fine Art. The goal of Pater's humanism was the perfection of the moral life through the idealization of sensuous beauty, "a sort of *moral* purity; yet, in the *forms* and *colours* of things" (*Imaginary Portraits*, 23).

## V  *"Diaphanéité"*

In attempting to define the harmony between man's sensuous nature and his moral character, Pater's earliest extant essay, "Diaphanéité," dated 1864 but published posthumously, represents a development of that ideal of "self-culture" which so outraged S. R. Brooke. The essay is a blueprint of the elusive Aesthetic personality in which all aspects of culture are merged. Such an ideal nature, elementally simple, is the regenerative principle, the creative spark, in human culture. In a sense all of Pater's Old Mortality essays seem to have shared a certain family resemblance. His first essay, one recalls, was a " 'hymn of praise to the Absolute,' " and the February 20 paper was preoccupied with the Divine Idea. Although Pater couched "Diaphanéité" in the serviceable phrases of Matthew Arnold and others, it is possible to envision his diaphanous hero as the perfected outcome of what for Fichte was a continuous struggle by which the self transcends its lower forms and identifies the external world as no longer foreign, but as its own and as that in which its life consists. The hero's "mind of taste lighted up by some spiritual ray within," his infinite striving after the moral ideal whereby "the veil of an outer life not simply expressive of the inward becomes thinner and thinner," and his embodiment of "a phase of intellect, of culture," (*Miscellaneous Studies*, 274 - 54 *passim*) are all ideas apparently taken from Fichte's lectures. Such a "clear crystal nature" is the final expression of the gradual expansion of soul in which, as Pater elsewhere described it, "the material and spiritual are fused and blent; if the spiritual attains the definite visibility of a crystal, what is material loses its earthiness and impurity" (*Appreciations*, 212; *Plato*, 135). In his first imaginary work, "The Child in the House," Pater describes just how "inward and outward" are "woven through and through each other into one inextricable texture" (*Miscellaneous Studies*, 173), but already here in "Diaphanéité" Pater is outlining this essential characteristic of the Aesthetic condition. That condition, as Schiller had described it in his twenty-second letter on aesthetic education, is not limited or one-sided; it is the harmony of all human powers, the highest perfection of culture.

Pater begins "Diaphanéité" by considering the possible character types—saint, artist, philosopher—that are akin to his yet-to-be-described hero before rejecting them all as lacking the essential simplicity of the type he envisions. This simplicity or "neutrality," as he calls it, is not a reflection of the "colourless uninteresting existence" of the man who has been neutralized by "suppression of gifts"; rather, it is the colorless all-color of those individuals among whose talents there is a "just equipoise." "In these," says Pater, "no single gift, or virtue, or idea, has an unmusical predominance" (252). Just three years later Pater wrote in "Winckelmann," his first Renaissance study, that the modern age demands "life in the whole" (*Renaissance*, 228), and the Aesthetic personality responds to this demand by living "not only as intense but as complete a life as possible" (188). "The proper instinct of self-culture," says Pater, examines every form of genius; it "struggles with those forms till its secret is won from each, and then lets each fall back into its place, in the supreme, artistic view of life. With a kind of passionate coldness, such natures rejoice to be away from and past their former selves, and above all, they are jealous of that abandonment to one special gift which really limits their capabilities" (229).

Winckelmann, like the ideal personality in "Diaphanéité," is a representative of what Pater considered the Renaissance man, whose refusal to be "classified" (27) by any narrow, one-sided philosophy or discipline makes him a reconciler of opposites, a harmonizer.

Both Carlyle and Pater had been inspired by Fichte's lectures on the ideal scholar and both saw the hero as having a revolutionary force, but whereas Carlyle's heroes (Cromwell, Frederick II) aim at action, not thought, Pater's heroes do not change the world in any violent way; rather, with the reverence in which Solomon's temple was built, their revolutionism "appears softened, harmonised as by distance, with an engaging naturalness, without the noise of axe or hammer" (*Miscellaneous Studies*, 254). Although contrasting the violence of Carlyle's Charlotte Corday with the harmonious revolutionism of the Aesthetic hero, Pater finds in Carlyle's heroine that intensity-death equation that his later work will characterize as the prelude to renewal: " 'What if she had emerged from her secluded stillness, suddenly like a star; cruel-lovely, with half-angelic, half-daemonic splendour; to gleam for a moment, and in a moment be extinguished; to be held in memory, so bright complete was she, through long centuries!' " (253). Since Pater's diaphanous heroes, as harbingers of change, can be seen as embodying the 1868 - 73 doctrine of Heraclitus' transmuting fire, here perhaps is the original version of the gem-like flame. In the 1864 "Diaphanéité" Pater elsewhere had anticipated the gem-star figure by noting that the "supreme moral charm" of the Aesthetic personality springs from "that fine edge of light, where the elements of our moral nature refine themselves to the burning point" (247 - 48). Later, in his "Winckelmann" essay, Pater echoed this image of the bright star when he wrote that the function of the culture hero is "to define, in a chill and empty atmosphere, the focus where the rays, in themselves pale and impotent, unite and begin to burn" (*Renaissance*, 214). So, too, only when he is able to pass "swiftly from point to point, and be present always at the focus where the greatest number of vital forces unite in their purest energy" can the young man of Oxford, like the man of the Renaissance, burn with a "hard, gemlike flame" (236). As the embodiment of the transmuting fire, as the epitome of harmonious, musical transition within history itself, he becomes the herald of "renaissance," of renewal: "A majority of such would be the regeneration of the world" (*Miscellaneous Studies*, 254).

## VI   *Brasenose College*

The college of Brasenose, which was to be identified with Pater's career, dates from 1509 and is architecturally bleak and severe. Its black and blistering façade, which fronts on the small square occupied by the Radcliffe Library, must have given scant comfort to Oxford's most aesthetic don. A certain bracing austerity was also observable in Pater's cramped room, but the deeply recessed oriel window looking out upon the Radcliffe Library brought a measure of distinction to his living quarters. Decorated with tasteful simplicity, his rooms contained only a few objects to provide the mind with impressions of beauty—engravings, books, and, in later years, some copies of beautiful Greek coins and a wide, blue china bowl filled with dried rose-leaves "presented by an old lady in the country from a special recipe, and sent every year as a present to him."[29] Edward Manson, who had Pater as his tutor in 1869, described the rooms as "panelled in a pale green tint, the floor was matted, the furniture was oak and severe in style, there were a few choice prints on the walls, choice books on the shelves, and a dwarf orange-tree, with real oranges on it, adorned the table." Manson described Pater at that time as being "slight and gracefully made, though a little round shouldered . . . and he walked 'delicately.' . . . He had one of those faces that laughter does not become. Laughter gave him a saturnine, Mephistophelean look. Report said that he had sat to Solomon the painter for the portrait of Judas Iscariot."[30]

Humphry Ward, recalling his first visit to Pater's rooms, described them as "small, freshly painted in greenish white, and hung with three or four line-engravings" from Michelangelo, Correggio, and Ingres—pictures more spontaneous than the finished oils in heavy frames that were the usual Oxford taste. Ward also observed that "the clean, clear table, the stained border round the matting and Eastern carpet, and the scanty, bright chintz curtains, were a novelty and a contrast to the oaken respectability and heaviness of all other dons' rooms at that day. The effect was in keeping with his own clear-cut view of life, and made, in a small way, 'the colours freshen on this threadbare world.' "[31] William Sharp, who visited the rooms some years later, described the "snug, inset, cushioned corner," and then used the phrase "delicate austerity" to suggest his over-all impression.

There was a quiet simplicity everywhere, eminently characteristic of the dweller; but one could see at a glance that this austerity was due to an imperious refinement, to a scrupulous selection. There were low-set bookshelves, filled with volumes which were the quintessential part of the library Pater might have had if he had cared for the mere accumulation of books. Most of them were the Greek and Latin classics, German and French works on aesthetics, and the treasures of French and English imaginative literature. To my surprise I noticed, in one section, several volumes of distinctly minor contemporary poetry; but these proved to be presentation copies, for which Pater always had a tender heart.[32]

Perhaps because his daily routine of creation, correction, and conversation partook of the same refined simplicity, Pater enjoyed a temperamental placidity unruffled by depression; he was "absolutely and always the same."[33] His mornings were given over to writing or lecturing; afternoons to correcting or walking and meditating on what he had written and would write the next morning; evenings were reserved for socializing. Commenting on the distractions that interfere with the creative process, Pater once advised a young man that the morning hours, from the time of arising, should be sacred: " 'One ought to come out of sleep into one's work like a ripe fruit from the tree into the hand.' "[34] Yet Pater always gave generously of his time to anyone who sought him out. "In spite of the many interruptions he suffered I never once saw his 'oak' shut," observed a colleague, who added that Pater's pupils would remember especially "his ready sympathy and pretended leisure,—for it was the extreme of his politeness to always appear to the visitor as having nothing to do; and his invariable change of seat from fire to window, that the caller might have the benefit of the only easy chair."[35]

But because he never considered himself a professional educator, Pater gave as little time as he could to the administrative affairs of his college. On one occasion, Mandell Creighton reports, he undertook the reading of the English essays for a scholarship examination. When the examiners met to decide on the outcome, Pater came without his list of marks, languidly commenting that the essays did not much impress him anyway. In an effort to help him recall such impressions as he could, the names were read out alphabetically. Shaking his head mournfully at each name, he murmured dreamily, "I do not recall him." "He did not strike me." Finally, the reader came to the name of Sanctuary. Pater's face brightened, "Yes!" he said, "I remember—I liked his name."[36] On another occasion when he was on the governing body at Brasenose, a statuary group, said to have been a work of John of Bologna, that represented Samson braining a Philistine was sold for lead scrap owing to the nudity of the figures, which inspired undergraduate pranks. Gosse tells that Pater, "from indolence, or else from indifference to late Italian sculpture, did not stir a finger to prevent this desecration, and in later years a perfectly unfailing mode of rousing him would be to say, artlessly, 'Was there not once a group of John of Bologna in the college?' However sunken in reverie, however dreamily detached, Pater would sit up in a moment, and say, with great acidity, 'It was totally devoid of merit, no doubt.' "[37]

About May, 1867, Pater delivered the first of his lectures at the college. "His way was not so much to search out the meaning of Aristotle or to help scholars to understand him," recalled one former student, "as to take a text and pour out, extempore, the thoughts which it suggested to himself—comparing or contrasting Aristotle with other philosophers. His manner in lecturing was to bend his head over the table at which he sat, and cover his eyes with his hands, not often looking up to ask a question."[38] Pater was also supposed to lecture on divinity to his pupils, but the students, discovering that he disliked the duty and tried to evade it when possible, made every effort to be present and punctual. Finally, he boldly discontinued his divinity lectures. Pater can be credited, however, with introducing archaeological lecturing to Oxford. As a former student recalled, Pater in 1878 "advertised a series of six lectures on archaic Greek art, . . . an epoch in the history of Oxford studies; for he was the first to give this practical expression to the idea that Greek art was a fitting lecture subject for a classical teacher."[39]

Besides giving lectures, his duties involved tutorials with students who produced essays for him. In 1963, the oldest surviving Brasenose graduate recalled that Pater corrected his essays very carefully, saying he would not spoil them like that did he not think them to be good and to merit careful attention.[40] Such care was not typical of most university tutors who simply listened to the essay as the student read it aloud, making unpremeditated verbal comments. Humphry Ward reports that Pater "was severe on confusions of thought, and still more so on any kind of rhetoric. An emphatic word or epithet was sure to be underscored, and the absolutely right phrase suggested." Ward added elsewhere that "I learnt still more from Pater in many a long walk on autumn afternoons, and more still in a delightful month that I spent, by his invitation, at Sidmouth in the Long Vacation of 1867. He lived in a little house overhanging the sea, and I had lodgings in the town, going to him

every morning with an essay, or to hear him discourse on the
*Republic* and the thousand subjects suggested by it.''[41] Another
Brasenose graduate noted: "He can never have been a very practical tutor so far as the 'Schools' were concerned, but in his quiet
way he had a profound influence on many who came in contact
with him. Along with his friend Dr. Bussell he used to give famous
dinners to undergraduates in the quaint green-panelled rooms
above the Bursary. Towards the end of his life 'he showed signs of
becoming a strict disciplinarian, and he used often to wish that Sunday morning chapel was made compulsory.' "[42]

Perhaps Pater's researches in the 1890s into the "unsparing discipline" (*Miscellaneous Studies*, 210) of Spartan education had
some influence, but for most of his career Pater's indulgence of the
undergraduates was notorious. He was generally a mitigating force
in any disciplinary action; and his observation, apropos of illicit
bonfires in the quadrangle, was simply that they lighted the spire of
St. Mary's so beautifully. Something of his Rousseauistic bias for
natural education and natural feeling doubtless colored his inter-
position once into a serious discussion about university reform in the
common-room at Brasenose: "I do not know what your object is. At
present the undergraduate is a child of nature; he grows up like a
wild rose in a country lane; you want to turn him into a turnip, rob
him of all grace, and plant him out in rows."[43] Once, when he was
asked if the horseplay of the undergraduates disturbed him, he
replied, "Oh! no; I rather enjoy it. They are like playful young
tigers that have been fed." At least as a teacher Pater was skillful in
dealing with the undergraduates. When Henry Jackson, who in
1870 had just begun to lecture on Plato at Trinity College, found
himself seated next to Pater at dinner in Brasenose, he remarked:
" 'I believe you lecture constantly on *The Republic*. How do you
get through it in time? It seems as though lecturing three times a
week for three terms, it would be impossible to deal adequately
within a year with all the problems and the fallacies.' 'Oh!' said
Pater, 'I always begin by telling them that Socrates is not such a fool
as he seems, and we get through nicely in two terms.' "[44]

## VII  *Sisters and Friends*

In 1869, Pater took a house in Bradmore Road; but he retained
his college rooms for occasional nights at Brasenose or for the lodging of a visitor. His sisters, returning from Heidelberg, settled with

him and kept house. Almost immediately opposite the Paters in Bradmore Road, which was then the newest quarter of the town and nearly as quiet as the country, lived the Humphry Wards. Mrs. Ward described the aesthetic atmosphere of the Pater home in the 1870s:

The drawing-room which runs the whole breadth of the house from the road to the garden behind was "Paterian" in every line and ornament. There was a Morris paper; spindle-legged tables and chairs; a sparing allowances of blue plates and pots, bought, I think, in Holland; . . . framed embroidery of the most delicate design and colour, the work of Mr. Pater's elder sister; engravings, if I remember right, from Botticelli or Luini, or Mantegna; a few mirrors, and a very few flowers, chosen and arranged with a simple yet conscious art. I see that room always with the sun in it, touching the polished surfaces of wood and brass and china, and bringing out its pure, bright colour.[45]

Those "furry creatures," the Pater cats, were another decorative touch in the home. It is reported that these cats, Persians for the most part, were lovingly tended until age and disease had destroyed nearly all semblance of the feline form.

The Misses Pater are said to have "dressed in advanced 'aesthetic' styles: Clara Pater 'in peacock blue serge ornamented with crewel sunflowers and an amber necklace,' and both in what Vernon Lee called 'fantastic applegreen Kate Greenaway dresses.' Hester ('Tottie') acted as hostess for the family, and seems to have been appreciably more domestic than her younger sister: observers comment on the excellence of her coffee and her needlework, not her conversation or intellectual accomplishments. Clara Pater, on the other hand, was known in the seventies as one of the best female conversationalists in Oxford and was a woman of considerable intellectual powers. She was active in the cause of higher education for women in Oxford, and, having taught herself Latin and Greek, became the first classics tutor at Somerville College."[46] Elizabeth Wordsworth, a sister of one of Pater's colleagues and the first principal of Lady Margaret Hall, called to mind in later years the graceful figure of Clara, "with her fine oval face and beautiful dark eyebrows and grey eyes; always arrayed in some becoming shade of blue, with the same slow movements and carefully pitched tones as her brother. It is simply impossible to imagine any of the Paters in a crowded railway station, or being jostled about, and losing their luggage, or running to catch a 'bus."[47]

Yet when the tutorial work of the term was over, Pater spent his long vacations abroad in Germany, France, or Italy with his sisters. With typical whimsical perversity he "used to pretend that he shut his eyes in crossing Switzerland, on his journeys to and from Italy, so as not to see the 'horrid pots of blue paint,' as he called the Swiss lakes."[48] Pater particularly loved the north of France, walking as much as possible (his only form of exercise) in order to fix exactly the fugitive impressions of topography and architecture. Describing a visit to Azay-le-Rideau he said (September 10, 1877): "We find always great pleasure in adding to our experiences . . . and return always a little tired indeed, but with our minds pleasantly full of memories of stained glass, old tapestries, and new wild flowers." Since the Paters preferred to absorb thoroughly a few places at a time, they never hurried from one impressive sight to the next.

In November, 1869, Pater published "Notes on Leonardo da Vinci," which, as the first of a series in the *Fortnightly Review* on Italian artists, was followed by his "A Fragment on Sandro Botticelli" in August, 1870, and then by "Pico della Mirandula" and "Michelangelo" in October and November, 1871. With the publication of these essays, Pater's reputation began to grow in places other than Oxford. He himself seems to have blossomed socially, entertaining and being entertained. His circle of acquaintants grew to include, besides the Mark Pattisons and the Humphry Wards (the wives were as talented as their husbands), such notables as Charles Dodgson, the author of *Alice in Wonderland* (1865), and A. C. Swinburne, whose *Poems and Ballads* (1866) were very much the *succès de scandale* of the decade.

Pater found Dodgson's humor a chief attraction, and the two spent many an amusing hour in Dodgson's rooms at Christ Church. Between Pater and Swinburne, the Old Mortality Society doubtless provided the initial link although Swinburne had left Oxford under somewhat of a cloud several years before Pater joined. But, given the lasting ties of the society, which held reunions until 1876, it is not surprising to learn that, even during his residence at Brasenose, Pater entertained Swinburne. Although he also formed friendships with Arthur O'Shaughnessy, Simeon Solomon, and other satellites of the Pre-Raphaelite circle, Pater was never more than merely acquainted with Dante Gabriel Rossetti. Theodore Watts-Dunton gossiped that Swinburne "took him round to see Rossetti, who disliked him extremely."[49] In later life even Swinburne denied more than a mere acquaintance with Pater. This probably derives from his self-righteous attitude toward their mutual friends, J. A. Symonds and Simeon Solomon, as well as his fear of being stigmatized with the disrepute of Aestheticism.

In the 1880s, Humphry Ward introduced the Paters to the young writer Violet Paget, known by her pseudonym as Vernon Lee. In her company, Pater seems to have opened himself more than with most of his friends or, with the exception of Hester and Clara, any woman. Violet Paget's initial impression of him as "a heavy, shy, dull looking, brown mustachioed creature over forty, much like Velásquez' Philip IV, lymphatic, dull, humourless," is immediately softened by his evident civility and lack of affectation. He is, she says, "a very simple, amiable man, avowedly afraid of almost everything."[50] Though residing on the Continent, she visited the Paters on her trips to England; enjoyed long discussions in Pater's study; and, at one "literary tea-drinking" in 1886 at the home of mutual friends, shared conversation with the Paters, Henry James, Andrew Lang, Thomas Hardy, George Moore, and others. As is usually the case, other friends who are of little or no significance for literary history were personally as important to Pater as his more famous contemporaries. One such was the shadowy figure of C. L. Shadwell, private pupil of Pater, Old Mortal, fellow and (later) provost of Oriel College, to whom Pater dedicated *Studies in the History of the Renaissance* and who served, not without a measure of editorial malpractice, as Pater's literary executor.

But apart from his sisters and those favored few closest to him, "the rest of the world found him affable and acquiescent," Gosse reports, "already in those remote days displaying a little of that Renan manner which trifled gracefully and somewhat mysteriously with a companion not entirely in sympathy."[51] Others who knew Pater also agreed that he had a wide circle of acquaintances but that he never had many intimate friends. Those closest to him often enjoyed his piquant and perhaps slightly malicious wit. Adept at matching undergraduates with their animal totems and mimicking their actions, Pater could also amuse companions by inventing little farcical dialogues. Mark Pattison, whose speech and peevish intonation Pater had a knack of imitating, proved ripe for parody. One scene had Pattison leaping from bed at midnight to confront a burglar with a revolver. "If it's books you want," cried Pater imitating the Rector's querulous voice, "I'm in your hands. Make a selection, but be merciful. But if you want silver, you'd better go over to ————'s. I'm a poor man and have nothing but plated goods, but ———— is rich and has the real thing!" Another of Pater's whimsical games, kept up for so many years that even close friends were deceived, involved a group of relations—Uncle Capsicum, Aunt Eugenia, Uncle Guava—whose names Pater borrowed from plants mentioned in a fashionable novel; he also invented Aunt Fancy, who fainted at the mention of the word "leg," and Aunt Tart for whom no worthy gift could ever be found.[52]

## VIII  *Inner Life*

Harmlessly droll as all this may have been, Pater's susceptibility to a beauty colored by the curious and strange often produced in his work elements of the macabre. The violence hidden under the tranquil surface of *Marius the Epicurean*—Faustina employing for her magic rites the blood of gladiator-lovers or the gruesome martyrdom of the Gallic Christians—raises the question whether such action is meant to function thematically or possibly indicates a diseased imagination. It could be argued that, thematically, the macabre serves as a Romantic counterbalance to Classic order, two tendencies that exist, according to Pater, in various degrees at all times and places and are united in perfect art. In Pater's narratives this Romantic macabre takes two main forms, ritual slaughter and sexual or pathological corruption. Broadly defined, images of slaughter occur in the *Ambarvalia, Confarreation* and martyrdoms of *Marius* as well as in the torture-execution of the boy Raoul in an unpublished portion of *Gaston de Latour* and again in the imaginary portraits in the dismemberment of Denys and the autopsy performed on Emerald Uthwart. Themes of sexual corruption find their apotheosis in Pater's description of the Mona Lisa but also appear in other *femmes fatales* and in the sinister males, Verus and Flavian. Several incurable consumptives, a plague (the *pestis Antoniana*), an exhumed saint, and a half-burnt cat account for the corporal corruption depicted. Pater's mythic archetype for the ritual slaughters is the annual dismemberment of the year-daimon, Dionysus; his archetype for corruption is the tainted "Medusean" beauty of the goddess of death, Persephone. As embodied in Dionysus and Persephone, the Romantic macabre is, clearly, an expression of the ceaselessly interacting antinomies of generation and decay within nature and the historical process.

Although Pater carefully guarded his inner, private life, some critics profess to find in his "deep, turbid, violent phantasy" an indication of "ungratified desire" owing to a latent homosexuality: "If for 'homo-erotic' we substitute the term once familiarly used in the more ancient universities, 'romantic friendship,' very obviously this is where Pater's allegiances lay, whatever the limits of their expression may have been."[53] Another recent critic also prefers to interpret Pater's celebration of the human image in life and art as homoerotic in nature. He quotes a sentence from the novel—"Marius believed that Cornelius was to be the husband of Cecilia; and that, perhaps strangely, but had added to the desire to get him away safely"—and he remarks: "The public reading would be that Marius, having affection for Cecilia, does not want to see her married to Cornelius; the opposite, of course, is the case. Marius, being fond of Cornelius, does not want to see him married to Cecilia."[54] There is nothing "of course" about this interpretation, but such support as it could be given might typically be found in a passage in the first edition of *Marius* which was toned down a bit when Pater revised the novel: "the person of Cornelius sanctioned or justified the delight Marius had always had in the body; at first, as but one of the consequences of his material or sensualistic philosophy" (*Marius*, II, 53).

External evidence for the "homoerotic" thesis comes from several acquaintances, such as Frederick Wedmore who mentions that once he appealed to Pater "to be moved by some singular exhibition of womanly beauty, more probably in Art than in Life" and received a cold response, Pater explaining that life at Oxford "had made him so much more familiar with the beauty of boyhood, the beauty of male youth."[55] In this connection Will Rothenstein, a young artist who sketched Pater in 1894, reported that "Pater made a practice of entertaining the football and cricket-playing undergraduates, while he rather ignored the young *précieux*. He gave regular luncheon parties on Wednesdays; each time I was invited, I met very tongue-tied, simple, good-looking youths of the sporting fraternity. But Pater's close companion, Bussell, was always of the party, to share Pater's slightly malicious enjoyment."[56] One might couple this observation with an entry (May 5, 1878) in Mark Pattison's unpublished diary alluding to suspicions of Oscar Browning's pederasty, in part for which he recently had been dismissed from his mastership at Eton: "To Pater's to tea, where Oscar Browning, who was more like Socrates than ever. He conversed in one corner with 4 feminine looking youths 'paw dandling' there in one fivesome, while the Miss Paters & I sate looking on in another corner—Presently Walter Pater, who, I had been told, was 'upstairs' appeared, attended by 2 more youths of similar appearance."[57] Finally, there is the amusing incident of Rodin's bronze, "The Man with the Broken Nose," which had been offered "on easy terms" to York Powell: "I thought that Pater would like the first refusal of it, I brought him to see it. Pater came in, and looked at it without a word, then gave a kind of shudder. He thought, you know, of the ideal of manly beauty as somewhere between nineteen and twenty-three. He said, thanking me very politely, 'I don't think I could *bear* to live with it!' "[58]

Gordon McKenzie, aware that Pater's early family experience was not unlike that found in cases of homosexuality, observes that the pattern of "the absent, neglectful father, the dominant, devoted mother, and the loving, loyal child" which emerges in Pater's mythological studies (e.g., "Hippolytus") represents a subconscious but revealing selection from available myths. However, McKenzie cautions that this view of family relationships "should not be taken in a simple post-Freudian way because the data are insufficient and conclusions based on them are almost certain to be false or misleading."[59] If one suspects that perhaps W. H. Mallock began a trend in 1876 by offering Oxford a rather too hasty explanation of Aesthetic philosophy in his satire of Pater's supposed sexual disequilibrium, then a similar caution might be applied to all those stories of Pater's enchantment with young men. Certainly followers of the rather out-dated cult of private meanings in Pater's work miss his very real thematic concern with the human form. The sentence describing Marius' "delight" in the body, for example, is meant to contrast him with the Emperor Aurelius who was "a despiser of the body." Another critic quotes the following, " 'You would hardly believe,' writes Pliny to his wife, 'what a longing for you possesses me,' " and cites the change in the third edition, ". . . writes Pliny—to his own wife!—. . ." (*Marius*, II, 111), as evidence of Pater's "emotional abnormality."[60] But surely this is meant to be taken ironically—the love implied by marriage had become in the age of Aurelius and Faustina the exception, not the rule.

Admittedly, Oxford's atmosphere of a celibate all-male society tended to warp normal sexual instincts. By 1870 two contrasting streams of masculine sentiment were especially evident at the more ancient universities: "one from the Oxford Movement with its undercurrent of emotional friendship as expressed by Newman and Faber; the other from the muscular Christianity of Dr. Arnold at Rugby School. . . . These two streams . . . were joined at the point in a friendship where emphasis is placed on overtones of self-sacrifice, and not on the practical advantages accruing. At this point Dr. Arnold's athletic comradeships, with their socially cohesive values, could interweave with Faber's religious comradeships."[61] Perhaps this unisexual environment took its toll in Pater's art in which the portrayal of women is particularly unconvincing, although dramatic limitations also impair his handling of the male figures. Typically, the attachment of Pater's hero to an accomplished friend or to a teacher or to a woman tends to follow a familial paradigm: brother, sister, father, or mother. Eroticism is not altogether lacking, however—the love of Aucassin for Nicolette is a heterosexual example; the love of Winckelmann for Friedrich von Berg is homosexual—but if one insists that Pater's most famous aesthete, Marius, is attracted sexually to his friend Cornelius, then one must note that he is attracted sexually to Cecilia in at least as intense a degree—as well as to all the other persons and, even, objects of beauty which fall within his ken. Clearly what the fiction reveals of Pater's inner life must be treated as gingerly as a Delphic utterance. And aside from the Oxford anecdotes revealing his envy of athletic good looks and scorn for the lack of intellect they usually implied, there is no biographical evidence to indicate abnormal behavior.

About 1877 Pater's path unfortunately seems to have crossed that of Richard C. Jackson, an eccentric figure who claimed not only to have been Pater's intimate friend from this year on, but to have been the model for the hero of *Marius the Epicurean*. This claim, together with a wealth of detail, was published in Thomas Wright's *Life of Walter Pater* (1907). The ascertainable facts suggest, however, that the friendship was a fantasy of Jackson's pathological imagination. In a letter to Wright, Jackson claimed that Pater had said to him: "Yours is a personality of which no creature is fitting to unlace your shoes."[62] Fortunately, Wright did not print this Messianic fantasy, but the material he did allow into his biography was sufficient to characterize Pater as a fawning sycophant. Few noticed the travesty, and the protestations of those who did went unheeded. Edward March, in *The Forum* (July, 1907) wrote: "It is unfortunate that this romantic story rests as it does on the practically unsupported word of Jackson himself who thus comes into Pater's life, so to speak, a dozen years after his death. Mr. Wright, with a childlike trust that might be touching in a less experienced biographer, has accepted the unsupported recollections of this *soi-disant* friend as sufficient to establish historical truth, however at variance with probabilities or with previously recorded facts."[63] But, despite such strictures, the record remained distorted until Germain d'Hangest's study (1961) first cast doubt on the whole relationship.

In later years Jackson became reclusive, starving himself to buy the works of art he coveted and deluding himself with the notion that he was a bishop of a Greek Church in England. It is likely that Pater and Jackson may indeed have met, for Jackson's fantasizing was doubtless prompted by some initial *donnée*, but that this pathetic figure succeeded in clouding Pater's reputation with an aura of emotional sickness indicates how willing most critics were to believe anything of an author whose works were so "decadent." Certainly Thomas Wright, whose biography attempts by this condescending exposure of Pater's character to prolong the early satiric stereotype and to destroy the idealized image given him in the posthumous tributes of Johnson, Gosse, Sharp, and Symons, must bear primary responsibility. It is safest to say that in Pater's work the erotic has been subsumed in the aesthetic, and perhaps Arthur Symons' comment is closest to the heart of the matter: "Pater seemed to draw up into himself every form of earthly beauty, or of the beauty made by men, and many forms of knowledge and wisdom, and a sense of human things which was neither that of the lover nor of the priest, but partly of both; and his work was the giving out of all this again, with a certain labour to give it wholly."[64] As for Pater's celibacy, it is best described as monastic in kind, for he was, in James Joyce's words, "a priest of eternal imagination" and would take for his mistresses none but the Ausonian Sisters. Beyond this, all one can say is that the lack of information about Pater's relationships will make any verdict on his psychology tentative. What, for example, should be done with the rumor which circulated Oxford that Pater had a metaphysical sin on his soul?

CHAPTER 2

# *Manifesto for the 1870s*

EVER since Pater had first read Ruskin's *Modern Painters*, his interest in the fine arts had been slowly germinating. "Ruskin, I never heard him mention," says Arthur Symons, "but I do not doubt that there, to the young man beginning to concern himself with beauty in art and literature, was at least a quickening influence."[1] Yet during his undergraduate years when he was not occupied with the study of the Classics, Pater's intellectual pursuits seemed chiefly directed toward philosophy. His visits to Germany, as well as the later influence of Benjamin Jowett and T. H. Green, tended to strengthen his preoccupation with German metaphysics. But in the summer of 1865, Pater paid his first visit to Italy in the company of C. L. Shadwell. Together they visited Ravenna, Pisa, and Florence, with the result that the art of Italy began to exercise as strong an influence on Pater as the metaphysics of Germany had previously. Subsequently, in 1866 when he read Otto Jahn's biography of J. J. Winckelmann, he recognized in the career of this German humanist sojourning in Italy the pattern of his own quest for an ideal beauty revealed in physical form. Winckelmann's character caught the antique spirit—a spirit that liberated the religious-moral side of man by subordinating it to the artistic world of the senses. Those qualities of Winckelmann's character worthy of emulation also could be found, Pater realized, in the artists of the Renaissance. From this time onward, he appears to have thought of the Renaissance as that period when aesthetic, religious, and practical concerns were harmoniously balanced, when wholeness and unity of spirit were restored after the limits imposed by the asceticism of the Middle Ages on heart and imagination had been destroyed.

I   Studies in the History of the Renaissance

In 1872 Pater combined his *Fortnightly* and *Westminister* essays with a "Preface" and with three new studies on Italian artists; this collection was published the following year as a book on Renaissance art. Framed by a "Preface" and a "Conclusion," the eight chapters of *Studies in the History of the Renaissance*—"Aucassin and Nicolette," "Pico della Mirandula," "Sandro Botticelli," "Luca della Robbia," "The Poetry of Michelangelo," "Lionardo da Vinci," "Joachim du Bellay," and "Winckelmann"—treat impressionistically the life and works of writers, painters, and sculptors from the thirteenth to the eighteenth century. Among the fine arts, only music and architecture are not included. Later, Pater did write the appreciative essays on the French cathedrals of Amiens and Vezelay; but, perhaps because in his day Renaissance music was a scholarly *terra incognita*, he never produced an essay on music—an unfortunate omission, considering his celebrated remark in "The School of Giorgione" (which was added to the third edition) that "all art constantly aspires towards the condition of music" (*Renaissance*, 135). The essays included in *The Renaissance* present similar artistic personalities devoted passionately to the creation of concrete beauty. Emblematic of this consummate Renaissance type is the Leonardesque frontispiece, a face enveloped in an aureole of hair, expressing the sexless wholeness of the diaphanous hero and suggesting the centrality of Leonardo's vision to the age in its entirety. In contrast to the medieval obsession with Scholastic subtlety and mortification of the flesh, the Renaissance artists are devoted to sensuous form; they desire "to escape from abstract theory to intuition, to the exercise of sight and touch" (184). The pre-existing Christianity of the Middle Ages, by developing the latent Romantic strain (the darker mysteries of the soul) in the newly recovered pagan art of the senses, produced in the hands of these gifted men the "larger and profounder music" (222) of Renaissance art. The Greeks, recognizing the centrality of the human form to the arts, had celebrated a sculptural outer image, the perfection of the body; under the influence of medieval inwardness, the Renaissance extended this humanistic ideal to the processes of thought, man's mental form. This recovery of the human image in a new guise, and its consequent enrichment, is the thematic link between the artists and works of art treated in the volume.

The unity of the Renaissance essays is, then, not merely chronological but developmental: the evolution of an ideal personality type from the twelfth century down to the nineteenth, from its first anonymous expression in the legend of Aucassin and Nicolette (depicting in contrast to medieval morality a Hellenic worship of the body and a celebration of the pleasures of nature and the senses) down to its description in the "Conclusion" and its embodiment in the modern reader. The connection which Pater visualizes between this ideal sensibility and the development of culture from generation to generation had been described initially by J. G. Herder and Goethe. Long before Wilhelm Dilthey, Herder had taught that there must be a reciprocal relation between individuals and the common cultural sphere, that the individual acquires his thoughts through tradition, speech, and external influences. This evolving cultural sensibility, which is passed onward in the lives of great artists, culminates in the modern era not in the activity of creating art, but in a historical understanding of the human image. With Goethe's diaphanous figure in the foreground, Winckelmann the historian is fittingly the subject of Pater's last chapter. After the sixteenth century there arose an artificial French classicism out of contact with the actual antique, but Winckelmann's modern historical sensibility perceived that the true human image can only emerge out of a recovery of the original Hellenic culture. This Hellenic harmony between man's sensuous nature and moral character Winckelmann conveyed to Goethe not only by his books, but also by his personal intensity in the service of sensuous beauty. Goethe, afterwards identifying the whole historical development of this harmony as that in which the life of the individual mind consists, embodies the final stage in what Pater calls "the growing revelation of the mind to itself" (230).

Pater's sources for the imaginative reconstruction of the lives of his Renaissance artists are shrouded in conjecture. One may say that he used his sources in two different (though not mutually exclusive) ways: either quarrying them for anecdotal and factual material or finding in them an attitude toward the past. Of the first sort, Pater draws upon Giorgio Vasari's famous *Lives of the Painters* (1568) for the sake of biographical detail, speaking of the work at different times as "brilliant" and as "gossip." He repeats Vasari's story of Leonardo's freed birds and of the silver horse's skull harp, for example. He also read there that Botticelli was accused of embracing a heresy of Palmieri, but cautiously hesitated to accept Vasari's uncorroborated word. Pater draws more precise and factual information from such later critics as Guasti on Michelangelo, Amoretti on Leonardo, Crowe and Cavalcaselle on Botticelli and Giorgione, and Jahn on Winckelmann. Although he mentions Ruskin nowhere in his works save once only in a letter to assert prior discovery of Botticelli (in the light of Crowe and Cavalcaselle neither Ruskin nor Pater can rightfully claim, as both did, to have been the English discoverer of Botticelli),[2] the most immediate influences on Pater's attitude toward the past, by way of reaction, are *The Stones of Venice* (1851, 1853) and *Modern Painters* (1843 - 60). Whereas Ruskin had celebrated the Middle Ages and denounced the Renaissance as a "foul torrent"[3] corrupting pure Christian faith with pagan sentiments, Pater protests the criticism of art by moral standards and aspires to reverse Ruskin's condemnation of the Renaissance as immoral and therefore unartistic.

Ever since his undergraduate days at Queen's College when he visited his sisters and aunt in Heidelberg, Pater had a special interest in the literary and philosophical life of Germany, his ideas coming indirectly through the writings of Matthew Arnold and Thomas Carlyle and directly from the German philosophers and Hellenists—Winckelmann, Herder, Goethe, Schiller, and others. Since he was a close student of the German interpreters of Romantic thought, their Hellenic catholicity of appreciation doubtless encouraged his celebration of Renaissance eclecticism, the blending of medieval and pagan elements. Also his tutor at Queen's, W. W. Capes, had introduced him the the writings of Edgar Quinet, the most "Teutonized" of nineteenth-century French historians. Quinet, together with such other French dissenters from the moralistic method of art criticism as Jules Michelet, Hippolyte Taine, and Joseph Ernest Renan, did not share Ruskin's devotion to the Gothic and disdain of the Hellenic. With reference to specific studies of the Renaissance, it is difficult to determine if Pater had read Jacob Burckhardt's *Civilization of the Renaissance* (1860), but Michelet's 1855 volume on the Renaissance in his *History of France* (1833 - 67) was certainly familiar to him. Both historians exalted the Renaissance as the ideal eclectic culture, a perception confirmed for Pater by Herder and German Romantic philosophy which posited all forms of life, hence all periods of history, as phases of the same unifying and harmonizing Divine Idea. Furthermore, Pater's emphasis upon the extreme limits of the historical phase, its earliest and latest flowering, his stress upon the continuity of cultural history, the innovative freshness in the work of his youthful heroes that is not iconoclastic but represents a harmonious melding of purpose with earlier and later trends, could owe much to either Burckhardt or Michelet.

The poems of Schiller and Goethe and the aesthetic writings of Hegel, Lessing, and Schelling additionally supplied Pater with the notion of cultural rebirth. Although the cyclic conception of history had been suggested by thinkers as early as Plato, Hegel's *Aesthetik* may have led Pater to view the historical process as an eternal cycle of death and rebirth in which earlier cultural phases are cumulatively recapitulated in present culture and anticipate yet higher stages in the future. In a sense, any attempt to pinpoint the cyclic-progressive idea or its associated metaphor of rebirth is impossible since the complex intellectual climate of the nineteenth century cannot be so easily simplified. Many of Pater's major contemporaries—Carlyle, Tennyson, Newman—utilized the cyclic image of death and rebirth to characterize the historical process; and one cannot help recalling Matthew Arnold's poignant image of himself in "Stanzas from the Grande Chartreuse" as wandering between two worlds, one dead and the other powerless to be born.

The most fanciful aspect of Pater's handling of the theme of cultural rebirth was his utilization of Heinrich Heine's light-hearted fable, "The Gods in Exile" (1853), to provide a unifying myth for the *Renaissance* volume. Heine's legend of the return of the pagan gods who had been exiled by the coming of Christianity gave a concrete and dramatic form to the idea of medieval repression and the Renaissance recovery of the life of the senses. The legend is found, with varying degrees of emphasis, in five of the chapters. Near the beginning of the essay on Pico della Mirandola, Pater quotes Heine's tale of " 'how the gods of the older world, at the time of the definite triumph of Christianity, that is, in the third century, fell into painful embarrassments . . . . They had then to take flight ignominiously, and hide themselves among us here on earth, under all sorts of disguises' " (31 - 32). The myth was particularly apposite because Pico's blending of antique Classicism with the medieval Romanticism could be exactly expressed by it: "It is because the life of Pico, thus lying down to rest in the Dominican habit, yet amid thoughts of the older gods, himself like one of those comely divinities, reconciled indeed to the new religion, but still with a tenderness for the earlier life, and desirous literally to 'bind the ages each to each by natural piety'—it is because this life is so perfect a parallel to the attempt made in his writings to reconcile Christianity with the ideas of paganism, that Pico, in spite of the scholastic character of those writings, is really interesting" (44).

Pater treats other figures in *The Renaissance* also in terms of Heine's myth. Aucassin and Nicolette, who, like Pico, fuse two antithetical cultures, owe their passionate love to "the return of that ancient Venus, not dead, but only hidden for a time in the caves of the Venusberg, of those old pagan gods still going to and fro on the earth, under all sorts of disguises" (24). Pater also describes Leonardo da Vinci as a kind of clairvoyant who, not unlike his own Saint John the Baptist, bears a "strange likeness to the Bacchus which hangs near it, and which set Théophile Gautier thinking of Heine's notion of decayed gods, who, to maintain themselves, after the fall of paganism, took employment in the new religion" (118). Botticelli's comely figures also echo the myth; they are "like angels, but with a sense of displacement or loss about them—the wistfulness of exiles, conscious of a passion and energy greater than any known issue of them explains" (55). Finally, in the Winckelmann essay Pater notes that the Romantic sadness of the Greeks anticipated the medieval "suppression of the sensuous" and their tranquil gods "seem already to feel that bleak air in which . . . they wander as the spectres of the middle age" (228). And Winckelmann himself is described as one whose nature is "like a relic of classical antiquity, laid open by accident to our alien modern atmosphere; . . . he seems to realise that fancy of the reminiscence of a forgotten knowledge hidden for a time in the mind itself; as if the mind of one, lover and philosopher at once in some phase of pre-existence, . . . fallen into a new cycle, were beginning its intellectual career over again, yet with a certain power of anticipating its results" (220, 194).

The supreme expression of the reborn gods is, of course, Pater's description of the ambiguous Mona Lisa who synthesizes the antinomies of the flux: animalism and lust merged with mysticism; the profane, Leda and Helen, merged with the sacred, Saint Anne and Mary; actual history merged with mythic history; ultimately, life merged with death, for like the goddess Persephone, Lisa also "has been dead many times, and learned the secrets of the grave" (125). Both Lisa and Persephone are older than the immemorial rocks, and the eyelids of both are a little weary and "shadowy" (*Greek Studies*,

149). In the final analysis they sum up the growth, decay, and renewal of nature and thus embody the principle of life and death continually transforming into each other. Pater's description of Lisa-Persephone is, even for him, uncharacteristically rich and "purple," and the epiphany of this goddess is clearly meant to structure the diverse portraits of *The Renaissance* by epitomizing the eternal renewal of the senses. Her nature is sinister only to the eye of the uncompromising spiritualist (a theme in Pater's later portraits, "Apollo in Picardy" and "Gaudioso, the Second"): "When the actual relics of the antique were restored to the world, in the view of the Christian ascetic it was as if an ancient plague-pit had been opened. All the world took the contagion of the life of nature and the senses" (*Renaissance*, 226).

Pater's earliest expression of this myth of the return of the exiled gods had appeared in the 1864 "Diaphanéité" essay, and its last expression in his work came in the unfinished imaginary portrait, "Gaudioso, the Second," which Pater was writing at his death. In the studies produced in the intervening years, the theme also occurred frequently. Its implication for *The Renaissance* and for Pater's other work generally is that the recovery of the old Classic desire for beauty and sweetness in an intense, passionate, and visionary age will produce, by the harmonious blending of Classic and Romantic qualities, the greatest works of art. This was how Pater understood the Renaissance "wholeness" and "completeness" of life which had gone back to its Hellenic sources "to be clarified and corrected" (199). This rebirth, for Pater, was a continuing process; and the narrow Victorian morality of his own time which associated sensuous delight with sinful pleasure also stood in need of just such a Hellenic clarification and correction. Although Pater declined to join Matthew Arnold in "bracing the moral fibre," he did hope to introduce a code of conduct based on a frank acceptance of the senses and the body and on liberty of thought and imagination. Just as paganism had returned, like the gods in exile, to temper and liberalize medieval Christianity, so a new call went out in 1873 for the return of those antique deities. Pater's real subject was not the history of the Renaissance, but the renascence of history—the continuous rebirth of culture, clarified and corrected in the hero's balancing of sense with spirit.

## II  *The "Conclusion"*

*The Renaissance* served upon its appearance as the manifesto of the Aesthetic Movement, and students at Oxford were often heard chanting its melodious passages in unison. No doubt part of the younger generation's enthusiasm for the book lay precisely in the older generation's somewhat indignant reaction to it. In particular, the "Conclusion" to the volume was responsible for the *succès de scandale* of Pater's criticism, for in it Pater proclaimed the gospel of flux—that what is real in our existence is not some supernatural world rather than visible creation, but the here and now in all its sensuous, fleeting beauty:

Every moment some form grows perfect in hand or face; some tone on the hills or sea is choicer than the rest; some mood of passion or insight or intellectual excitement is irresistibly real and attractive to us,—for that moment only. Not the fruit of experience, but experience itself, is the end. A counted number of pulses only is given to us of a variegated, dramatic life. How may we see in them all that is to be seen in them by the finest senses? How shall we pass most swiftly from point to point, and be present always at the focus where the greatest number of vital forces unite in their purest energy? To burn always with this hard, gemlike flame, to maintain this ecstasy, is success in life. (*Renaissance*, 236)

The passionate observation of nature, the sense of the transience of all beauty, the moment isolated from the flux—there seems to be, as some have thought, the old *carpe diem* in its urgent tones.

The first printing of the "Conclusion" was not in *The Renaissance* itself; it had appeared as the last three pages of the 1868 *Westminster Review* article, "Poems by William Morris." The essay was unsigned and iconoclastic, and for this reason Pater may himself never have alluded to it later. Moreover, a number of early critics, Pater's friends and biographers who supplied checklists of his writings, knew only vaguely that such an article had been written and were unable to supply many precise details. Pater formed two important essays out of the Morris review: "Aesthetic Poetry," which made its single reappearance in the first edition of *Appreciations* (1889), and the "Conclusion" itself. Because "Aesthetic Poetry" was permanently suppressed by Pater in all editions subsequent to its initial 1889 appearance—as Lionel Johnson incredulously reported, Pater said " 'there were things in it; which some people, pious souls! thought profane, yes! profane' "[4]—it had a relatively brief textual history compared with the five revisions given to the "Conclusion." A close comparison of the 1868 "Conclusion" with the 1873 version in the first edition of *The Renaissance* reveals thirty-eight points of variance: twenty-seven alterations in punctuation, nine verbal emendations, and two remaining changes of intent. Small though most of the alterations are—a comma for a dash, a dash for a comma—they do prove that the 1873 essay was republished with careful, indeed anxious, consideration.

Of the two changes in intent, the first concerns the omission of one entire paragraph. Following the sentence ending "that strange perpetual weaving and unweaving of ourselves," the following short paragraph is found in the 1868 article: "Such thoughts seem desolate at first; at times all the bitterness of life seems concentrated in them. They bring the image of one washed out beyond the bar in a sea at ebb, losing even his personality, as the elements of which he is composed pass into new combinations. Struggling, as he must, to save himself, it is himself that he loses at every moment."[5] Having described the flux of physical and mental life, Pater here states boldly that at every moment of our existence each of us is losing what the drowning man loses—identity as an individual. The analogy was probably cut because drowning suggested the desperation but not the day by day recurrence of the loss. But unfortunately the phrase "at first," adds something that is present only by implication in the later 1873 version; namely, that the sense of desolation and bitterness concomitant with this view is not a permanent one. In a way of thinking parallel to that of the Buddha, Pater implies that the shock is only temporary; the true effect is a sharpening of intensity, a recovery of life within the dimensions of the here and now.

The second substantive emendation is a translation in English of a passage from Victor Hugo's *Les Misérables* which is given a different stress in the second version. Pater first describes the young Rousseau, who, believing himself mortally ill, dedicated with renewed energy his remaining time to art. Then, in the 1868 version, he writes: "Well, we are all *condamnés*, as Victor Hugo somewhere says: we have an interval and then we cease to be" (312). In 1873, this statement becomes: "Well, we are all *condamnés*, as Victor Hugo says: *les hommes sont tous condamnés à mort avec des sursis indéfinis:* we have an interval, and then our place knows us no more" (212). It is clear that *"condamnés"* by itself does not make its point; whereas the complete quotation explains to what and under what conditions we are all condemned. The indefiniteness of the reprieve is now stressed. Pater also changes "we cease to be" to "our place knows us no more," suggesting that *being* may not, in fact, altogether cease.

The most important change, however, is one that does not appear in the text itself because it marks a change in context. The 1868 conclusion to a study of Morris' Pre-Raphaelite poetry is made to serve in 1873 as a "Conclusion" to a study of the Renaissance, a period no longer imbued with those medieval qualities so much admired by Morris and the Pre-Raphaelite Brotherhood. In the never-reprinted paragraph of 1868 that served as the transition between the review of Morris' poetry and the material that became the "Conclusion" to *The Renaissance,* Pater implied a link between recent scientific theories and Aesthetic philosophy. The real subject of the "Conclusion" is neither Morris' poetry in 1868 nor the historic Renaissance in 1873, but a problem deriving from the new science being proclaimed in Pater's time by men such as Darwin, Spencer, and Huxley; namely, because "the modern world is in possession of truths, what but a passing smile can it have for a kind of poetry which, assuming artistic beauty of form to be an end in itself, passes by those truths and the living interests which are connected with them, to spend a thousand cares in telling once more these pagan fables as if it had but to choose between a more and a less beautiful shadow?" The modern reader demands that poetry apply scientific principles to pressing social problems; he considers Aesthetic poetry to be old-fashioned. But ironically it is this modern reader who is passé, for modern science implies the impossibility of arriving at any fixed principles, and thus beauty for its own sake is a justifiable alternative. That the Aesthetic life can actually be a life lived in accord with scientific formulations and that *l'art pour l'art* is premised on the most up-to-date theories—this is what the "Conclusion" wished to prove. "Let us accept the challenge," Pater continued, "let us see what modern philosophy, when it is sincere, really does say about human life and the truth we can attain in it, and the relation of this to the desire of beauty."[6]

### III   *Art and History*

It is entirely possible that the "Conclusion" may originally have been written in 1865 or 1866 as an essay for the Old Mortality Society, Pater challenging the Old Mortals' physical and psychic sense of fixed identity by describing their fundamental continuity with the perpetual flux—the human body as the confluence of random physical forces soon parting and the psyche as a web of impressions continually weaving and unweaving. In this modern conception of life, Pater saw an identity with the ancient philosophy of Heraclitus. "The seeds of almost all scientific ideas might seem to have been dimly enfolded in the mind of antiquity" (*Plato*, 18), writes Pater, and he quotes Heraclitus' dictum, "All things give way: nothing remaineth," as the epigraph to the "Conclusion." "The principle of disintegration, the incoherency of fire or flood," Pater noted in his chapter on Heraclitus in *Plato*, "are inherent in the primary elements alike of matter and soul. . . . The principle of lapse, of waste, was, in fact, in one's self. 'No one has ever passed twice over the same stream.' Nay, the passenger himself is without identity. Upon the same stream at the same moment we do, and do not, embark: for we are, and are not" (15 - 16). And as with man's body and psyche, so also with the "original products of human genius" (or "art" one may say, for Pater treated every philosophic system as an aesthetic object) in which "the seemingly new is old also, a palimpsest, a tapestry of which the actual threads have served before, or like the animal frame itself, every particle of which has already lived and died many times over" (8).

This ancient Heraclitean belief that all existence is the momentary product of a ceaseless alternation of generation and destruction is especially relevant to Pater's portrayal of the human condition. In his own time, Pater might have found the Heraclitean idea expressed in John Tyndall's or T. H. Huxley's addresses. In his 1868 "On the Physical Basis of Life," Huxley described the basic protoplasm of life as the result of physical elements perpetually recombining:

Under whatever disguise it takes refuge, whether fungus or oak, worm or man, the living protoplasm not only ultimately dies and is resolved into its mineral and lifeless constituents, but is always dying, and, strange as the paradox may sound, could not live unless it died. . . . All work implies waste, and the work of life results, directly or indirectly, in the waste of protoplasm. Every word uttered by a speaker costs him some physical loss; and, in the strictest sense, he burns that others may have light—so much eloquence, so much of his body resolved into carbonic acid, water, and urea. It is clear that this process of expenditure cannot go on for ever. . . . By and by, I shall probably have recourse to the substance commonly called mutton. . . . A singular inward laboratory, which I possess, will dissolve a certain portion of the modified protoplasm; the solution so formed will pass into my veins; and the subtle influences to which it will then be subjected will convert the dead protoplasm into living protoplasm, and transubstantiate sheep into man.[7]

This is the new Eucharist for the nineteenth century, the perpetual transubstantiation of carbon, hydrogen, oxygen, and nitrogen.

For Pater as for Huxley and Heraclitus, the physical body (or every manifestation of anything that seems in itself distinct and individual) always exists as a result of the forces that are in continuous motion in the cosmos. And if the body is the confluence of random forces soon parting and the psyche is a solipsistic nexus of fleeting impressions, then the distinction that the man in the street supposes is so easy to make between the physical or mental self and the not-self proves illusory. Instead of the stable paradigm of a sharply bounded circle of self within the larger circumference of not-self, Pater suggests a paradigm of process in which there is no enduring circle of self (only an asterisk, a star-bright center) since at every moment the self is being defined anew as the elemental threads (physical properties or mental impressions) are added and subtracted. Within the flux there is simply a succession of selves, each of which contains only "a relic" (*Renaissance,* 236) of the self that preceded it. Any given person or thing—Pater, let us say—is but a centripetal crossing of elements beginning in 1839 and shifted by the centrifugal thrust of the flux moment by moment, year by year, until finally in 1894 the constituents are too radically altered to have any viable coherence left. What temporarily remains of that nexus of elements is then buried in Holywell Cemetery, Oxford, and eventually reappears in "the springing of violets from the grave" (234).

One is tempted to say that in siding with the Empiricists Pater denied that the flux is an intrinsically rational process. A philosophical purist neither in temperament nor method, Pater at no point in his career defined with precision his own notions, yet for him existence was both meaningful and rationally directed. But unlike Enlightenment rationalists, who were inclined to locate the meaning of history in a transcendent or Absolutist system of valuation, the Romantics and, increasingly, the Victorians typically qualified the traditional idea of a time-transcending, eternally complete Deity. Certainly British Empiricism and French Positivism, representing a protest against rationalism in metaphysics and a consistent appeal to direct experience, suggested to Pater that the values, ideals, and purposes that metaphysics and religion traditionally imposed upon existence are to be found in the empirical reality of the historical process itself. Throughout history, he says, there have been certain recurrent ideas that must possess always a definite fixed charm or power of stimulus over the imagination. These ideas must surely one day find their justification in some empirically realizable equivalent, otherwise how could one explain their persistence? The most enduring of such ideas, which since the time of Heraclitus has been present in philosophy, is that of a universal intelligence in things. And the empirical reality of this "Logos" or Absolute, says Pater, is really an actual body of persons: "The idea of a sleepless reason which assists and rounds our sleepy, intermittent, intelligence, in which the eternal . . . ideas of things have a durable, permanent, free, independent existence, lending itself and lifting for a little time our transient, individual intelligence, for us actually translates into that conception of collective humanity." Pater extends to Pascal the credit for being the first to conceive of humanity as the Logos. And for his own century, Pater says that the two opposite schools which have divided speculative activity between them—Hegelian Idealism and Comtean Positivism—are at one in this conception of humanity. In Comte's "Grand-être," which is the society of the dead, and in Hegel's "Absolute," which is the collective life of the whole human race, two opposite poles of philosophy meet each other halfway.[8]

Apart from the technical sense of viewing all reality as of-the-nature-of-consciousness, Pater's personalistic Idealism, in sympathy with Kant, Leibnitz, and Lotze and in contrast with Hegel and Fichte, may be termed qualitatively pluralistic insofar as it views the universe as composed of unique selves; it is numerically monistic because it describes the many selves as expressions of the Absolute which becomes self-conscious in and through the historical self-consciousness of mankind. As against orthodox Hegelianism and in agreement with the Oxford Personalists, Pater implies that the Absolute, far from negating finite selves, has indeed no meaning except in experienceable qualities of human selves. But above all—and this is not only Pater's clearest point of divergence from Hegel but his closest approximation to the historical method of Wilhelm Dilthey—Pater de-emphasizes speculative metaphysics in favor of a critical study of the principal modes of experience. Both Dilthey and Pater begin with the radical empiricism of psychological introspection, that is, with lived experience and its memories. Then, by virtue of the self's direct experience of relations and connections, the phenomenological historian passes from autobiography to biography and, finally, by "retracing in his individual mental pilgrimage the historic order of human thought"

(*Marius*, I, 134), approaches cultural history. As Dilthey observed: "The power and breadth of our own lives and the energy with which we reflect on them are the foundation of historical vision. It alone enables us to give life back to the bloodless shadows of the past. Combined with an infinite desire to surrender to and lose one's self in the existence of others, it makes the great historian."[9]

Pater's book, one realizes, is an achievement of original temperament—a vision of culture and a sense of style. It reflects neither Hegel's metaphysical approach to art nor Ruskin's moral approach nor, for that matter, the historical approach preferred by Mrs. Mark Pattison. Reviewing *Studies in the History of the Renaissance*, she remarked that its title was "misleading" because "the historical element is precisely that which is wanting, and its absence makes the weak place of the whole book." The work, she found, lacked "true scientific method" and "is in no wise a contribution to the history of the Renaissance."[10] But Pater's purpose is never some "actual revival" of the past era: "such vain antiquarianism is a waste of the poet's power," he says, for "the composite experience of all ages is part of each one of us: to deduct from that experience, to obliterate any part of it . . . is as impossible as to become a little child, or enter again into the womb and be born. But though it is not possible to repress a single phase of that humanity, which, because we live and move and have our being in the life of humanity, makes us what we are, it is possible to isolate such a phase, to throw it into relief, to be divided against ourselves in our zeal for it; as we may hark back to some choice space of our own individual life" (*Appreciations* [1889], 223 - 24). Like Dilthey, Pater founded his vision of history on a contemplation of his own life; and applying the principle that only his subjective impressions could truly be known, Pater abdicated the role of authoritative art historian that Mrs. Pattison demanded of him.

"The function of the aesthetic critic," writes Pater, "is to distinguish . . . [the] special impression of beauty or pleasure" (*Renaissance*, ix) produced by the aesthetic object. Owing to this concern with subjective impressions, the essays in *The Renaissance* interpret cultural history in terms that are suggestive and private, and their judgments are not meant to reflect a defensible critical position. But although Pater's theories are often incorrect, his evocations of distinctive artistic qualities, on the other hand, are astute and vivid, though sometimes he relied too confidently on first impressions or memory—in the first edition he substituted a "bat" for the "rabbit" which he initially supposed to have been creeping about the cheek of Leonardo's Medusa, and in the "Conclusion" he confused Rousseau's pleasure in a work by Bernard Lamy with an earlier mention of Voltaire in the *Confessions*. But such minor slips hardly matter, for nowhere does Pater conceive of historical writing as merely the compilation of a vast number of authoritative facts pertaining to an artist's work or life; indeed, he made decreasing use of documentation in successive revisions of *The Renaissance* and in the essay on Leonardo actually disparaged with the epithet "Antiquarianism" not only the hastily assembled facts of Houssaye but also the painstaking work of Amoretti. Seemingly preferring to utilize legends about the artist rather than established facts, he occasionally wrote about work the artist did not execute: "in what is connected with a great name, much that is not real is often very stimulating. For the aesthetic philosopher, therefore, over and above the real Giorgione and his authentic extant works, there remains the *Giorgionesque* also—an influence, a spirit or type in art" (147 - 48). Preferring stimulating readings to textually accurate ones, Pater in his essay on Michelangelo freely chose his quotations from both the corrupt 1623 edition of the poems as well as from the authoritative version established by Guasti.

## IV   *Reception of* The Renaissance

Although *The Renaissance* with its seeming neopagan hedonism—the "deification of passion," as it was called in the *Saturday Review*—lay outside the Christian tradition of Oxford, certain readers hailed it with praise. Swinburne, to whom Pater sent a copy, wrote John Morley a few weeks after its publication: "I admire and enjoy Pater's work so heartily that I am somewhat shy of saying how much, ever since on my telling him once at Oxford how highly Rossetti as well as myself estimated his first papers in the *Fortnightly*, he replied to the effect that he considered them as owing their inspiration entirely to the example of my own work in the same line."[11] And Morley, who as editor of the *Fortnightly* had accepted those first papers, praised the book warmly in a review. He noted that the revived study of pagan art and poetry in *The Renaissance* was a protest similar to Tractarianism against the mechanical formalities and narrow popular creeds and equally a return to an older manifestation of the human spirit—to Greece rather than to the primitive church. Perhaps some indication of

Morley's own agnosticism appears when he notes that the fact that such "a serious writer should thus raise aesthetic interest to the throne lately filled by religion, only shows how void the old theologies have become."[12] And J. A. Symonds in an *Academy* review praised the style as having "scarcely a superfluous word or a hasty phrase," although privately Symonds' opinion of Pater was that "There is a kind of Death clinging to the man, wh[ich] makes his music (but heavens! how sweet that is!) a little faint and sickly. His view of life gives me the creeps, as old women say. I am sure it is a ghastly sham; & that live by it or not as he may do, his utterance of the theory to the world has in it a wormy hollow-voiced seductiveness of a fiend." Upon reading Pater some years later, Symonds reversed his opinion of the style also, for he found himself as he said, "wandering about among the precious sentences just as though I had lost myself in a sugar-cane plantation."[13] Others also were less enchanted by Pater's prose; they considered such emotion-charged words as *tender, lovely,* and *sweet* to be too sugary; and they were also rankled by Pater's philosophy of life. Margaret Oliphant, reviewing the volume in *Blackwood's Magazine,* found it "pretentious" and "artificial" and its author suffering from "some fundamental incompetence—some impotency of the mind and imagination."[14] George Eliot, who agreed firmly with Margaret Oliphant's hostile review in *Maga,* noted that the book "seems to me quite poisonous in its false principles and criticism and false conceptions of life."[15]

The hothouse world of Oxford, however, seems to have been even more outraged by the volume than the world at large. A few weeks after its publication, John Wordsworth (the clerical grandnephew of William Wordsworth and Pater's colleague, former student, and a fellow Old Mortal) wrote to Pater on March 17, 1873:

After a perusal of the book I cannot disguise from myself that the con-cluding pages adequately sum up the philosophy of the whole; and that that philosophy is an assertion, that no fixed principles either of religion or morality can be regarded as certain, that the only thing worth living for is momentary enjoyment and that probably or certainly the soul dissolves at death into elements which are destined never to reunite. . . . Could you have known the grief your words would be to many of your Oxford contem-poraries you might even have found no ignoble pleasure in refraining from uttering them. . . . The difference of opinion which you must be well aware has for some time existed between us must, I fear, become public and avowed, and it may be my duty to oppose you.

Indeed, like some heretical early Christian treatise, *The Renaissance* even received an episcopal condemnation from John Mackerness, bishop of Oxford, who in his *Charge Delivered to the Clergy of the Diocese of Oxford* devoted a good part of his address to the "current school of unbelief," citing extracts from the "Conclusion," and adding, "can we wonder that some who played an honourable part in Oxford life a generation since, refuse to let their sons imbibe lessons so alien from the lore they learned? Can you wonder that to young men who have imbibed this teaching the Cross is an offence, and the notion of a vocation to teach it an unintelligible craze?"[16] Actually, Pater did all that he could to remove unnecessary hesitation in the minds of young men that he was counseling about the fitness of a religious vocation. But, notwithstanding, the prejudice against him was so great that in 1874 Jowett moved to block Pater's way to the coveted office of proctor. Jowett's stinging epigram for Pater, "the demoralizing moralizer,"[17] accompanied, for good measure, the loss of the post and its £ 300-350 stipend. Two years later Pater became a candidate for Matthew Arnold's previously held professorship of poetry, but the opposition that developed was so bitter that Pater withdrew his name from consideration. Again, in 1885, after Ruskin's resignation of the Slade professorship, Pater's name was in contention for the fine arts position, but he was passed over by the electors.

In 1876, as Pater was preparing for the second edition of *The Renaissance*, W. J. Courthope, under the guise of a review of a Wordsworth edition, attacked the "emasculated principles of art" propounded by the "Conclusion," decrying what he called "the effeminate desires which Mr. Pater, the mouthpiece of our artistic 'culture,' would encourage in society."[18] Possibly the best known hostile reaction was W. H. Mallock's *roman à clef, The New Republic*, which was first serialized in *Belgravia* from June to December, 1876, and which satirized a number of well-known people, Pater among them. Burlesquing Pater as Mr. Rose, Mallock has Lady Ambrose shrilly complain: "He always seems to talk of everybody as if they had no clothes on." It is reported that Pater was more amused by Mallock's burlesque than pained; however, the caricature precisely anticipated the manner of Oscar Wilde and may not always have been taken in the spirit of satiric intensification. Many readers of Pater came to suppose that he could indeed remark in a languid monotone:

"I rather look upon life as a chamber, which we decorate as we would decorate the chamber of the woman or the youth that we love, tinting the walls of it with symphonies of subdued colour, and filling it with works of fair form, and with flowers, and with strange scents, and with instruments of music. And this can be done now as well—better, rather—than at any former time: since we know that so many of the old aims were false, and so cease to be distracted by them. We have learned the weariness of creeds, and know that for us the grave has no secrets. We have learned that the aim of life is life; and what does successful life consist in? Simply," said Mr. Rose, speaking very slowly, and with a soft solemnity, "in the consciousness of exquisite living—in the making our own each highest thrill of joy that the moment offers us—be it some touch of colour on the sea or on the mountains, the early dew in the crimson shadows of a rose, the shining of a woman's limbs in clear water, or . . . ."
Here unfortunately a sound of "Sh" broke softly from several mouths.[19]

When tea is served in the garden, these insinuations that Mr. Rose is a homosexual surface again when he helps Lady Grace's page, "a pretty boy with light hair," to arrange tumblers. Elsewhere Mr. Rose bargains animatedly to buy a pornographic book and describes in baroque detail " 'a delicious walk' " he took by the river, " 'hoping I might see some unfortunate cast herself from the Bridge of Sighs. It was a night I thought well in harmony with despair. Fancy,' exclaimed Mr. Rose, 'the infinity of emotions which the sad sudden splash in the dark river would awaken in one's mind—and all due to that one poem of Hood's!' "[20]

Mallock and the others had done their work effectively; for, as a result of such public censure, Pater suppressed the supposedly hedonistic "Conclusion" in the second edition of *The Renaissance* when it appeared in 1877. Feeling he had been deliberately misrepresented, Pater complained wryly to Gosse, "I wish they wouldn't call me a 'hedonist,' it produces such a bad effect on the minds of people who don't know Greek."[21]

## V   *Editions of* The Renaissance

Pater's publisher, Alexander Macmillan, proposed a second edition of *The Renaissance* as early as November, 1876; and Pater gladly accepted. In 1872, an amusing, polite but stubborn battle had occurred over the first edition, for Pater planned his volume as a total aesthetic experience that was addressed to the eye as well as to the mind. Evidently wishing his book to be artistic, he had proposed an "old-fashioned binding in paste-board with paper back and printed title, usual, I think, about thirty years ago, but not yet gone quite out of use" (November 2, 1872). Macmillan had replied that a return from cloth to paper boards and labels, which soiled easily, would be "like a recurrence to the *fig-leaf*." But Pater answered on November 11 that, "for a book on art to be bound quite in the ordinary way is, it seems to me, behind the times; and the difficulty of getting a book bound in cloth so as to be at all artistic, and indeed not quite the other way, is very great. I prefer in all cases the paper label, as the lettering is clumsy on a cloth binding, especially when as in this case the volume is a thin one . . . . I should like, with your permission, to select the kind of paper I think nicest, providing it is not more expensive than that ordinarily used."

However, lecturing Pater on the fundamentals of art, Macmillan had persisted in imposing his authority, citing a Glasgow publisher who had attempted using the old-fashioned binding and

been obliged to abandon it for cloth. He still uses paper labels—and gives a duplicate label to be stuck on when the old gets dirty! This is droll, to say the least of it. The bookseller or possessor has to remove the old one and get paste—which he possibly has not at hand—and repaste the clean one on. The *recurrence* has nothing admirable in it to me.

The use of inferior, unuseful materials cannot be needful to the realisation of any art which is of much value—at least I cannot see how. Gold lettering on cloth was an immense advance on the old paper boards, and was welcomed as such. I remember the period of change. I still possess books which are done up in smooth cloth with paper labels, and value them historically—just as I would value Adam's original fig-leaf, if I could find it.

But I will most gladly cede my tastes to yours as far as possible. I send you by this post a book in a style of binding which I devised for the author, and which he liked. His tastes were "artistic." He is an intimate friend of Mr. Burne-Jones and others who think in that line. Also the paper of the book is made to imitate the old wire-wove paper, which can only now be got in this mock rib, which is really rather pleasant to my own eye.[22]

In the end Pater had capitulated to Macmillan's prudent aesthetics, writing on November 13: "The volume you send seems to me a beautiful specimen of printing, and I should much like to have the same sort of paper."

Pater also evinced ominous signs in 1876 of wanting to dictate the format of the second edition when he replied to Macmillan's proposal: "I should like the new edition to be as perfect as possible." He then added that he would like to include an engraved vignette. In the same letter of November 15, 1876, he suggested the amended title of *The Renaissance, A Series of Studies in Art and Poetry, A New Edition.* Hopefully he added, "Also, perhaps the price might be raised." The price was indeed raised from 7s. 6d. to 10s. 6d.; and, though Pater's suggestion for the title was accepted, it was simplified to *The Renaissance: Studies in Art and Poetry.* The change of title followed upon Mrs. Pattison's criticism that the book was not an historical study. In the interests of accuracy, Pater also retitled his first essay "Two Early French Stories," for he had added the tale of Amis and Amile to that of Aucassin and Nicolette. This additional material may in part have been prompted by Pater's concern not to shorten an already "thin" volume, for the most significant alteration he planned for the second edition was to be the suppression of the offending "Conclusion." His discretion may have been owing not only to the continuing suspicion and hostility that clerical Oxford directed toward the don whose corrupting maxims were quoted by the marveling young, but possibly also to such peripheral scandals as the conviction of his homosexual friend Simeon Solomon (the Uffizi has a striking 1872 drawing of him by Solomon) which may have increased Pater's fear of confirming the image of Mr. Rose. But above all Pater's move to suppress the "Conclusion" was owing to John Wordsworth's letter: "Could you indeed have known the dangers into which you were likely to lead minds weaker than your own, you would, I believe, have paused." When, in the third edition, Pater restored the "Conclusion," he had toned down its iconoclastic contents by judicious substitutions of crucial words, adding in a footnote that it had been "omitted in the second edition of this book, as I conceived it might possibly mislead some of those young men into whose hands it might fall . . . . I have dealt more fully in *Marius the Epicurean* with the thoughts suggested by it" (*Renaissance*, 233). Wordsworth's "leading weaker minds into danger," echoing as it does in Pater's "misleading young men," must have been sharpened for Pater by a final ironic circumstance: Wordsworth had been elected in 1876 to the very proctorship for which he had been passed over.

Pater followed the publication of the new edition with minute attention. On January 30, 1877, he suggested: "The page might, I think, be shortened by one line . . . which to my eye is better for a broad space at the foot." On February 24, 1877, the proofs were near correction point, but Pater was still concerned about the binding and was not wholly satisfied with those offered him. On March

10 he prepared the advertisement and wanted it inserted in "your list of forthcoming books" in his "exact form." And three days later he suggested that, since "the subject of the vignette has no recognised name, being only a small drawing;—the words of the advertisement might run,—'with a vignette after Leonardo da Vinci, engraved by Jeens'; and in any gossip on the subject it might be described as being from a favourite drawing by L. da V. in the Louvre." Unknown to Pater, this drawing—"a face of doubtful sex, set in the shadow of its own hair, the cheek-line in high light against it, with something voluptuous and full in the eyelids and the lips," as Pater described it in his essay on Leonardo (115)—was an erroneous ascription to the artist. But Pater, enchanted with the proof of the vignette, wrote on March 31: "I . . . think it the most exquisite thing I have seen for a long time—a perfect reproduction of the beauty of the original, and absolutely satisfactory in the exactness and delicacy of its execution. My sincere thanks to Mr. Jeens. I should like to see an impression in red, that I may judge the colour. I suppose it ought to have a morsel of tissue paper inserted to cover it."

When, however, an early printing of the book was sent to him, he replied on April 26, 1877, with a rush of objections: the title page was insecurely fixed and the letters were not bitten in enough; the sheets were irregularly folded, making the margins unequal; the "Preface" was printed out of level with the rest of the book and smudged by the hands of the bookbinder; the vignette should have been pasted on, its attribution to Leonardo da Vinci was omitted, the name of the engraver was indistinct and it was printed awry, not exactly midway between the printing above and below it. But a month later, when the book came out, it was well bound, and despite some remaining flaws the volume must have pleased Pater, for several years later, when *Marius* was about to appear, he wrote to Macmillan: "I should like the volume to be, in size, quality of paper, and binding, precisely similar to the second edition of my Essays, which though simple in form, is, I think, a model of what such a book should be, as regards that matter" (September 14, 1884).

When in 1888 the third edition of *The Renaissance* appeared, two significant additions were made. The essay, "The School of Giorgione," printed in *The Fortnightly Review* (October 1877), was added; and the suppressed "Conclusion" was restored. Although Pater seemed to have planned originally to include the Giorgione study in the first edition, he canceled it after it was in proof, embodying some of its parts in the "Preface." Now, having been rewritten for the *Fortnightly*, it made its first appearance in the third edition. The "Conclusion" also was restored, showing the impact of criticism following its appearance in 1873, as well as further stylistic revision. Of the forty-one alterations made in the "Conclusion" for the third edition, five revisions remove offending allusions to religion; indeed, the words *religion, religious,* and *morality* are entirely absent and secular equivalents are substituted: "speculative culture," "abstract theory," "enthusiastic activity." Finally, instead of saying that the wisest spend their interval in art and song rather than in moral or religious activity, Pater inserted a biblical qualifying phrase, "at least among 'the children of this world,'" and left the adherents of art and song with some degree of priority, but allowed the status of those who are not among the children of this world to be taken as the reader wished. Thus, while maintaining his position on the relativity of experience, Pater had withdrawn anything which might extend the argument to the world of religion.

This sort of precautionary editing had already taken place in the second edition in the "Winckelmann" portrait where implicit and explicit anti-Christian remarks had been excised. An inconspicuous line from the essay on Michelangelo best illustrates this progressive softening in Pater's language up to 1888. In the first edition, he spoke of "the soothing influence which . . . the catholic church has often exerted over spirits [souls, 1871] too noble to be its subjects." In the second edition, the phrase "catholic church" became "Roman church" (elsewhere, "Roman Catholic church"); also he began capitalizing the third personal pronoun referring to God or Christ). In the third edition, he succumbed to a capital "C" for "Church" also, following, as he consistently did in the fourth edition, the high Anglican usage by saying "the Roman Church." Furthermore, in the 1888 edition the phrase "spirits too noble to be its subjects" was softened to "spirits too independent to be its subjects" (*Renaissance,* 94). Such alterations should not obscure the fact that Pater's assurance had grown sufficiently to allow him to restore the "Conclusion"; more remarkable still was the increased frankness in his treatment of a long quotation from Fauriel's version of *Aucassin et Nicolette* with which he concluded his opening chapter. Though cautiously (and awkwardly) left untranslated in the first edition, this glowing description of the pleasures of Hell

was timidly replaced in the second edition with an evasive statement calling it "a passage in which that note of rebellion is too strident for me to translate it here, though it has its more subdued
echoes in our English Chaucer"; but in the third edition he canceled
the evasive comment and replaced it with a half-page condensa-
tion of the original passage, in plain English.

Collation between the third edition (1888) and the fourth (1893),
the last to be published in Pater's life, shows that he made a
thorough revision yet once more. The "Conclusion," for example,
displays eighteen points of difference. The majority are concerned
with polishing and refining expression: four alterations of punctuation, nine changes of single words, four minor adjustments of phrasing, and one last modification for the sake of contemporary expec-
tations—"the love of art for art's sake" becomes "the love of art for
its own sake." Curiously, seven years after Pater's death, certain unexplained variants were introduced in the fifth edition of 1901
which closely follows the third edition, but gives a few fourth edition revisions and introduces several emendations (possibly not attributable to the errors of the printer) found neither in the third nor
fourth editions. Similarly, although the posthumous 1898 fourth
edition of *Marius* preserves a host of verbal changes, it fails to
preserve nearly a tenth of the changes in punctuation made for the
definitive edition. This suggests either deliberate editing by
someone after Pater's death or otherwise more than one set of
proofs for each of these last supervised editions. Perhaps Shadwell
inadvertently used these earlier sets of proofs for the posthumous
texts of 1898 and 1901. Although the text of *The Renaissance* in the
standard 1910 Library Edition is based on the final edition in
Pater's lifetime, that of *Marius* follows the corrupt 1898 posthumous
text.

CHAPTER 3

# *The Hero in* Marius the Epicurean

A lengthy, twelve-year interval elapsed between the publication of *Studies in the History of the Renaissance* in 1873 and the appearance of Pater's second book, *Marius the Epicurean,* in 1885. Besides arranging for the second edition of *The Renaissance* (1877), Pater was occupied during this period in publishing essays, reviews, and sketches and in experimenting with various literary projects before settling upon the composition of *Marius.* He considered doing a series of Shakespeare studies, which he began with "A Fragment on Measure for Measure" (1874) in the *Fortnightly Review;* and he meant to follow it with the study on which he was working in 1875 of "Love's Labour's Lost." But about this time his attention turned toward Greek myth; and the first of his Greek studies, "The Myth of Demeter and Persephone," was given in two public lectures for the Birmingham and Midland Institutes in November, 1875, and published the following year in the *Fortnightly.* This lecture, too, was to have been the first essay in a projected series to be called *Dionysus and Other Studies.* Although the type for the volume had been set, Pater changed his mind and asked Macmillan to cancel it and paid £ 35 to cover the printing expenses. His third plan was to publish a series of imaginary portraits. On April 17, 1878, Pater wrote to George Grove, editor of *Macmillan's Magazine,* as follows: "I send you by this post a M.S. entitled *The House and the Child,* and should be pleased if you should like to have it for Macmillan's Magazine. It is not, as you may perhaps fancy, the first part of a work of fiction, but is meant to be complete in itself; though the first of a series, as I hope, with some real kind of sequence in them, and which I should be glad to send to *you.* I call the M.S. a portrait, and mean readers, as they might do on seeing a portrait, to begin speculating—what came of him?" A second portrait, entitled "An English Poet," was begun but never finished.

I   *The Art of the Imaginary Portrait*

Prior to the publication of "The Child in the House," Pater had written in *The Renaissance* of historical personages mythically; he had also written in his Greek studies of mythical figures historically. But in "The Child in the House" he created his first *imaginary* portrait—a weaving of history and myth around an imaginative motif. These imaginary portraits occupy a significant place in the history of British fiction; for as nineteenth-century fiction expanded in scope and evolved in technique, it carried with it a sort of penumbra of experiments in which definitely fictional elements were applied in works that could not qualify as stories or as novels by any conventional definition. There was a wide range of nineteenth-century "semi-fiction," such as Robert Southey's *Colloquies on Society,* John Wilson's *Noctes Ambrosianae,* Carlyle's *Sartor Resartus,* Arnold's *Friendship's Garland,* and Walter Savage Landor's *Imaginary Conversations* (which together with Sainte-Beuve's *Portraits contemporains* perhaps supplied Pater with his "imaginary portraits" classification)—all of which formed a context for what Edmund Gosse has called Pater's "delicate essays in criticism by fiction."[1] Whereas Pater's work may most nearly be related to certain stories of Rossetti and Morris (anticipating perhaps Yeats' "Romantic Mythologies"), the usual procedure of readers confronted by work outside the traditional generic categories has been to multiply names. *Marius the Epicurean*—"an Imaginary Portrait of a peculiar type of mind in the time of Marcus Aurelius," as described by Pater in a letter (July 22, 1883) to Violet Paget—is called "ideological" or "critical" or "ruminative" fiction; the shorter portraits are called "character studies," "narrative" or "fictive" essays, "prose romances," "prose idylls," and sometimes "récits," "fabulae," or "rêveries."

One might note that the distinguishing characteristic technically of this genre of Aesthetic portraiture is its emphasis not on action, but on significant acts of perception, not on immediate gesture and utterance, but on their psychological equivalents, that is, finely discriminated "sensations and ideas" (the subtitle of *Marius*). One might even argue for a flexible understanding of Pater's fiction that would include many of the quasi-historical portraits in *The Renaissance* and elsewhere. The creative latitude is somewhat greater in the imaginary portraits, but the aesthetic, literary, and fictional portraits each depict a similar Aesthetic temperament. The aim of Pater as critic and as writer of fiction was always the realization of the living personality behind the philosophic idea or work of art: "all true knowledge," he writes, "will be like the knowledge of a person, of living persons," adding that "human persons and their acts" are visible representations "of the eternal qualities of 'the eternal' " (*Plato*, 146, 268). And again Pater reminds one: "If in reading Plato, for instance, the philosophic student has to reconstruct for himself, as far as possible, the general character of an *age*, he must also, so far as he may, reproduce the portrait of a *person*" (*Plato*, 124 - 25). One can see, then, a strong resemblance and continuity between the objective of Pater's critical writings and the goal which he held out for his imaginary portraits: "Imaginary—and portraits: they present not an action, a story; but a character, personality, revealed especially in outward detail."[2]

If the prospective critic expects of these Aesthetic portraits the sort of low-mimetic "formal realism" found in some of the historical fiction of Pater's contemporaries, he is bound to be frustrated. Pater's is a style expressive of feelings and attitudes because his subject is not outward events, but inward vision. This interior quality of his fiction owes much to Rossetti's sketch, "Hand and Soul" (1850). Rossetti's hero, Chiaro dell' Erma, entertained from the first a "longing after a visible embodiment of his thoughts." Chiaro finds fame in his service of beauty; he faithfully transcribes reality; but, dissatisfied, he turns to didactic moralizing and loses his audience. He discovers that his faith had not failed him, but that his abstract moralizing had, when his soul lays a charge upon him: "Chiaro, servant of God, take now thine art unto thee, and paint me thus, as I am, to know me . . . and so shall thy soul stand before thee always and perplex thee no more."[3] The vocation of the artist is, therefore, to body forth neither an artificial value system nor a set of real-life occurrences, but rather an inner vision, a complete *dramatis personae* of the soul. Pater draws this same distinction as Rossetti between fact and the artist's "imaginative sense of fact" when speaking of Wordsworth's vision: "For just in proportion as the writer's aim, consciously or unconsciously, comes to be the transcribing, not of the world, not of mere fact, but of his sense of it, he becomes an artist, his work *fine* art. . . . And further, all beauty is in the long run only *fineness* of truth, or what we call expression, the finer accommodation of speech to that vision within" (*Appreciations*, 9 - 10).

With Rossetti, then, Pater agrees that the artist's vocation is to present a kind of spiritualized autobiography. But, like Dilthey, Pater also conceives of the artist as dramatizing the essential continuity between his own consciousness in the present and that of other selves existing in the past—dramatizing the continuity of mind within the empirical reality of history by re-creating in language or other artistic media an inner vision expressive of "a common mental atmosphere." By portraying character, not action, Pater is really giving a personification of the common artistic atmosphere in which his hero lives—Renaissance or Antonine Italy, for example. Writing of the Greek ideal in his essay on Winckelmann, Pater notes that "from a few stray antiquarianisms, a few faces cast up sharply from the waves, Winckelmann, as his manner was, divines the temperament of the antique world, and that in which it had delight" (*Renaissance*, 208 - 209). The faces of Pater's heroes float just so upon the culture of their age. Marius' "sensations and ideas" are conveyed through a variety of literary genres collectively far richer than actual lived experience: a Platonic fable in the form of a translation of Apuleius' tale of Cupid and Psyche; stanzas from the second-century Latin poem, the *Pervigilium Veneris;* orations by Marcus Aurelius and Cornelius Fronto; translations of two dialogues by Lucian, *The Hermotimus* and *The Halcyon;* selections from the *Epistle of the Churches of Lyons and Vienne;* and various historical quotations, epitaphs, hymns, and so forth. Pater's novel is one in which the background, the *Zeitgeist* of the second century, has become the foreground by virtue of its personification in Marius.

The idea of a personality as a fantastically complex palimpsest woven from the flux was implied in the "Conclusion" to *The Renaissance.* As was noted earlier, Pater, in describing the "perpetual weaving and unweaving of ourselves" (236), depicted human identity as a crossing—a centripetal nexus or node—of the elemental threads necessary for the creation of life. This conception underlies Pater's discussion of how Dionysus became the "spiritual form" of leaves and dew—"the name of Dionysus recalled to the Greek mind, under a single imaginable form, an outward body of flesh presented to the senses, and comprehending, as its animating soul, a whole world of thoughts, surmises, greater and less experiences; . . . the image of an actual person, in whom, somehow, all those impressions of the vine and its fruit, as the highest type of the life of the green sap, had become incorporate" (*Greek Studies,*

10, 37). Possibly Pater's most famous example of the "spiritual form" is his description of the Mona Lisa. From Leonardo's childhood, writes Pater, Mona Lisa's face had been "defining itself on the fabric of his dreams" (*Renaissance*, 124). Like Rossetti's Chiaro who painted the manifestation of his soul, so Pater's Leonardo found the face of his dreams in La Gioconda's house. She is his "ideal lady" into whose beauty is condensed "all the thought and experience of the world." She becomes thereby, like all the Aesthetic heroes, a face cast up sharply from the waves of history; in her "spiritual form" the growth, decay, and renewal of nature and of culture is personified. Refined from actual life by Leonardo's art and afterwards rerefined by Pater's critical-imaginative skills, Mona Lisa becomes the visionary emblem of Pater's fraternity with Leonardo and of Leonardo's continuity with the historical process. Later, in *Marius the Epicurean*, Pater similarly dramatizes this unity of personality with history; but whereas in *The Renaissance* he chooses merely to reimagine the goddess whom Leonardo himself beheld, in the novel Pater portrays autobiographically in Marius the aesthetic sensibility linking his present consciousness to the historic past objectified in St. Cecilia and her church.

## II  "The Child in the House"

"The Child in the House" is a transitional work between *The Renaissance* and *Marius*. In it, reminiscent of the Romantic poet who discovers in nature the sacred light of his own inwardness, Pater portrays his own artistic sensibility as uniting for mutual enrichment an inner and outer reality. As an autobiographical account of how he came to be the advocate of a kind of Keatsian "Life of Sensations" or (to switch from Keats to Wordsworth and adapt the subtitle of *The Prelude*) as an introduction to "the growth of an artistic mind," Pater's portrait consists almost entirely in a series of vivid childhood impressions that shape the faculty of imagination, the artistic sensibility of the adult mind. Although it has its foundation in actual recollections, the portrait idealizes Pater's childhood so that the inessential and incongruous aspects are excluded. In those impressions which inscribe themselves indelibly upon his consciousness, Pater-Florian experiences the accumulation of discrete moments in a single vivid and ideal instant—an inner, powerfully personal sense of time. Pater is especially indebted to Wordsworth for identifying this more-than-temporal consciousness and locating its source in childhood. The operative passage, to which Pater alludes in his essay on Wordsworth, is found in Book XII of *The Prelude:*

> There are in our existence spots of time,
> That with distinct pre-eminence retain
> A renovating virtue, whence . . . our minds
> Are nourished and invisibly repaired.
> . . . . . . . . . . . . . . . . . . . . . . . . . . . . . . . . . .
> This efficacious spirit chiefly lurks
> Among those passages of life that give
> Profoundest knowledge to what point, and how,
> The mind is lord and master—outward sense
> The obedient servant of her will. Such moments
> Are scattered everywhere, taking their date
> From our first childhood.

These Wordsworthian "spots of time" are similar to the Paterian "moment of vision" during which the natural object, as it moves into the consciousness, is "enriched by the whole colour and expression of the whole circumjacent world, concentrated upon, or as it were at focus in, it" (*Plato*, 158).

In an encounter with a hawthorn, Florian's creative imagination is born: "A garden gate, usually closed, stood open; and lo! within, a great red hawthorn in full flower, embossing heavily the bleached and twisted trunk and branches, so aged that there were but few green leaves thereon—a plumage of tender, crimson fire out of the heart of the dry wood. . . . For the first time, he seemed to experience a passionateness in his relation to fair outward objects, an inexplicable excitement in their presence, which disturbed him, and from which he half longed to be free" (*Miscellaneous Studies*, 185 - 86). Childhood's preaesthetic environment (natural beauty, not yet artistic beauty) has prepared in him a receptivity to the beauty of aesthetic objects that someday he will apprehend in a fashion similar to the hawthorn blossoms. Describing this adult experience, Pater says that Giorgione's art consists in "profoundly significant and animated instants, a mere gesture, a look, a smile, perhaps—some brief and wholly concrete moment—into which, however, all the motives, all the interests and effects of a long history have condensed themselves, and which seem to absorb past and future in an intense consciousness of the present. Such ideal instants [are] . . . exquisite pauses in time, in which, arrested thus, we seem to be spectators of all the fulness of existence, and which are like some consummate extract or quintessence of life" (*Renaissance*, 150). Childhood in particular is charged with such luminous moments and is therefore crucial to the maturation of the artist who will batten on such revelatory experiences. This is why Pater suggests that da Vinci's Mona Lisa harked back to images in Leonardo's childhood (an intuition which for other reasons earned Pater approval in Freud's psychoanalytical study of Leonardo); from childhood "those shadowy recollections," as Wordsworth calls them in his "Intimations Ode," flow out to "uphold us."

Yet out of childhood also flow impressions of pain and fear. The child of *The Prelude* who "grew up / Fostered alike by beauty and by fear" (Book I) is given in the Paterian setting a more disturbing awareness: "with this desire of physical beauty mingled itself early the fear of death—the fear of death intensified by the desire of beauty" (*Miscellaneous Studies*, 189 - 90). This relation of death to beauty had been previously noted in the concluding paragraphs of the 1868 Morris review (thus bringing the "Conclusion" and "The Child in the House" into close thematic association) in which Pater described "the pagan spirit" of Morris' poems—their "continual suggestion, pensive or passionate, of the shortness of life; this is contrasted with the bloom of the world and gives new seduction to it; the sense of death and the desire of beauty; the desire of beauty quickened by the sense of death."[4] Although aesthetic appreciation is enhanced by life's transience, Florian has not yet been able to reconcile himself to the ongoing process that will rejoin to the flux all manifestations of beauty, his own life included; he is haunted by those "waxen, resistless faces" (190) in the Munich cemetery subsiding without the vivifying flame back to their first elements.

The child's is a world of dreams—dreams of beauty potentially frustrated by death. But for the artist and for such as live in the spirit of art, moments of aesthetic ecstasy offer a way of expanding the brief interval of life. To live in these luminous moments of more-than-temporal dimension is to breach that "wall of custom" (177) behind which, in the words of the "Conclusion," the mind commonly keeps "as a solitary prisoner its own dream of a world" (*Renaissance*, 235). The child's house, standing "among high garden-walls" (*Miscellaneous Studies*, 176), possesses the same ambivalence as the wall of custom; it can be either a vitalizing or deadening influence, depending on Florian's success in progressively identifying its externalities as no longer foreign but as that in

which his dreams consist. The open gate through which the child
passes to obtain the vision of the hawthorn is just such an escape
from potential entrapment—an escape that is also foreshadowed in
the release of the starling and symbolized in the rescue of the pet
bird from the closed house. That the cagelings symbolize Florian's
soul is evident from Pater's subsequent use of the image to describe
Marius' freeing of his trapped birds, at the request of his mother,
because his soul itself, so she told him, was like a bird to be carried
unsoiled across a crowded marketplace (*Marius*, I, 22). This image
occurs again in the first of Pater's portraits written after *Marius* in
which the narrator glimpses a bird caught in a stone church and
compares its plight to her own entrapment in time.

"The Child in the House" had opened with Florian's sympathetic act of helping an aged man (a Wordsworthian figure of
humble dignity) along the road with his burden; it closes with his
charitable rescue of the helpless bird. Set within the framework of a
dream-vision, the images of the old man and bird, together with the
child, the house, and the road, suggest the symbolic theme of stages
in life's pilgrimage. At one point Pater described the lifeless body as
"a worn-out garment left at a deserted lodging" (*Miscellaneous
Studies*, 190), and several passages in his later writings amplify this
soul-body - body-house analogy: " 'The house in which she lives
. . . is for the orderly soul . . . only an expansion of the body; as
the body, according to the philosophy of Swedenborg, is but a
process, an expansion, of the soul.' . . . So it must needs be in a
world which is itself, we may think, together with that bodily 'tent'
or 'tabernacle,' only one of many vestures for the clothing of the
pilgrim soul, to be left by her, surely, as if on the wayside, worn-out
one by one, as it was from her, indeed, they borrowed what momentary value or significance they had" (*Marius*, II, 92 - 93). Pater
utilized this relation again in his essay on Rossetti in which he
echoes the concluding drama of Florian's childhood—"the house
one must quit, yet taking perhaps, how much of its quietly active
light and colour along with us!—grown now to be a kind of raiment
to one's body, as the body, according to Swedenborg, is but the raiment of the soul" (*Appreciations*, 214).

If men rise on stepping stones of their dead selves to higher
things, it is only natural that at the close of the portrait the deserted
house should strike Florian "like the face of one dead"
(*Miscellaneous Studies*, 196). The narrative has returned to the
physical house from which both Florian's actual life and mental

journey began, and with his departing act of charity a new stage in his development is symbolized. At the end of the "Winckelmann" essay, Pater had required of modern art that it satisfy the spirit. "And what does the spirit need in the face of modern life? The sense of freedom" (*Renaissance*, 231). By his recovery of the pet bird, Florian is, in effect, rescuing his expanding, maturing soul from the trap of a limited world of natural beauty in order to deliver it into the larger sensuous domain of artistic beauty. Throughout the portrait, recurrent images of reflected light as well as references to pictures of sacred personages suggest that Florian's goal is to find in the forms of culture the ideal reflection of the human image, himself spiritualized. Although leaving behind the house and its edenic garden, Florian gains through cultural experience the greater vision of that "sacred double" which is "at once the reflex and the pattern" (*Miscellaneous Studies*, 194) of that diaphanous selfhood the child had only glimpsed.

Arthur Symons reports that Pater told him that "The Child in the House" was designed "to be the first chapter of a romance which was to show 'the poetry of modern life,' something, he said, as Aurora Leigh does."[5] Perhaps Symons misunderstood Pater's idea of a "series" or possibly Pater changed his plan; at any rate had not the composition of *Marius* intervened, the unfinished "English Poet" would have been the second serial installment. Although Pater considered including the orphaned "Child in the House" in his 1887 collection of *Imaginary Portraits*, he chose to omit it because, as he wrote William Sharp on May 23, 1887, "I . . . found it would need many alterations, which I felt disinclined to make just then. I hope it may be included in some future similar series." Symons recalled that as late as 1889 Pater "still spoke of finishing it"—the poetic romance of modern life that replaced the idea of a series—but "he was conscious that he could never continue it in the same style, and that it would not be satisfactory to rewrite it in his severer, later manner."[6] In 1894, Pater made minor alterations for a private printing of the portrait to be sold at a summer "fête" at which a performance of *Alice in Wonderland* was to be given in the Worcester College gardens. And so "The Child in the House" stands as the first installment in a never-completed series; it is accompanied only by the unfinished gods-in-exile tale of an English poet begotten by Dionysus upon a young girl who first saw his image when she found a long-lost Roman coin. What other plans Pater may have had for that aborted series will never be known.

The tentative, uncertain direction of Pater's literary program between *The Renaissance* and *Marius* may well have been the result of a defensiveness over the supposedly hedonistic philosophy propounded in the "Conclusion" which did not allow him to pursue his projects free of anxiety. It has become fashionable to interpret "The Child in the House" as a backing away from the espousal in *The Renaissance* of a private life of exquisite sensations and a turning toward the social, collective ideal of sympathy that culminated in *Marius*. The basis for this interpretation is that the portrait appeared only a year after the offending "Conclusion" had been suppressed and that Pater felt the need to produce a "corrective" to the doctrines of 1873. But although the note of sympathy is struck in "The Child in the House," Pater's main aim is to defend the morality of aesthetic ecstasy itself by dealing in a semi-autobiographical way with the philosophy of his first volume. Certainly for hasty readers of *The Renaissance* the cause of the gem-like flame seemed to leave little room for the ideal of sympathy, but Pater's cautionary stress upon Winckelmann's narrowness in pursuit of beauty and his correlative emphasis upon Pico's humanistic sympathy might have suggested to Pater's more reflective readers that his "art-for-art's sake" pronouncements were shapings of the phrase directed against a dominant Ruskinesque aesthetic didacticism.

By treating consecutive stages (childhood and school) in the development of the Aesthetic personality, "The Child in the House" and "An English Poet" seem to anticipate *Marius*, which also deals with the issues raised in the "Conclusion," albeit transposed historically to the second century, by depicting stages in the growth of an Aesthetic personality. In a sense "An English Poet" seems to be a transitional work occupying a halfway house between fictionalized autobiography and the more objectively fictional portraits of the 1880s. On the one hand, it is still allied to the personal events of Pater's life; but, on the other, it has a more elaborate setting and more developed sequence of actions. Already Pater is striking out toward *Marius* by moving away from the loose structure of linked impressions in "The Child in the House." Yet that first portrait appeared at a crucial juncture in his literary development. On one of those small scraps of paper which he habitually used to compose notes to himself, Pater wrote: "Child in the House: voilà, the germinating, original, source, specimen, of all my *imaginative* work."[7]

### III "A Fourth Sort of Religious Phase"

To determine exactly at what time Pater's attention turned toward the creation of *Marius the Epicurean*, the major literary work of his career, is difficult. Although prior to 1881 he may have contemplated writing a portrait set in Roman times, the Brasenose library records show that his research did not begin until spring of that year. Between December, 1882, and January, 1883, Pater spent a month in Rome engaged in background research for his novel; he devoted "all this time to the galleries and churches and was so tired in the evening he was quite unfit for social intercourse" (February 24, 1883). The novel itself is dated 1881 - 84 and was published by Macmillan in two volumes in March, 1885. To be free to work on *Marius*, Pater had resigned his Brasenose tutorship, although this meant a considerable loss of income; he continued, however, as lecturer and, until his death, he held the office of dean. The deanship, though largely honorary, entitled Pater to a canopied stall near the college chapel altar, and during term-time every Sunday morning and evening without fail, he could be seen in this conspicuous seat in reverent meditation. Pater was, however, a bit pained that the governing body of the college acquiesed with such alacrity in his resignation of tutorial duties, possibly implying that his colleagues had not been wholly satisfied with the discharge of his responsibilities. But, freed from the petty interruptions to which a tutor is always liable, Pater could allocate more time to the planning and execution of his literary projects. Apparently, he did not mean *Marius* to stand alone, for on January 28, 1886, he wrote to an American correspondent that the novel "is designed to be the first of a kind of trilogy, or triplet, of works of a similar character; dealing with the same problems, under altered historical conditions. The period of the second of the series would be at the end of the 16th century, and the place France: of the third, the time, probably the end of the last century—and the scene, England." Pater's unfinished second novel, *Gaston de Latour*, was to have been the sixteenth-century French study; of the third novel, only a few unpublished fragments exist. Each volume of the trilogy would have dealt with the problem of religious belief—with the impact of the relative spirit on moral absolutes in the age in which the hero lived.

The problem of spiritual crisis seems in the 1880s to have superseded Pater's earlier concern in the 1870s with the worship of beauty. These two interests are related; but, in contrast to *The*

*Renaissance*, the tone of *Marius* is not so iconoclastic; and the attention given to the problem of religious development is, therefore, proportionally greater. To a degree, *Marius* is undeniably autobiographical, and one may say of the Pater revealed in its pages, as Pater had said of Blaise Pascal in an unfinished essay, that he stands "as if at the very centre of a perpetually maintained tragic crisis holding the faith steadfastly, but amid the well-poised points of essential doubt all around him and it. It is no mere calm supersession of a state of doubt by a state of faith; the doubts never die, they are only just kept down in a perpetual *agonia*" (*Miscellaneous Studies*, 77). This tendency to examine critically revealed religion had brought Pater initially in the 1870s to the skeptical conclusion that truth is relative and that in matters of belief suspended judgment is the most reasonable attitude. He inherited here a tradition that originated with Pyrrho of Elis, founder and inspirer of the skeptical schools of Greek philosophy, which was transmitted to nineteenth-century England through Sextus Empiricus, the Church Fathers, the medieval Nominalists, Pico della Mirandola, Pascal, Sir Thomas Browne, Montaigne, and others. Victorian skepticism, though not revived exclusively by *The Origin of Species*, might nevertheless conveniently be dated from this 1859 watershed. A decade later Henry Sidgwick observed:

We are growing . . . more sceptical in the proper sense of the word: we suspend our judgment much more than our predecessors, and much more contentedly: we see that there are many sides to many questions: the opinions that we do hold we hold if not more loosely, at least more at arm's length: we can imagine how they appear to others, and can conceive ourselves not holding them. We are losing in faith and confidence: if we are not failing in hope, our hopes at least are becoming more indefinite; and we are gaining in impartiality and comprehensiveness of sympathy.[8]

That same year the eminent man of science, John Tyndall, was urging the idea upon the students at University College, London, that "there are periods when the judgment ought to remain in suspense, the data on which a decision might be based being absent. This discipline of suspending the judgment is a common one in science, but not so common as it ought to be elsewhere. . . . We ought to learn to wait. We ought assuredly to pause before closing with the advances of those expounders of the ways of God to men, who offer us intellectual peace at the modest cost of intellectual life."[9]

In the 1880s, Pater showed himself less a Pyrrhonist than a

"probabilist"—a form of skepticism that Sextus Empiricus had distinguished from the absolute skepticism of Pyrrho. Skeptical probabilism, while believing that certainty exists nowhere, accepts the sufficiency of probable truth in governing practical actions. Faith, for Pater, is hope in the actuality of "the Great Possibility" (*Essays*, 35); and his creation of the Aesthetic hero is an attempt to define this hopefulness that is possible in a strongly rationalistic age. Marius the Epicurean, his most famous aesthete, was clearly an answer to religious skepticism. In the *Athenaeum*, a reviewer wrote of *Marius* that Pater "observed to a friend at Oxford, in an intimate conversation soon after it appeared, that it was written 'to show the necessity of religion.' "[10] This statement is also supported by Pater's letter of July 22, 1883. In referring to an article by Violet Paget in which three types of rationalistic unbelief are delineated—optimistic Voltaireanism, aesthetic pessimism, and militant, humanitarian atheism—Pater wrote the author that he considered the composition of *Marius* to be "a sort of duty" because "I think that there is a fourth sort of religious phase possible for the modern mind, over and above those presented in your late admirable paper in the Contemporary, the conditions of which phase it is the main object of my design to convey." If one wished, one might say the Aesthetic hero embodied this "fourth sort of religious phase" which, minimally stated, is a form of hopeful agnosticism or probabilistic skepticism. The extent of Pater's eventual concession to Christianity is perhaps best gauged by a passage he wrote as an introduction to a translation by C. L. Shadwell of Dante's *Purgatorio*. To Pater,

An age of faith, if such there ever were, our age certainly is not: an age of love, all its pity and self-pity notwithstanding, who shall say?—in its religious scepticism, however, especially as compared with the last century in its religious scepticism, an age of hope, we may safely call it, of a development of religious hope or hopefulness, similar in tendency to the development of the doctrine of Purgatory in the church of the Middle Age:—*quel secondo regno / Ove l'umano spirito si purga:*—a world of merciful second thoughts on one side, of fresh opportunities on the other, useful, serviceable, endurable, in contrast alike with that *mar si crudele* of the *Inferno*, and the blinding radiancy of Paradise.[11]

Although Pater wrote this in 1892, toward the close of his life, it represents those qualities of religious hopefulness which the temperament of his Aesthetic hero is meant to embody. Pater's heroes, imaginary and historical alike, are neither figures of nihilism in an age of disbelief nor saints in an age of faith; rather, they are questors after religious hope in a skeptical age.

## IV   Marius: *Part the First*

As it stands, *Marius the Epicurean* is an autobiographically colored study of a Roman youth who serves as amanuensis to the emperor Marcus Aurelius; and if one looks not for a plot line, but for a cumulative pattern of successively ever more significant moments of perception, the novel will not disappoint. Marius' quest for the vision of Ideal beauty, foreshadowed in the allegory of Cupid and Psyche, develops in terms of four religions (two of which may be called religious philosophies) that are associated with four personalities: the religion of Numa with the mother of Marius, Epicureanism with Flavian, Stoicism with Aurelius, and Christianity with Cornelius. Each of the four books into which the novel is divided depicts an expansion of Marius' initial dreamy awareness as a child at White-nights of the "possibilities" for vision. Pater parallels Marius' mental journey from illusion through sadness to vision with a physical journey from home to city and from city to church. The addition of the physical journey suggests that the object of Marius' quest is not some purely intellectual assent to Christianity; it implies, rather, a movement outward from a mental world of dreams toward an actual vision of those dreams incarnated materially. Marius undergoes a process of discovering in the world of physical sensations the clarification and meaning of his earliest experiences of mother love and home (though this is not to suggest that in some simplistic psychosexual way he is looking for Mother).

This quest for the identification of inner vision with outer manifestation is presented and analyzed through a pattern of subtle comparisons and contrasts. Chief among the contrasts is the dialectic between Venus (and her varied manifestations as Faustina and assorted courtesans) and Psyche. Marius does not so much reject the harlot in order to find the virgin as perceive that in Cecilia corruption and purity coalesce in the same manner as, mythically, Persephone and Kore coalesce within the great mother Demeter. Whereas in *The Renaissance* the epiphany of Persephone-Kore in the guise of Lady Lisa only tentatively structured the loosely-knit portraits, in *Marius* it becomes the dramatically unifying event. Burying her child in the underworld of the catacombs, Cecilia (anticipated in the dolorous figure of Marius' mother) is not less than Lisa an expression of the ceaselessly interacting antinomies of generation and decay. Like Chiaro who painted the manifestation of his soul or like Leonardo who found the face of his dreams in La Gioconda's house, so this female embodiment of Marius' gradually evolving inner vision of ideal beauty is beheld at last. In his last book, *Plato and Platonism,* Pater asks rhetorically of Socrates, who had always discounted visual experience, "Ah, good master! was the eye so contemptible an organ of knowledge after all?" (97). As he lies dying, Marius does not assent intellectually to Christianity, yet certain sensitive readers will perceive that in Pater's scheme vision is faith. "One learns nothing from him," Pater quotes Goethe as remarking about Winckelmann, "but one becomes something" (*Renaissance,* 185). In precisely that sense, Marius assents to nothing but "becomes something." In the Christian villa, where he has been abandoned by soldiers on his way to trial and certain execution, Marius experiences in his last moments, with the vision of Cecilia fresh in his mind, a sense of his continuity with the historic process; that is, with Cecilia's church as it will come to be in history. By a finer sense of vision as a transforming instrument than Socrates or certain recent critics of the novel itself will allow, Pater has his early Christians bury Marius as a martyr. Although set in the second century, *Marius* is Pater's essay toward defining those qualities of religious hopefulness possible in Victorian England so many centuries later.

As a sensitive young boy, born about A.D. 147 but very much like Pater himself, Marius grows to adolescence on the Tuscan estate, White-nights, in an atmosphere of pagan piety and rural simplicity. In its physical aspects the family villa suggests something of that inherited "vesture of the past" (*Plato,* 72) which clothes each succeeding generation. Personified with a "face," White-nights is not only a clothing of the body in the same way that the body is raiment for the soul, but is itself nearly indistinguishable from its surroundings, its forms continually growing and dying, weaving and unweaving as the years go by, like a natural organism in evolution: "Two centuries of the play of the sea-wind were in the velvet of the mosses which lay along its inaccessible ledges and angles. . . . The pavement of the hall had lost something of its evenness; but, though a little rough to the foot, polished and cared for like a piece of silver, looked, as mosaic-work is apt to do, its best in old age" (*Marius,* I, 19). This identity between the villa and its environing flux is suggested especially by Pater's description of the "sea-wind" in the "mosses" which lay along the "angles" of the villa. It is almost as if the angles of the building had been sculpted not by human hands but by nature, the contours of the wind-shaped mosses marking out the villa's angles. One should compare this with the later description of Marius' withdrawal into the Sabine hills outside Rome where the old temples were "seemingly of a piece with the ancient fundamental rock" (II, 65). Nearly all the buildings in the novel reveal a close integration with nature, yet also are expressive of the personal values of their inhabitants. Thus White-nights objectifies the religion of Numa; the villa at Tusculum objectifies Epicureanism; Aurelius' chambers objectify Stoicism; Cecilia's house objectifies Christianity; and the dusty villa where Cornelius and Marius pause on their journey to Rome objectifies the Empire, the world itself.

Although White-nights, like Florian's house, came to be a part of the child's life, "inward and outward being woven through and through each other into one inextricable texture" (*Miscellaneous Studies*, 173), for the young Marius the dream within has not as yet found its incarnation in the vision without. The name *White-nights* itself implies, Pater says, "nights of not quite blank forgetfulness, but passed in continuous dreaming, only half veiled by sleep" (*Marius*, I, 14). The goddess of this veiled, twilight state is Persephone, who holds "the poppy, emblem of sleep and death by its narcotic juices, of life and resurrection by its innumerable seeds, of the dreams, therefore, that may intervene between falling asleep and waking" (*Greek Studies*, 148 - 49). Keats' "Ode to a Nightingale" ("Was it a vision, or a waking dream?/Fled is that music:—Do I wake or sleep?") and Wordsworth's "Intimations Ode" (lines 58 - 77 especially) provide Pater with familiar Romantic parallels. For Keats the quest for a vision of ideal beauty is continually frustrated by the intrusion of the conceptual mind, and for Wordsworth "the glory and the dream" of childhood lasts only until the "prison" of adulthood closes upon the growing boy. For Marius, too, the seeds of man's inexorable fate are already contained within his paradise of White-nights. Taking a walk one day, Marius encounters breeding snakes which taunt him with the spectre of his own death and with the ironic insinuation that their sinister ugliness might be the ultimate reality—might, indeed, survive his quest for truth in beauty. In all their intimations of death, insanity, temptation, evil wisdom, moral depravity, and twisted sexuality, the writhing serpents so repugnant to him embody that dread darkness of his own "humanity, dusty, and sordid," the suffering aspect of man, a "lower side of the real world" (*Marius*, I, 23 - 24). Marius' aspirations are no longer fulfilled by a simple delight in the sensuous forms of nature; the disembodied dreams of his soul have become delirium.

While still a child, Marius is taken to Aesculapius' temple for what, elsewhere, Pater had called a cure of "overwrought spiritualities" by a return to the "life of the senses" (*Appreciations* [1889], 224). The quiet, fresh atmosphere of the college and the teachings of Galen, the Roman physician, offer an antidote to the gloomy ritual slaughters of Marius' hereditary religion and expand his original ideal of the family worship of Numa into an awareness of the larger human community. As an expression of the continuity of mind within the flux, synthesizing the antinomies of life and death, innocence and corruption, the ongoing community or city of mankind provides the key to Marius' escape from the trap of physical nature into a larger, yet still entirely sensuous and visible, form. On his last morning at the temple, Marius looks through a hidden opening: "What he saw was like the vision of a new world, by the opening of some unsuspected window in a familiar dwelling-place. . . . It might have seemed the very presentment of a land of hope, its hollows brimful of a shadow of blue flowers; and lo! on the one level space of the horizon, in a long dark line, were towers and a dome: and that was Pisa.—Or Rome, was it?" (*Marius*, I, 40). Marius discovers that the dwelling place of this world, so familiar and seemingly unenchanted, may afford a hopeful vision to the questing soul, but its indeterminacy ("Pisa.—Or Rome?") indicates the distance he must still cover before that vision is clearly perceived.

Soon after the death of his mother, Marius moves to Pisa to go to school. "As in that gray monastic tranquility of the villa, inward voices from the reality of unseen things had come to him abundantly; so here . . . it was the reality, the tyrannous reality, of things visible that was borne in upon him" (I, 47). Marius begins his education at Pisa on the very principles laid down in his creator's famous "Conclusion" to *The Renaissance*, reading Heraclitus and cultivating direct sensation. Perhaps Pater is recalling that Pisa was the city where Rossetti's young hero, Chiaro dell' Erma, came to study art and discovered the beauty and passion of the world. At any rate, Marius' transition from White-nights to Pisa is, in Pater's scheme, illustrative of that "law of the life of the human spirit" which Pater in 1868 had described as the "reaction from dreamlight to daylight" by which, through escape into the life of the senses, the Renaissance overthrew the monastic "reign of reverie" (*Appreciations* [1889], 221 - 22, 216).

At school, Marius finds the life of the senses epitomized in his friend Flavian, who seems almost to anticipate the characters in Oscar Wilde's *Dorian Gray*; and one might say of Flavian, as Pater remarked of Lord Henry Wotton, that "he has too much of a not very really refined world in and about him."[12] Flavian embodies that as yet unresolved dialectic of beauty and corruption which runs throughout the novel: "How often, afterwards, did evil things present themselves in malign association with the memory of that beautiful head, and with a kind of borrowed sanction and charm in its natural grace! To Marius, at a later time, he counted for as it were an epitome of the whole pagan world, the depth of its corruption, and its perfection of form" (*Marius*, I, 53). Because of his experience at the temple of Aesculapius, Marius has an ideal of beauty rooted in the golden mean which "made him revolt with unfaltering instinct from the bare thought of an excess in sleep, or diet, or even in matters of taste, still more from any excess of a coarser kind" (I, 34).

Marius' desire for a beauty without taint or flaw is heightened by the discovery of the story of Cupid and Psyche in Apuleius' *Metamorphoses*. This tale is closely interwoven with the history of his mental development and forms no mere digression. The allegorical quality of the legend is strengthened by the elimination of irrelevant personifications and by the suppression of the earthy humor of the original. Something of Apuleius' exuberance and preciosity is nevertheless recaptured by the neologisms and archaisms of Pater's style, which echoes the Latin vocabulary ("*clemens quidam sonus*" is rendered "a sound of a certain clemency" [I, 67]) and which borrows the elegant Elizabethan phrases of William Adlington's famous 1566 translation ("three daughters exceeding fair" [I, 61]). As an "allegory" (I, 61), the quest of Psyche (the mortal soul) for Cupid (divine love) emerges as a preview of Marius' own quest for the vision of ideal love in tangible form. Pater here again may well be mindful of Chiaro dell' Erma's revelation at Pisa that the vocation of the artist is to body forth the inner vision of his soul and its divine aspirations. Exactly this idea of an epiphany of the divine in visible form is conveyed in Marius' re-enactment of Apuleius' mythic quest.

Soon after reading this story with Marius, Flavian falls ill of a plague brought back to Italy by the armies of Lucius Verus and Marcus Aurelius which have returned from a campaign into the eastern reaches of the Empire. When Marius asks his dying friend (in what is the only real dialogue in the entire novel) if he will be comforted to know that someone will weep over his grave, Flavian responds: "Not unless I be aware, and hear you weeping!" (I, 119). The type of immortality here considered is that which Marius' mother had provided for her deceased husband, "that secondary sort of life which we can give the dead, in our intensely realised memory of them—the 'subjective immortality,' to use a modern phrase, for which many a Roman epitaph cries out plaintively" (I, 20). Pater himself had used just this phrase, "subjective immortality," in his Old Mortality essay of twenty years before when he was more strongly under the influence of Auguste Comte and similar humanistic religious philosophers. In a sense, Pater's main effort in 1885 is to suggest that this purely humanistic view offers little else than simple annihilation and to show just where and how the consoling faith in a Christian immortality could gain admittance into the gloomy Antonine-Victorian world.

## V   Marius: *Parts the Second and Third*

To Marius, the death of Flavian comes almost as a negative epiphany, presenting the greatest menace yet to the ever-widening horizon of his vision. Death is Marius' central problem, from the deceased father in the opening pages of the novel to his own death at the conclusion, and the action is designed to answer the question of how he can cope with this ineluctable fact. Initially, Marius thinks he has surmounted the threat by a total commitment to a life of the senses; but, on the seventh day of his journey from Pisa to Rome, as he is climbing a winding mountain road and just as his thoughts reach their most perfected state, a heavy mass of falling rock suddenly plunges down the slope so close behind him that, like Achilles or Eve, "he felt the touch upon his heel" (I, 166).

This startling revelation of the nearness of death shakes his carefully developed philosophy of Epicureanism, which could hardly have explained the meaningfulness of being crushed to extinction

under the landslide: "A sudden suspicion of hatred against him, of
the nearness of 'enemies,' seemed all at once to alter the visible
form of things. . . . His elaborate philosophy had not put beneath
his feet the terror of mere bodily evil; much less of 'inexorable fate,
and the noise of greedy Acheron' " (I, 166). At the moment of
realization that Epicureanism cannot provide an answer to pain and
death, Marius meets Cornelius of the Twelfth Legion—the famed
Christian "Thundering" Legion as Xiphilinus says it later came to
be named. The undercurrent of gloom in Marius' childhood religion
of Numa and in the religious philosophies of antiquity is absent in
Cornelius' Christianity, for his religion differs from the other
systems in that it can deal with the problems of suffering and death.
In all other aspects, as Pater is at pains to show, Christianity finds its
roots in the pre-existing value systems of the pagan world; however,
Cornelius, as the embodiment of the new joy, has nothing of the
despair of Flavian, the Epicurean turned hedonist, or of the moral
coldness of the emperor, who will permit bloodshed to escalate from
the games in the amphitheater to the final slaughter of the
Christians.

Stopping on the way to Rome at the villa of an absent friend,
Cornelius dons his military dress—a figure of action in the empty
house. The Roman Empire, like the house, has grown "dusty" and
is emptied by plague; but, as Marius gradually comes to realize,
"new hope had sprung up in the world of which he, Cornelius, was
a depository, which he was to bear onward in it" (II, 209). "Every
object of his knightly array," Marius later reflects, "had seemed to
be but sign or symbol of some other thing far beyond it" (I, 233).
Although Pater had observed in a work of Romanino the figure of
St. Alessandro, a young patrician converted to Christianity from the
Roman army (*Miscellaneous Studies*, 105), Cornelius' name looks
back to another early Christian warrior, the centurion who was bap-
tized with his household by Peter. Cornelius is the answer to
Marius' old, vague fear of some shadowy adversary in the dark, for
he is the Pauline embodiment of that new knighthood that battles
not against flesh and blood, but against the rulers of the darkness of
this world.

Arriving in Rome, Marius finds its welter of competing religions
to be mainly gross superstition; and, although Aurelius patronized
them all, being a shrewd politician, he had his own religion too.
Shortly after his arrival, Marius listens to a discourse by Aurelius,
almost every sentence of which Pater borrowed directly from the

*Meditations,* but so selected and combined as to drive home Aurelius' awareness of the shortness of life, the closeness of death, and the vanity of existence. Stoicism, despite all the awareness of evil with which Pater endows it, fails as utterly as did Epicureanism in solving the problem of suffering and death. Aware of evil, the emperor simply ignores it, committing the cardinal "sin of blindness." After the events in the amphitheater, Marius concludes that Aurelius, who could complacently watch the public spectacle of suffering animals, was "his inferior now and for ever on the question of righteousness. . . . Surely evil was a real thing, and the wise man wanting in the sense of it, where, not to have been, by instinctive election, on the right side, was to have failed in life" (*Marius,* I, 241 - 43). The emperor fails to inspire others with his high but remote moral standards—his wife is unfaithful, his son dissolute—and his citadel of indifference offers him no protection when his child becomes ill and dies.

Marcus Cornelius Fronto, Aurelius' aged teacher of rhetoric, takes Marius an important step toward defining the object of his quest, the Celestial City, and promotes in him a more receptive frame of mind in which to apprehend it. In his rich and novel style, Fronto presents to Marius the idea that "the world is as it were a commonwealth, a city" (II, 10). This idea of the community of all men gives rise to the idea "of that new, unseen, Rome on high" (II, 11). Fronto's *urbs beata* builds on Marius' earlier vision at the temple of Aesculapius. Just as Marius could not then quite envision the city, so he now leaves the lecture hall perplexed as to how that city is actually to be found—"Where were those elect souls? . . . . Where was the comely order?" (II, 12)—and he sees Cornelius riding by "with that new song he had heard once before floating from his lips" (II, 13). Following the encounter with Fronto, Marius realizes that his earlier philosophy of the senses would lack theoretic completeness unless it matched the outer life with inward possibilities and ideals that as yet cannot be wholly experienced. One way for him to expand the narrow interval of present sensation is to ally oneself with some system larger than one's limited, immediate experience: "The mere sense that one belongs to a system—an imperial system or organisation—has, in itself, the expanding power of a great experience; as some have felt who have been admitted from narrower sects into the communion of the catholic church; or as the old Roman citizen felt" (II,26). This idea of expanding experience by allying oneself with a larger external

structure lies at the heart of Pater's philosophy, and because the
aesthetic object represents "the summing up of an entire world of
complex associations under some single form" (II, 128), the pursuit
of art is the most effective means to achieve that expansion. In
Marius' story, the ritual of the Mass and the vision of Saint Cecilia
serve as the turning point in his quest for the Divine Idea in concrete form and action.

Having described Marius' attainment of a less rigid state of mind,
Pater now reintroduces him into the presence of Aurelius, who
carries forward Fronto's vision of the *urbs beata*. But Aurelius'
helplessness in the face of evil—indeed, his toleration of it—shows
Marius that Stoic thought provides "no real accommodation of the
world as it is, to the divine pattern of the *Logos,* the eternal reason,
over against it" (II, 51). Marius could not help noting that Aurelius'
philosophy, with its "forced and yet facile optimism, refusing to see
evil anywhere, might lack, after all, the secret of genuine cheerfulness" (II, 52), and that it contrasted oddly with the joy of
Cornelius, whose cheerfulness was "certainly united with the bold
recognition of evil as a fact in the world" (II, 53). Inevitably, then,
the *urbs beata* remains for Aurelius, even "in his clearest vision of
it, a confused place" (II, 40). This vision lacks in content, for
Aurelius is without love and cannot understand that man's capacity
to triumph over suffering by compassionate participation gives to
the human community its heavenly pattern. This contentless vision
is ironically echoed by the physical circumstances of the interview.
In order to raise funds for the war, Aurelius sells the imperial furniture and lives alone in the hollow rooms: "in his empty house, the
man of mind, who had always made so much of the pleasures of
philosophic contemplation, felt freer in thought than ever" (II, 36).
But the freedom is illusory, and Aurelius remains a prisoner locked
in his own dream of a world since the chamber, nearly "win-
dowless," has only "a quite medieval window here and there" (I,
216) that lets in light. Pater draws a far harsher portrait of the
bemused emperor than was common in the nineteenth century
(*vide* Ernest Renan, Matthew Arnold, and lesser-known writers)
since it was vital to his purposes to establish Stoicism as an inade-
quate substitute for the religion that Marius seeks.

The emperor's "blindness" contrasts ironically with Marius'
mystic experience in the final chapter of the third book. On a trip to
Tibur, Marius feels in the garden of an inn located in the Sabine
hills an inexplicable but overwhelming sense of gratitude to

someone not physically present. This sense of a mystical companion is tied to his quest for the ideal city, and he speculates:

Might not this entire material world . . . be . . . but . . . a creation of that one indefectible mind, wherein he too became conscious, for an hour, a day, for so many years? . . . The purely material world, that close, impassable prison-wall, seemed just then the unreal thing, to be actually dissolving away all around him: and he felt a quiet hope, a quiet joy dawning faintly, in the dawning of this doctrine upon him as a really credible opinion. It was like the break of day over some vast prospect with the "new city," as it were some celestial New Rome, in the midst of it. (II, 69 - 70)

The Wordsworthian mood of this passage suggests the mind's mastery of outward sense; in the language of "Tintern Abbey," the individual becomes "a living soul: / While with an eye made quiet by the deep power / Of harmony, and the deep power of joy, / We see into the life of things." Even Pater's chapter title, "The Will as Vision," recalls Wordsworth's delineating of those moments when "The mind is lord and master—outward sense / The obedient servant of her will."

Pater clearly wishes to add to Marius' "sensations and ideas" a third determinant, "will." He repeats the Hartleian-Associationist subtitle of his novel to stress the modification of that philosophy here: "Himself—his sensations and ideas—never fell again precisely into focus as on that day, yet he was the richer by its experience" (II, 71). John Locke, and after him David Hartley, both denied the mind's creativity by implying that although sense impressions could be linked and combined, simple sensations could only be built into idea-complexes; they could provide no escape from the deterministic prison of mechanical casuality. The "will" as a determining agent, however, belongs not to the sensations and ideas of the empirical ego, which acts in time, but (to borrow a Kantian distinction) to the noumenal ego to which all temporal predicates are inapplicable. Pater is not so much rejecting as supplementing the empirical tradition by supplying a transcendental activity to the mind in order to gain that "sense of freedom" (*Renaissance*, 231) or its equivalent so sought after by modern man. This is not an escape from the senses but an expanding of experience by an act of perception that recognizes in external structures the existence of "a general consciousness, a permanent common sense, independent indeed of each one of us, but with which we are, each one of us, in communication" (*Plato*, 151). In neo-Hegelian terms this is the Absolute Self that underlies and includes all the narrow, limited selves, constituting what Wordsworth calls the "One great society alone on earth, / The noble Living and the noble Dead."[13] Marius' sense of a divine assistant is a personal equivalent to this unity of selves; and since the only elements of truth and beauty touching man's being appear to derive from this spiritual community, the only reasonable basis for life must be a search "for the equivalent of that Ideal, among so-called actual things—a gathering together of every trace or token of it, which his actual experience might present" (*Marius*, II, 72). Although Marius' vision has passed beyond the bounds of his immediate visible experience, he nonetheless seeks to locate in the world that ideal city that Stoicism despaired of finding amid so much sin and suffering.

## VI    Marius: *Part the Fourth*

The pace of the novel quickens as Pater builds toward the climax. The fourth book opens with contrasting scenes, the first presenting the pagan house where Marius meets the idol of his youth, Apuleius, and the second describing the Christian home where Marius first sees Saint Cecilia, the second-century martyr. The action of the first chapter is an elegant supper party given by a wealthy dilettante to honor Apuleius, author of the Golden Book in which Marius had found the legend of Cupid and Psyche. After the party and in view of a distant fire—"the disintegrating Heraclitean fire" which "had taken hold on actual life, on men's very thoughts, on the emotions and the will" (*Plato*, 107)—Apuleius expounds to Marius a neo-Platonic theory of intermediary beings that link the human world to the divine. As much as he would like to, Marius cannot accept Apuleius' guesses in the darkness; he demands visible evidence: "he must still hold by what his eyes really saw" (*Marius*, II, 90). But Marius can concede that Apuleius is something better than a mystical quack; his speculations "bore witness, at least, to a variety of human disposition and a consequent variety of mental view . . . regarding . . . a world, wider, perhaps, in its possibilities than all possible fancies concerning it" (II, 91).

If this chapter shows how dead Marius' own childhood neo-Platonism was for him, the next chapter indicates how much more meaningful religion may become when the acknowledged "possibilities" are matched by evidence more concrete than that marshaled by Apuleius. One afternoon Marius and Cornelius visit a house situated where a branch of the Via Latina intersects the Via

Appia. This house at the crossroads also marks the moment of choice and vision in Marius' pilgrimage. Contrasting with the soft decadence of the literary party at the villa at Tusculum, the church in Cecilia's house reflects the calm purity and stability that Marius so vainly sought in the Heraclitean conflagration of the empire. Pater's portrayal of Cecilia was inspired by the virgin martyr of that name, the patron saint of music depicted by Raphael as holding her invention, the organ. All the arts aspire to the "condition of music," language itself passing finally into a "strain of music," and the music of the early Mass everywhere dominates these later chapters. Cecilia herself, a latter-day Orpheus, expresses the principle of musical "harmony" (I, 131) or "antiphonal rhythm" (*Plato*, 17) within the perpetual flux, representing thereby the continuity of cultural tradition. In her church the older pagan art was not destroyed by the newer Christian decorations, but harmonized in "the old way of true Renaissance—the way of nature with her roses, the divine way with the body of man, and it may be with his very soul—conceiving the new organism, by no sudden and abrupt creation, but rather by the action of a new principle upon elements all of which had indeed lived and died many times" (*Marius*, II, 95 - 96). Marius, sensing here the continuity of his beautiful religion of childhood, is no stranger to the scene before him: "That intelligent seriousness about life, the absence of which had ever seemed to remove those who lacked it into some strange species wholly alien from himself, accumulating all the lessons of his experience since those first days at White-nights, was as it were translated here, as if in designed congruity with his favourite precepts of the power of physical vision, into an actual picture" (II, 96 - 97).

As Marius descends and emerges again from the catacombs of the holy family Cecilii, references to Hercules and Orpheus, as well as to Jonah, combine to suggest a metaphoric re-enactment of "escape from the grave" (II, 103)—an escape anticipated in the legend of Cupid and Psyche and foreshadowing the novel's conclusion. In contrast to the dying *Campagna* around, cited as victim of the ravages of the plague, stands this garden and its "bold paradox" (II, 102) which treats death as birth. Although the religion of White-nights had celebrated the seasonal cycle, here birth, death, and rebirth seem to constitute the essence of a more refined, less primitive, religious hope. Epitomizing this new hope is Saint Cecilia's temperate and "virginal beauty" (II, 106) which "brought reminiscences of the serious and virile character of the best female statuary of Greece. Quite foreign, however, to any Greek statuary was the expression of pathetic care, with which she carried a little child at rest in her arms. Another, a year or two older, walked beside, the fingers of one hand within her girdle" (II, 105). The image of Cecilia recalls not only those Renaissance paintings of the Madonna with children but also the figure of the Great Mother, Demeter. In Demeter, as Pater described her, the blending of the contrasting phases of life and death, innocence and corruption, are represented by her two daughters, Kore and Persephone. As an embodiment of both the growth and decay of the earth, Demeter typifies "fertility as arisen out of death" (*Greek Studies*, 147). Saint Cecilia, burying her child in the underworld of the catacombs, represents like Kore-Persephone-Demeter the ceaselessly interacting antinomies of generation and decay. Her face is stamped on Marius' memory, and he feels as though "that visionary scene was the close, the fitting close, of the afternoon's strange experiences. . . . The old longing for escape had been satisfied by this vision of the church in Cecilia's house, as never before" (*Marius*, II, 105 - 106). He calls it a "new vision," undoubtedly thinking of the visions of the temple of Aesculapius and of the inn-garden, both of which have now been superseded.

The Christmas Mass that Marius shortly thereafter unexpectedly witnesses provides the ritualistic context for his vision of Cecilia and her dead child. Indeed, many years before he had planned *Marius*, Pater anticipated this association of the sacrament with the house and its catacombs. Mandell Creighton recalled how one evening after dinner in 1873 Pater digressed from discussion of ecclesiastical matters "to a dreamy monologue about the beauty of the reserved Sacrament in Roman churches which 'gave them all the sentiment of a house where lay a dead friend.' "[14] On that evening a heated theological argument had ensued; nevertheless, the motif of the body or bodies within the house remained Pater's chosen way of dramatizing the renewal of life. At the Christmas Mass, Marius does not feel himself the uncomfortable spectator of a slaughter as he had at the agricultural festival of the *Ambarvalia* or later during Rome's celebration of Lucius Verus' marriage. Marius perceives in the sacrificial figure of Christ "towards whom this whole act of worship still consistently turned—a figure which seemed to have absorbed, like some rich tincture in his garment, all that was deep-felt and impassioned in the experiences of the past" (II, 134)—the potential within history itself for renewal. As Christ stands in relation to his Church, so Cecilia stands to her community, transmuting the pagan fertility rites and the decayed chthonian beauty of Faustina and assorted courtesans, redeeming Marius from the snakes, the plague, and the grave. Despite its rather Victorian "assertion of the ideal of woman, of the family, of industry, of man's work in life" (II, 114), Cecilia's spiritual community is the heavenly city made visible, a more inclusive society than White-nights, yet still entirely concrete and historical. Through his vision of the church in Cecilia's house, Marius escapes his finite condition and participates with the Christian community in its larger historical existence.

In the following chapter, "A Conversation Not Imaginary," Pater counterbalances the warmth of the Mass with a chilling contrast. Indebted to Landor's *Imaginary Conversations*, particularly the dialogue betwen Lucian and Timotheus, Pater's "conversation" is a shortened and sharpened translation of Lucian's *Hermotimus*. Its Pyrrhonistic import is that metaphysical speculation is hopeless, that skepticism is the only reasonable philosophy, and that man is helpless because he has been given no divine revelation. Pater turned Lucian's adult protagonist into a mere schoolboy, perhaps to suggest in the fragile optimism of Hermotimus something of the naive young Pater-Marius himself. Although the mature Marius can appreciate the destructive criticism that Lucian levels against the various sects, he is not led into Lucian's skepticism, but recalls to mind the revelation of Christ to the fleeing Apostle Peter, giving him strength to return to Rome and his martyrdom. Developing the idea of a revelation, the next chapter rejects as insufficient—either for the second century or, for that matter, the nineteenth—the traditional idea of a god who literally returns. In the privacy of his diary, Marius wonders what would literally be gained by an actual return, as was envisioned, for example, in the religion of Numa. What is needed to offset the ever-present sorrow of this life is perhaps not so much the return of a god as love among men, a love that would itself reveal God.

In March, 1886, not long after *Marius* had been published, Pater wrote a review of Mrs. Humphry Ward's translation of Henri-Frédéric Amiel's *Journal Intime*. Much of what Pater said in that review concerning Amiel's failure to accept "the Church of history" is applicable to Marius' vision of the historic church itself as a revelation of the divine. Amiel, says Pater, failed to bring such beliefs as he did hold into connection with the facts, the venerable institutions of the past—with the lives of the saints. By failure, as we think, of that historic sense, of which he could speak so well, he got no further in this direction than the glacial condition of rationalistic Geneva. "Philosophy," he says, "can never replace religion." Only, one cannot see why it might not replace a religion such as his: a religion, after all, much like Seneca's. "I miss something," he himself confesses, "common worship, a positive religion, shared with other people. Ah! when will the Church to which I belong in heart rise into being?" To many at least of those who can detect the ideal through the disturbing circumstances which belong to all actual institutions in the world, it was already there. (*Essays*, 33 - 34)

In an earlier letter to Mrs. Ward (December 23, 1885), Pater had touched on precisely this same point when he criticized Amiel's limited vision. "To my mind," Pater wrote, "the beliefs, and the function in the world, of the historic church, form just one of those obscure but all-important possibilities, which the human mind is powerless effectively to dismiss from itself; and might wisely accept, in the first place, as a workable hypothesis."

Unlike those of Amiel, Marius' beliefs are brought into connection "with the lives of the saints" as he once more attends Mass the following spring and listens to Eusebius' *Epistle of the Churches of Lyons and Vienne*. Abridged and rearranged by Pater, this letter, dating from the persecutions of A.D. 177, testifies as vividly as any document can to a vision or a revelation that directly answers the inexorable sorrow of the world. Martyrdom seems unmistakably "the overpowering act of testimony that Heaven had come down among men" (*Marius*, II, 214). As witness to a love stronger than death on which the Christian community is based, the blood of the Gallic martyrs becomes the revelation for which Marius had been half prepared. At this juncture, he journeys home to White-nights to visit his family mausoleum. Wandering through its dusty interior, he identifies himself closely with those around him by seeing himself almost as one or another of the dead.These generations of ancestors laid away in the sterile vault represent Marius' own dead heritage. He is pained by the unnatural air of neglect, in strong contrast to the Christian graves he had seen: "With a vain yearning, as he stood there, still to be able to do something for them, he reflected that such doing must be, after all, in the nature of things, mainly for himself. His own epitaph might be that old one— . . . *He was the last of his race!*" (II, 207). As the last of his race, Marius stands between past generations and those of the future. Aware of

the Christian belief in the resurrection of the body, he buries the
remains of his ancestors in the Christian manner as a symbol of
hope for the future which the past may possess.

The title of the concluding chapter—"Anima Naturaliter
Christiana"—is taken from Tertullian's *Apologeticum* and describes
the state that Marius' soul has reached: "the soul by nature
Christian." As Marius returns to Rome, by the same route he had
taken as a young man, he is accompanied by Cornelius who, as the
"unseen companion" now manifest, is a representative of Christian
humanity. All of Marius' hope for the future is concentrated in the
person of Cornelius: "Identifying himself with Cornelius in so dear
a friendship, through him, Marius seemed to touch, to ally himself
to, actually to become a possessor of the coming world; even as happy parents reach out, and take possession of it, in and through the
survival of their children" (II, 209 - 10). But Marius arrives this
time not at the old Rome but at the ideal community he had sought
so long. At Lucca, he and Cornelius are caught in an earthquake
and are arrested as its cause by the supersititious inhabitants.
Marius, partly in love with Cecilia but believing Cornelius destined
to be her husband, substitutes himself for his friend and bribes the
soldiers to release him. On the way to Rome, Marius becomes sick
and is left by his guards to die at a Christian farmhouse. As he lies
mortally ill, he momentarily thinks his death ironic because it is not
a spectacular martyrdom; he has hardly been conscious of any decision at all: "We wait for the great crisis which is to try what is in us:
we can hardly bear the pressure of our hearts; . . . at last, the great
act, the critical moment itself comes, easily, almost unconsciously"
(II, 212 - 13). And yet his taking Cornelius' place is the "great occasion of self-devotion" (I, 18) for which Marius trained himself all
his life. In his depression he does not at first see his sacrifice as
organically determined through a host of prior decisions
culminating in his act at White-nights aligning the generations of
his past, the pagan world, with the hope of Christianity. Gradually,
out of his depression, it becomes clear to him that he has arrived at
the "new city" in the Christian community, part of which is now
ministering to him. His recent captivity and approaching death
dwindle in significance beside the possibilities of escape and life
represented in this new society. The peace, the pleasant fragrance
of new-mown hay, even the sunlight, make it seem as though "he
was lying safe in his old home" (II, 126)—a fulfillment of that
childhood "ideal of home, which throughout the rest of his life he

seemed, amid many distractions of spirit, to be ever seeking to regain" (I, 22).

At his death, Marius is still like the questing soul, Psyche, who in Apuleius' story descends into the realm of the dead to beg a boon from Persephone, goddess of death. This was Psyche's last labor before Love comes down and makes her his. The moment of revelation is at hand, and Pater emphasizes the possibilities beyond death:

Throughout that elaborate and lifelong education of his receptive powers, he had ever kept in view the purpose of preparing himself towards possible further revelation some day—towards some ampler vision, which should take up into itself and explain this world's delightful shows. . . . Surely, the aim of a true philosphy must lie not in futile efforts towards the complete accommodation of man to the circumstances in which he chances to find himself, but in the maintenance of a kind of candid discontent, in the face of the very highest achievement; the unclouded and receptive soul quitting the world finally, with the same fresh wonder with which it had entered the world still unimpaired, and going on its blind way at last with the consciousness of some profound enigma in things, as but a pledge of something further to come. . . . For a moment he experienced a singular curiosity, almost an ardent desire to enter upon a future, the possibilities of which seemed so large. (II, 219 - 21)

Like Psyche, Marius hopes to find his ideal; and, as she took along the bread that guaranteed her safety, so Marius, as he embarks upon his last quest, has the bread placed gently between his lips: "In the moments of his extreme helplessness their mystic bread had been placed, had descended like a snow-flake from the sky, between his lips" (II, 224).

## VII   Early Christian Conversion

*Marius the Epicurean* belongs to a long line of antiquarian philosophical novels depicting the religions and philosophies of ancient times: it shares with Charles Kingsley's *Hypatia* (1853) a paralleling of antiquity with Victorian England; it includes with J. H. Newman's *Callista* (1856) elements of autobiographical religious development; it takes from Edward Bulwer's *Pompeii* (1834) the cataclysmic denouement; and it finds in Cardinal Wiseman's *Fabiola* (1854) the possibility of becoming a true believer without formally joining the church. The seriousness with which Pater applied "the historical method" led him to synthesize for his novel a startlingly wide range of ancient and post-Apostolic literature. He researched minutely such ancient accounts as Dion Cassius' *Roman History* and the *Scriptores Historiae Augustae*, occasionally drawing inspiration from such Latin translations as Samuel Jebb's *Aristeides* and Thomas Gataker's *Marcus Aurelius* as well as such English translations as H. A. J. Munro's *Lucretius*, C. F. Crusé's *Eusebius*, and the *Apuleius* of William Adlington as well as that of the Bohn Classical Library. Pater also drew facts and phrases from such nineteenth-century studies as W. A. Becker's *Gallus* (1838), Charles Merivale's *History of the Romans* (1850 - 64), J. S. Northcote and W. R. Brownlow's edition of Giovanni de' Rossi's *Roma Sotterranea* (1869), E. B. Taylor's *Primitive Culture* (1871), Gaston Boissier's *La Religion Romaine* (1874), W. W. Capes' *The Roman Empire of the Second Century* (1877), Philip Schaff's *History of the Christian Church* (1883), and William Smith's various biographical and antiquarian dictionaries.[15]

But unlike conventional historical novels on early Christian times, *Marius* avoids sentimentality and melodrama in favor of psychological development. Eschewing the trite sensationalism inherent in gladiatorial-amphitheater and martyrdom spectacles, Pater uses such scenes functionally to define character; most significantly, he tones down the improbably sudden conversion to Christianity of the usual fictional hero. Although true belief without a formal act or confession of faith also has precedents in the historical religious novel, Pater's readers often deny that Marius ever reaches a state of grace. "Not what I do, but what I am, under the power of this vision . . . is what were pleasing to the gods!" (*Marius*, I, 154)—such is Marius' motto and such the manner in which his vision of Cecilia must be understood. Whereas Roman religion "had, indeed, been always something to be done, rather than something to be thought, or believed, or loved" (I, 181), Marius finds the sight of Christian worship is itself a religious awakening of the soul: "vision, the *seeing* of a perfect humanity, in a perfect world . . . —he had always set that above the *having*, or even the *doing*, of anything. For such vision, if received with due attitude on his part, was, in reality, the *being* something" (II, 218). By increasingly significant acts of perception which focus and sharpen the original ideal of home and love experienced at Whitenights (the Temple of Aesculapius, the love of Cupid and Psyche, Fronto's visionary city, the Sabine inn, the church in Cecilia's house), Marius moves from the isolation of dream to the sympathetic participation of vision. Although stopping short in his last hours at the edge of the final revelation, Marius is aware of a momentum generated carrying him from dream to vision and into the future, and it is this force of expectant vision that defines "the sort of religious phase possible for the modern mind."

Because Marius attains to Christianity within the primitive church of the apostles and martyrs, not the church of the *Summa Theologiae*, it would be unhistorical to expect from him a theologically reasoned assent. Indeed, Pater deliberately sought that phase of Christianity in which the sources of religious assent had not yet become entangled in the dogmas of the theologians. Together with the Victorian agnostics, Pater realized that elaborate doctrinal arguments were vulnerable to precisely their own sort of rationalizing; only the apologetical power of that personal vision by which primitive Christianity first conquered the pagan world could answer to the temper of Victorian unbelief. Mrs. Humphry Ward recalled that not long before Pater began *Marius* in 1881 she

once said to him in *tête-à-tête*, reckoning confidently on his sympathy, and with the intolerance and certainty of youth, that orthodoxy could not possibly maintain itself long against its assailants, especially from the historical and literary camps, and that we should live to see it break down. He shook his head and looked rather troubled. "I don't think so—" he said. Then, with hesitation—"And we don't altogether agree. You think it's all plain. But I can't. There are such mysterious things. Take that saying 'come unto me, all ye that are weary and heavy laden.' How can you explain that? There is a mystery in it—something supernatural."[16]

Everyone who knew Pater well has testified to the evident *rapprochement* with Christianity that took place in his thought from the late seventies on. In his observations to Mary Ward, Pater clearly separated himself from such earlier occasions as when he blurted out, pressed controversially one evening at a dinner party at his home by the High Church wife of a well-known professor, that no reasonable person could govern his life by the opinions or actions of a man who died eighteen centuries ago—at which the shaken professor and his wife hurriedly departed. Perhaps something of the influence of J. H. Newman gradually came to fruition in Pater's thought. In Pater's insistence upon the role of will and personality in Marius' religious belief, in his emphasis upon the authority of a religious-humanistic tradition, and in his grounding of assent in a convergence of probabilities, there is a correspondence with the ideas in several volumes of Newman's sermons and in his *Grammar of Assent* (1870). In the Christian community, says Pater, there are a number of individuals who experience relative to a divine person feelings of loyalty and gratitude. This loyalty of conscience may coexist with a great deal of intellectual skepticism, as in the faith of Pascal. In others who illustrate the extreme point of skepticism, such as Montaigne and Mill, concessions to religion are manifested merely in a suspension of judgment; yet even this concession on the part of humanism to the religious explanation of things seems significant. For Pater the outstanding contemporary representative of the loyal conscience was Newman. When in his old age Newman was guest of honor at Trinity College for a weekend (probably in May, 1880), among the literary people invited to meet him was Pater, who told Newman that he would come to St. Aloysius' Church, the Jesuit Oxford parish, to hear him preach. Newman answered, "I hope you will not come out of curiosity." Better to follow the service the next day, so the story goes, Pater carried a most beautifully illuminated medieval missal bound with the appropriate liturgical color of the season.[17]

It was not Newman's defense of the Roman church, but his development of the psychological notion of a faith founded on certain temperamental qualities, his willingness to accept the legitimacy of belief on approximate evidence, which intrigued Pater. In his last volume Pater analyzes that characteristic "dialogue of the mind with itself" (*Plato*, 183) which produces, like the ceaselessly interacting antinomies of history, not an absolute and eternal knowledge, but a truth which, "precisely because it resembles some high kind of relationship of persons to persons, depends a good deal on the receiver; and must be, in that degree, elusive, provisional, contingent, a matter of various approximation, and of an 'economy,' as is said" (187). Yet Pater also applauds the condemned Socrates for affirming the religious ideal of immortality as "an immovable personal conviction, which, he says, 'came to me apart from demonstration, with a sort of natural likelihood and fitness.'" Pater comments: "The formula of probability could not have been more aptly put. It is one of those convictions which await, it may be, stronger, better, arguments than are forthcoming; but will wait for them with unfailing patience" (95). Although he shared neither Socrates' serenity nor Newman's conviction, perhaps it is not too much to claim that in *Marius* Pater was trying to locate within the web of connections that makes up the character of society and history just that stronger, better argument for the immortality of the soul. Yet precisely because the evidence is by nature experiential, not metaphysical, the proof is in no way absolute. For Pater, the skeptical probabilist, "the doubts never die, they are only just kept down in a perpetual *agonia*."

## CHAPTER 4

# The Hero in the Short Portraits

AFTER *Marius* had appeared, Pater and his sisters moved in August, 1885, to London, taking a house facing Holland Park at 12 Earl's Terrace, Kensington. Pater did not settle again in Oxford (though during term-time he was in residence at Brasenose College) until 1893, after his experiment of living the life of a London man of letters clearly had become counterproductive.

## I *London Years*

Violet Paget, though delighted with the simplicity with which the Paters entertained the "fashionable Bohemian element," found their new home outwardly rather drab and "triste."[1] And Frank Harris recalled his surprise upon arriving for dinner the first time: "It was an ordinary, little, middle-class English house; no distinction about it of any kind. I had expected . . . something that would suggest this man's lifelong devotion to art. . . . Not a sign of this; hardly a hint. The house might have belonged to a grocer; might have been furnished by one, only a grocer would not have been content with its total absence of ornament, its austere simplicity." Pater himself, says Harris, "was only about five feet nine or ten in height, stoutly built though neither muscular nor fat; but he moved slowly, deliberately, and so conveyed the feeling of weight. When he took off his hat the impression was deepened; . . . a great domed forehead, massive features, closed eyes and mouth hidden under a heavy dark moustache."[2] Another observer described Pater as looking like "a retired artillery officer in reduced circumstances,"[3] an impression that has been disputed, although both Frank Harris' description and the well-known photograph by Elliott and Fry lend some credence to the image.

The hallmark of Pater in his London years, as Lawrence Evans notes, is "the dissipation of already scarce productive energies in extensive book-reviewing and social life." As a writer, Pater "has promised or undertaken too much, in too many diverse kinds. . . . Whether it was the expense of his Kensington establishment (he remarked to Symons that he wrote short reviews in the *Guardian, Pall Mall Gazette*, etc., 'just to pay a little bill'); whether he struggled too obligingly to satisfy some at least of the editors who clamoured for contributions; or whether his reach merely exceeded his grasp, Pater seems beleaguered, straining almost beyond his means. It may be that *Gaston de Latour*, undertaken in the midst of this, was the main victim of Pater's overcommitment."[4] Further, according to George Moore, Pater as a social man of letters "accepted invitations from almost everybody who invited him." Moore describes one droll scene in which Pater is seated at a dinner party "between two ladies whose bosoms overflowed their bodices, large full-blown roses, exchanging peaceable and amiable remarks, doing his best to keep them both entertained." Pater, says Moore, came to London because "he wanted to live, to join up, to walk in step, without, however, giving himself away, and I think all his friends experienced a certain sense of relief when they heard that he had returned to Oxford."[5]

During his London years, Pater not only revised the studies originally published in periodicals that he intended to include in books, but he often conflated them as well, and afterwards revised the successive issues of each book. The essays on Coleridge and Wordsworth are positively protean. For example, in 1889 Pater reprinted in *Appreciations* an altered version of the 1874 *Fortnightly* "Wordsworth" and that same year produced for the *Athenaeum* and the *Guardian* two reviews of the recently published *Recluse*, simplified versions of the 1874 article, differing only slightly from each other. Seven excellent works of short fiction were also produced during this period, several of which Pater had begun even before *Marius* was brought to completion. In 1887 four of these stories were collected from *Macmillan's Magazine* where they first appeared and published under the title *Imaginary Portraits*: "A Prince of Court Painters" (1885), "Denys l'Auxerrois" (1886), "Sebastian van Storck" (1886), "Duke Carl of Rosenmold" (1887). Their style, according to Symons, was "the ripest, the most varied and flawless, their art the most assured and masterly, of any of Pater's books: it was the book that he himself preferred in his work, thinking it, to use his own phrase, more 'natural' than any other."[6] According to Arthur Symons, "as far back as 1889 Pater was working towards a second volume of *Imaginary Portraits* of which *Hippolytus Veiled* [1889] was to have been one. He had another subject in Moroni's *Portrait of a Tailor* in the National Gallery, whom he was going to make a Burgomaster; and another was to have been a study of life in the time of the Albigensian persecution. There was also to be a modern study: could this have been *Emerald Uthwart* [1892]? No doubt *Apollo in Picardy*, published in 1893, would have gone into the volume."[7] Taken as a group, after the fashion of *The Renaissance* essays, these portraits may be rearranged according to the historical periods in which their central figures are set in order to show the same temperament "under altered historical conditions" (Pater's phrase for his projected "triplet" of novels). All seven portraits present some variant of the problem of self and society, the solution of which, as in *The Renaissance* and *Marius,* resolves itself into a conception of the historicity of human life. The role of the Aesthetic heroes in the portraits that follow is to reveal by their diaphanous condition the continuity of the finite self with the Self in history, a prelude to cultural renewal.

## II  *"Hippolytus Veiled"*

Set in the mythic past of Greece and inspired by a lost play of Euripides, "Hippolytus Veiled" tells of the chaste love of Hippolytus for the goddess Artemis. Pater prefaces his retelling of this mythic tale with an elaborate parallel between the dawning of the Italian Renaissance and the first Greek cultural flowering. He laments, however, the lack of contemporary accounts of the early growth of art in Greece. Evoking the image of a soldier nostalgically recalling the days of his youth, gone forever in the chaos of the Peloponnesian war, Pater takes the reader back to an even earlier period of transition: "in those crumbling little towns, as heroic life had lingered on into the actual, so, at an earlier date, the supernatural into the heroic" (*Greek Studies,* 160). Pater's story begins soon after Theseus' seduction of Antiope, the Amazon queen. Theseus, who has already tired of his stolen mistress and his new son, has hidden mother and child in a small village "as men veil their mistakes or crimes. They might pass away, they and their story, together with the memory of other antiquated creatures of such places, who had had connubial dealings with the stars" (163). Hippolytus, the country-bred son of Antiope, is afterwards wooed by Phaedra, his stepmother and Theseus' queen, who lives in

Athens and worships Aphrodite in sensual luxury. Jealous that he guards his sacred love from her lust, Phaedra tells her husband a false story and causes him to place a fatal curse upon Hippolytus so that Poseidon frightens his horses with a tidal wave and the young charioteer is dragged to his death on the rocks. Hippolytus anticipates the Greek genius for harmonizing, as in the best antique statuary, the controlling and humanizing impress of intellectual light (Self) with the variety and fragmentation of the life of the senses and the imagination (finite self).

The old stone home of Antiope and Hippolytus, located on a bypath to Eleusis and surrounded by olive trees, was once owned by a king and was once visited by a goddess, whose chapel is situated nearby. Pater's essay on "Demeter and Persephone," written some years before "Hippolytus," reveals that the deity who veiled her godhead in human form to dwell in the crude stone house when it belonged to Celeus, king of Eleusis, was none other than Demeter. Even the wellspring next to which Demeter rests is found in the story of Hippolytus who unstops it when he returns to its rightful place the image that belonged to the chapel. But the curious fact is that Hippolytus worships this goddess under the name of Artemis, not Demeter. The explanation for this confusion is that Hippolytus' Artemis is actually the primitive Titan goddess Hecate who, as ally of Zeus in the war with the giants, continued to be honored on Olympus and subsequently was identified with Artemis and also with Demeter and Persephone. As the double of Persephone and interchangeable with her mother Demeter, Hippolytus' Artemis is not only "the assiduous nurse of children, and patroness of the young" (168) but also the goddess of death.

In Pater's version of the old legend, Hippolytus has pledged himself to the *Magna Mater,* becoming, in mythic terms, her year-daimon. The year-daimon, whose annual cycle of death and rebirth governs the seasons, takes from the Great Mother his origin, being called her son, though he is simultaneously raised to divine status as her consort. His transfer of the wedding ring from Phaedra, his stepmother and would-be mistress, to Artemis indicates his dual role as son and consort of the *Magna Mater:* "Phaedra's young children draw from the seemingly unconscious finger the marriage-ring, set it spinning on the floor, and the staid youth places it for a moment on his own finger for safety. As it settles there, his step-mother, aware all the while, suddenly presses his hand over it. He found the ring there that night as he lay; left his bed in the darkness, and again, for safety, put it on the finger of the image, wedding once for all that so kindly mystical mother" (179). Small wonder that Phaedra finds Hippolytus, as the consort of Artemis-Demeter, difficult to seduce. Hardly naive, he seems "a wily priest rather, skilfully circumventing her sorceries, with mystic precautions of his own" (181). Because he withstands her blandishments, Phaedra's lust turns to fury. To show the ideality of Hippolytus' flawless character, Pater describes his expulsion as similar to that of the biblical Joseph. Theseus then expends "one of three precious curses (some mystery of wasting sickness therein) with which Poseidon had indulged him" (182) upon the unfortunate youth.

A wasting sickness afflicts Hippolytus, and the world around him seems to become part of Phaedra's unholy chapel: "his wholesome religion seeming to turn against him now, the trees, the streams, the very rocks, swoon into living creatures, swarming around the goddess who has lost her grave quietness. He finds solicitation, and recoils, in the wind, in the sounds of the rain; till at length delirium itself finds a note of returning health" (183 - 84). In thematic terms, Hippolytus' sickness represents his failure to find the Divine Idea incarnated in finite and sensuous form. Unlike Leonardo da Vinci, who at long last found the face of his dreams in La Gioconda's house, and unlike Marius, who finally beheld in Cecilia the beatific vision of antiquity, Hippolytus discovers in Athens only the grotesqueness inherent in the extremes of the Romantic temperament—an adulteress and her divine whore. "Reverie, illusion, delirium; they are the three stages of a fatal descent both in their religion and the loves of the middle age," remarks Pater *apropos* of a set of circumstances that might have been Hippolytus' own. Describing medieval religion as a "beautiful disease or disorder of the senses," Pater explains that the objects of love, the ideal but sensuous form of God, "was absent or veiled, not limited to one supreme plastic form like Zeus at Olympia or Athena in the Acropolis, but distracted, as in a fever dream, into a thousand symbols and reflections." With the visible object gone, the emotions were directed instead toward an imaginary object, giving rise to a "passion of which the outlets are sealed," so that the senses redound upon the mind and "the things of nature begin to play a strange delirious part" (*Appreciations* [1889], 216 - 18).

Hippolytus' bodily senses and emotions have awakened but, lacking a suitable sensuous outlet from the narrow prison of the finite self, remain disordered. For Pater, the Renaissance, as "a reaction from dreamlight to daylight," overthrew this "reign of reverie" by an escape into the older Classical life of the senses. Yet Athens, representing like Marius' city of Pisa an immersion in the sensuous, cannot supply any external structure of sufficient scope to contain the visionary dreams of the soul. In *Marius*, Flavian seemingly suffers the "fever dream" of Pisan entrapment so that his companion may discover at Rome in Cecilia and the ritual of the Mass the religious-aesthetic outlet for senses "grown faint and sick" (*Marius*, II, 129). Cecilia and the Mass, the Zeus at Olympia, the Mona Lisa—these are structures adequate to contain the dreams and passions of the spirit. Thus Hippolytus, unable to locate the object of his love in the myriad-minded life of Athens, finally realizes, as do later Marius and Chiaro and Leonardo, that Artemis as the epiphany of the historical process structures the sensuous world of Phaedra according to the dreams of the spirit. In line with this revelation of the mind to itself, Hippolytus' childhood happiness grows to be "a shade less unconscious than of old" (*Greek Studies*, 185). Hippolytus attains, with the dawning of self-consciousness, the diaphanous state; he becomes, like the Zeus at Olympia, a physical embodiment of inward light, thereby pointing the way toward the eventual triumph of Greek sculpture.

When Theseus' remaining curses take effect and Hippolytus is dragged home to his death by his horses, the violent end of this youth, who has ritually consecrated his virility to the Great Mother, becomes a giving, after the manner of the year-daimon himself, of the very blood and members of his body to fructify her—a self-sacrificial marriage consummated by his torn, bleeding body. But because Pater's Hippolytus is greater than the mere year-daimon of primitive myth, fructification of the goddess does not bring his physical resurrection; instead, the Greek artistic awakening comes as an indication of the renewal of his spirit. What Pater wrote about the "exquisite early light" of the Italian awakening is important in this connection. He noted that "the choice life of the human spirit is always under mixed lights, and in mixed situations; when it is not too sure of itself, is still expectant, girt up to leap forward to the promise."[8] The world of Hippolytus has just this "veiled" or twilight quality indicative of the "mixed lights" in the first moments of promise just before the break of day. Borrowing his image from Tennyson, Pater had written in *The Renaissance* that "Goethe's culture did not remain 'behind the veil': it ever emerged in the practical functions of art, in actual production" (*Renaissance*,

230). In that moment when hero and humanity become mutually creator and created, the burning of the divine fire erupts into history and a Renaissance has begun.

### III   *"Denys l'Auxerrois"*

The thirteenth century in France occupied Pater in a half dozen studies, primarily because it exhibited "a Renaissance within the limits of the middle age itself—a brilliant, but in part abortive effort to do for human life and the human mind what was afterwards done in the fifteenth" (*Renaissance*, 1). Often considered one of Pater's most striking portraits, "Denys l'Auxerrois" depicts the lad Denys, as a reincarnation of the old Greek god Dionysus, triumphantly revitalizing life in the thirteenth-century city of Auxerre. The first-person narrator, who gradually discerns this story as he examines old stained glass and tapestries, describes with rich pictorial detail the turning of Denys' summer gaiety into winter madness. Suspected of committing wanton acts of destruction, he is at last torn apart by his townsmen, but not before he has reconciled in his own person the dreams of the spirit with the life of the senses. Pater's story of Denys is an extension of Heinrich Heine's theme of the gods in exile, and the similarities between the myth of Dionysus and Pater's parable of the Classical revival are numerous. Studying old records, Pater additionally found in the history of Auxerre some real-life counterparts for the events in the Dionysus legend. The pains that he took to fuse myth and fact in this portrait indicate that he did not approach his story with the idea of imposing some fabricated pattern on reality from the outside; but rather, sought such a mythic pattern within reality itself.

Denys' story turns on the Pisa - White-nights, Athens - Eleusis antithesis, Auxerre being presented by the cultivated English gentleman who introduces the narrative as the balance between the summer sensuousness of Troyes and the winter spirituality of Sens. Auxerre, he says, "is perhaps the most complete realisation to be found by the actual wanderer" of the town "in which the products of successive ages, not without lively touches of the present, are blended together harmoniously, with a beauty *specific*—a beauty cisalpine and northern" (*Imaginary Portraits*, 48). This triadic image of the town serves to introduce the triad embodied in the figure of Denys himself. He, like the god Dionysus, has a *"Doppelgänger"* (*Greek Studies*, 44), for he is a two-sided figure closely linked to the natural cycle of the seasons, the embodiment both of summer vitality and of winter death. In the portrait, Pater divides Denys' life into three parts: in the first year, he is the summer Dionysus; in the second, he is the winter Dionysus; in the third, he is no longer merely Dionysus, but a symbol of the rebirth of higher culture—renaissance.

The significance of Denys' appearance is suggested by Pater's review in 1875 of John Addington Symonds' *Renaissance in Italy*; for Pater quoted a colorful passage telling how some workmen of the fifteenth century "had discovered a Roman sarcophagus while digging on the Appian Way, . . . and inside the coffin lay the body of a most beautiful girl of fifteen years, preserved by precious unguents from corruption and the injury of time." The story, said Symonds, is a sort of "parable of the ecstatic devotion which prompted the men of that age to discover a form of unimaginable beauty in the tomb of the classic world."[9] Pater draws on Symonds' parable when he tells how in the thirteenth century, while building the great cathedral of Saint Etienne at Auxerre, the masons unearthed "a finely-sculptured Greek coffin of stone, which had been made to serve for some later Roman funeral . . . . Within the coffin lay an object of a fresh and brilliant clearness among the ashes of the dead—a flask of lively green glass, like a great emerald" (*Imaginary Portraits*, 56). In contrast to the ashes, the flask, Phoenix-like, glows with new life; and from that moment a sort of golden age seemed to dawn "and the triumphant completion of the great church was contemporary with a series of remarkable wine seasons" (57).

This rebirth of the golden age centered in the person of Denys, for the lad was in reality, though quite unaware of it, the old wine-god Dionysus whose appearance was heralded by the discovery of the flask within the tomb. Denys is rumored to be the illegitimate son of the count of Auxerre; and, like the English poet in Pater's unfinished portrait, the inference is that he was born after the manner of Dionysus himself—from the union "of a god with a mortal woman," the mother dying in childbirth, and ignorant of the glory of her son (*Greek Studies*, 44). Denys is seen in public for the first time at the cathedral ball-playing on Easter, and his appearance at his market stall in town occurs at about this time also. That Easter should be the date of the appearance of the old wine-god Dionysus suggests that Denys reconciles in his person Christian and pagan traditions. With his appearance, there is a renewal of life; for we are told that "the sight of him made old people feel young again" (*Imaginary Portraits*, 60); and his influence at the ball game in the cathedral dramatically bears this out. All things are so infused with the joy of the summer Dionysus that "it seemed there would be winter no more" (62); and, indeed, the winter of that year is not described. Pater simply notes that Denys "had fled to the south from the first forbidding days of a hard winter which came at last" (65).

The second year opens with the reappearance of Denys at the Easter fair, with exotic oriental wares that he had brought back from the south. But Denys is different; for, upon his return, "he ate flesh for the first time, tearing the hot, red morsels with his delicate fingers in a kind of wild greed" (64 - 65). "The wise monk Hermes," writes Pater, "bethought him of certain old readings in which the wine-god, whose part Denys had played so well, had his contrast, his dark or antipathetic side; was like a double creature, of two natures, difficult or impossible to harmonise" (66). This duality Dionysus shares with Demeter, whose summer and winter phases are embodied in Kore and Persephone; in the Eleusinian mysteries he is even associated with the *Magna Mater* herself. In his "Study of Dionysus," Pater described this "darker side of the double god of nature, obscured behind the brighter episodes of Thebes and Naxos, but never quite forgotten" (*Greek Studies*, 42). The figure of "Dionysus Zagreus," hunter of life, concentrates "into itself all men's forebodings over the departure of the year at its richest, and the death of all sweet things in the long-continued cold" (47).

So the second winter comes to Auxerre: "Those fat years were over. It was a time of scarcity . . . . And then, one night, the night which seemed literally to have swallowed up the shortest day of the year, a plot was contrived by certain persons to take Denys as he went and kill him privately for a sorcerer" (*Imaginary Portraits*, 67 - 68). But the attempted murder is mysteriously transformed into its opposite—a feast in his honor. The reason, as given in Pater's "Study of Dionysus," is that the winter solstice was the traditional date for the propitiation of the god and the beginning of his return: "Yearly, about the time of the shortest day, just as the light begins to increase, and while hope is still tremulously strung, the priestesses of Dionysus were wont to assemble with many lights at his shrine, and there, with songs and dances, awoke the new-born child after his wintry sleep, waving in a sacred cradle, like the great basket used for winnowing corn, a symbolical image, or perhaps a real infant" (*Greek Studies*, 43 - 44).

However, the third year opens not with a "new-born child" but with a shrunken body, not with a resurrection but with its ghastly parody—exhumation:

At last the clergy bethought themselves of a remedy for this evil time. The body of one of the patron saints . . . must be piously exhumed, and provided with a shrine worthy of it . . . . The pavement of the choir, removed amid a surging sea of lugubrious chants, all persons fasting, discovered as if it had been a battlefield of mouldering human remains . . . . At last from a little narrow chest, into which the remains had been almost crushed together, the bishop's red-gloved hands drew the dwindled body, shrunken inconceivably, but still with every feature of the face traceable in a sudden oblique ray of ghastly dawn. (*Imaginary Portraits*, 68 - 69)

The clergy of Auxerre do not understand what is really needed, and this morbid exhumation is in sharp contrast to the opened coffin at the beginning of Denys' story. But the gruesome spectacle has an effect on the deranged lad: it "seemed indeed to have cured the madness of Denys, but certainly did not restore his gaiety. He was left a subdued, silent, melancholy creature" (69). Denys has now reached the third stage of his development: first gay, then mad, he is now melancholy. He is like the town of Auxerre itself, "its physiognomy is not quite happy—attractive in part for its melancholy" (51), or like "the image of Demeter enthroned, chastened by sorrow, and somewhat advanced in age, blessing the earth, in her joy at the return of Kore" (*Greek Studies*, 136).

In this third period, Denys abandons vinedressing and becomes a monk in cowl. He inspires the illumination of a manuscript of Ovid—"it was as if the gay old pagan world had been *blessed* in some way" (*Imaginary Portraits*, 71)—and turns his effort toward the building of the first organ, which "became like the book of his life: it expanded to the full compass of his nature, in its sorrow and delight. . . . It was the triumph of all the various modes of the power of the pipe, tamed, ruled, united" (72). The organ is given its first trial that following winter at the end of the third year at the marriage of the lady Ariane. Pater hints that Denys may be the half brother of Ariane, who is called Ariadne in Greek myth and is a seasonal goddess similar to Dionysus, and that he himself very nearly becomes her husband. He is thus assimilated into the persons of both the bride and bridegroom. The harmonious organ music and the marriage which reconciles the two feuding houses symbolize his antagonistic inner moods coalescing in the vision of Ariane, in the historical process. Denys then enacts her cycle of generation and destruction, renewing the life that the clergy of Auxerre had been unable to bring forth.

When Denys takes the part of hunted Winter in a fertility pageant, his scratched lip bleeds, the blood drives the people to a frenzy, the mob tears his flesh to shreds, and the men stick pieces of it into their caps. In the cult of Dionysus, such human sacrifice was a frequent practice: "That the sacred women of Dionysus ate, in mystical ceremony, raw flesh, and drank blood, is a fact often mentioned, and commemorates, as it seems, the actual sacrifice of a fair boy deliberately torn to pieces, fading at last into a symbolical offering (*Greek Studies*, 48). In his discussion of the frenzied disciples of the winter god in "The Bacchanals of Euripides," Pater had noted concerning Dionysus that, paradoxically, the responsibility for his slaughter

must be transferred to him, if we wish to realise in the older, profounder, and more complete sense of his nature, that mystical being of Greek tradition to whom all these experiences—his madness, the chase, his imprisonment and death, his peace again—really belong. . . . Dionysus *Omophagus*—the eater of raw flesh, must be added to the golden image of Dionysus *Meilichius*—the honey-sweet, . . . if we are to catch, in its fulness, that deep undercurrent of horror which runs below, all through this masque of spring, and realise the spectacle of that wild chase, in which Dionysus is ultimately both the hunter and the spoil. (78 - 79)

In the rending of Dionysus, bride and bridegroom, hunter and hunted, one watches death destroying itself, transforming itself into its opposite.

Implied in this cyclic pattern of the god who lives, dies, and is reborn is "the hope of a possible analogy, between the resurrection of nature, and something else, as yet unrealised, reserved for human souls; and the beautiful, weeping creature, vexed by the wind, suffering, torn to pieces, and rejuvenescent again at last, like a tender shoot of living green out of the hardness and stony darkness of the earth, becomes an emblem or ideal of chastening and purification, and of final victory through suffering" (49 - 50). Denys symbolizes this "type of second birth," and the "shoot of living green" that springs from the "stony darkness of the earth"

echoes the green flask in the ashes of the stone coffin. He, like the
vine itself, is springing "out of the bitter salts of a smitten, volcanic
soil, . . . a wonder of freshness, drawing its everlasting green and
typical coolness out of the midst of the ashes" (26).

## IV   "Apollo in Picardy"

The hero of "Apollo in Picardy" is Prior Saint-Jean, a medieval
monk who is revitalized like the townsmen of Auxerre by the spirit
of an old Greek god. Staying for his health with his young companion Hyacinth at a monastic grange, the prior meets the handsome
herdsman Apollyon, a medieval Apollo. After accidentally killing
Hyacinth with a discus, Apollyon vanishes and leaves the prior
wrongly accused of the boy's death. Confined to his room as mad,
Prior Saint-Jean pines away under a grief mercifully tempered with
hope. Whereas Denys l'Auxerrois' fate encompassed the whole
mythic cycle of life and death, Pater here varied the archetype by
apportioning death to Hyacinth and the penalty to the prior and by
leaving Apollyon as merely the instrument of change.

The portrait opens with Prior Saint-Jean and Hyacinth leaving
their cloistered routine to travel to the "valley of the monks" which
is actually an enchanted valley of Apollo. The prior feels uneasy in
his new environment: "These creatures of rule, these 'regulars,' the
prior and his companion, were come in contact for the first time in
their lives with the power of untutored natural impulse, of natural
inspiration" (Miscellaneous Studies, 156). The prior is quite convinced of the evil of Apollyon whom he encounters there; he
believes him "immersed in, or actually a part of, that irredeemable
natural world he had dreaded so greatly ere he came hither."
Apollyon seemed to have "an air of unfathomable evil about him as
from a distant but ineffaceable past, a sort of heathen understanding with the dark realm of matter" (158 - 59). The prior's
Gnosticism had its origin in the historical development of the
church. In Marius the Epicurean, Pater wrote that the barbarian in-
vasion, though it could not kill the church, did suppress the culture
of the pagan world with the result that "the kingdom of Christ was
to grow up in a somewhat false alienation from the light and beauty
of the kingdom of nature, of the natural man, with a partly mistaken tradition concerning it, and an incapacity, as it might almost
seem at times, for eventual reconciliation thereto" (Marius, II, 29).

In his portrait of Pico della Mirandola, Pater had noted that certain Renaissance scholars attempted to reconcile Christian and Greek values but that "an earlier and simpler generation had seen in the gods of Greece so many malignant spirits, the defeated but still living centres of the religion of darkness, struggling, not always in vain, against the kingdom of light" (*Renaissance,* 30). Thus in Prior Saint-Jean's "earlier and simpler generation" Apollo is appropriately called by the name of "a malignant one in Scripture, Apollyon" (*Miscellaneous Studies,* 152), the angel of the bottomless pit. Heinrich Heine's theme of the gods in exile again fits Pater's purpose here. Heine had written that at the triumph of Christianity the old temples and statues could not be spared, "for in these still lived the old Greek Joyousness which seemed to the Christian as devildom. In these temples he saw not merely the subjects of a strange cultus and a worthless and erroneous faith which wanted all reality, but the citadels of actual devils, while the gods whom the statues represented existed for him in reality, but as the devils themselves."[10] Apollo, under his Bunyanesque appellation, becomes one of the devil-gods in exile.

Yet Apollyon is irresistibly attractive despite his obvious involvement with the natural order. The prior is drawn to Apollyon against his will, and the reader soon begins to perceive that the prior's mind itself is the distorting element in the valley of the monks. "Like Prospero's enchanted island, the whole place was 'full of noises.' The wind it might have been, passing over metallic strings, but that they were audible even when the night was breathless" (148). Apollo's lyre, the source of this Pythagorean music, is included in the portrait to symbolize the perfect harmony between the physical and spiritual aspects of life. Only to the apprehensive medieval mind is this world at all sinister. Even the twilight in which Apollyon lives is only that of the Hyperborean Apollo, though it also suggests that enchanted darkness of "Hippolytus Veiled," the twilight in the first moments of promise just before the dawn. Indeed, the air, says Pater, "might have been that of a veritable paradise, still unspoiled" (150); and Apollyon is the unfallen man, "the old Adam fresh from his Maker's hand" (149). For this reason, both the prior and the novice grow younger, the influence of the place bringing out a certain "boyish delight" (150) in both of them.

But the impact of the natural order on the cold and repressive medieval world is almost catastrophic. The twelfth and final volume of the prior's epic work—"a dry enough treatise on mathematics, applied, still with no relaxation of strict method, to astronomy and music" (143)—presented "a strange example of a cold and very reasonable spirit disturbed suddenly, thrown off its balance, as by a violent beam, a blaze of new light, revealing, as it glanced here and there a hundred truths unguessed at before, yet a curse, as it turned out, to its receiver, in dividing hopelessly against itself the well-ordered kingdom of his thought" (143). Under Apollyon's tuition, the prior begins illustrating the Pythagorean singing of the planets. It is as if William Blake's "Rossetti manuscript" had been anticipated in the twelfth century, though the volume also suggests the nervous breakdown suffered by Hippolytus when the bodily senses awaken but the balance, the unity of inner and outer worlds, proves elusive. As an interim task, the prior supervises the erection of a barn which, under the influence of Apollo, turns into a kind of Greek temple. It is Apollo with his harp who builds the monastic grange, just as in antiquity he built the walls of Troy by marvelous musical powers that moved huge blocks of stone. The reader here is reminded of Denys' organ music and the church at Auxerre, another suddenly completed structure symbolizing a harmonious fusion of Christianity with Greek sensuousness.

Prior Saint-Jean also was forced to break off unconsummated the Midnight Mass of the Feast of the Nativity because of the disruptive influence of Apollyon, who had seemingly become the officiating priest. But as the prior himself must have known, Christmas day is not without echoes of the old Mithraic celebration of the victory of light over darkness. Apollyon, consequently, is also identified with Christ, and thus in the valley of the monks he kept the sheep, "was an 'affectionate shepherd,'. . . would bring them back tenderly upon his shoulders. Monastic persons would have seen that image many times before" (158). Such an image had stood in the church in Cecilia's house, and it expressed a religious ideal not ascetic, but "serene, blithe and debonair," representing the moral life "as a harmonious development of all the parts of human nature, in just proportion to each other" (*Marius*, II, 114, 121).

But the ascetic ideal had won ascendence, and the medieval mind, estranged from nature, could no longer enjoy sensuous beauty. The prior's delirium is another instance of that "beautiful disease or disorder of the senses" characteristic of the medieval mind, infusing all nature with "the maddening white glare of the sun, and tyranny of the moon." But inevitably that medieval entrapment of the senses gives way to a Renaissance liberation where there is no delirium or illusion, no experiences of mere soul while the body and the bodily senses sleep, or wake with convulsed intensity at the prompting of imaginative love; but rather the great primary passions under broad daylight. . . . This simplification interests us . . . chiefly because it explains . . . a transition which, under many forms, is one law of the life of the human spirit, and of which what we call the Renaissance is only a supreme instance. Just so the monk in his cloister, through the "open vision," open only to the spirit, divined, aspired to, and at last apprehended a better daylight, but earthly, open only to the senses. (*Appreciations* [1889], 221)

At the close of the portrait, the prior has been thrown back upon "the great primary passions"—tragic sorrow over the death of the lad Hyacinth—and apprehends that "better daylight."

As in many of Pater's portraits, "Apollo in Picardy" reaches its climax in a violent death. In *Plato*, Pater tells his readers that the Lacedaemonians met when the blue Hyacinths faded "to celebrate the death of the hapless lad who had lent his name to them, Hyacinthus, son of Apollo, . . . greatly beloved of the god, who had slain him by sad accident as they played at quoits together delightfully, to his immense sorrow. That Boreas (the northwind) had maliciously miscarried the discus, is a circumstance we hardly need to remind us that we have here, of course, only one of many transparent, unmistakable, parables or symbols of great solar change, so sudden in the south, like the story of Proserpine, Adonis, and the like" (*Plato*, 229). The death of Hyacinth, killed by an "icy blast of wind" (*Miscellaneous Studies*, 168), is that of a year-daimon. This is why Apollyon is both kind to animals and also slays them; creation and destruction are inextricably linked. There is no birth without death, and this hope of resurrection is implied in the various images of circularity that reflect the elemental cycle over which Apollo is the sovereign lord: in the trees, "moaning in wild circular motion" (168); in the instrument of death itself, the discus; and in the figure of the thrower, with his round, halo-like tonsure, "the disk in his right hand, his whole body, in that moment of rest, full of the circular motion he is about to commit to it" (167). When Apollyon departs northward the next day, he carries the awakening of nature to a winter land; and the prior, who takes his place, is accused of the murder of Hyacinth. Just as the shock of the exhumation of the saint threw Denys into a subdued and melancholy mood in which joy and sorrow coexisted, so the prior finds hope in the midst of desolation. He, like Denys, reminds one of Demeter at the return of Kore, "chastened by sorrow, . . . blessing the earth" (*Greek Studies*, 136).

The grieving prior is last seen confined to a room from which he can glimpse (almost like St. John after whom he is named) the new heaven and new earth of the senses to which he desires to return. In an image recalling the valley that the young Marius saw from the temple of Aesculapius—"a land of hope, its hollows brimful of a shadow of blue flowers" (*Marius*, I, 40)—the prior also gazes out over the monks' valley, mistaking "mere blue distance, when that was visible, for blue flowers, for hyacinths, and wept at the sight; though blue, as he observed, was the colour of Holy Mary's gown on the illuminated page, the colour of hope, of merciful omnipresent deity" (*Miscellaneous Studies*, 170 - 71). No longer does the prior shudder at the view. Only the pain of Hyacinth's death could break through the narrow asceticism that barred his consciousness from the elemental passions and sensations of the natural world. By coincidence, the necessary permission to return to the valley arrives on the day of the prior's death, suggesting that he himself will not enjoy the fruits of his vision. Indeed, Pater implies much the same of Pico and the fifteenth century in which he lived. The century was, he says, "great rather by what it designed than by what it achieved. Much which it aspired to do, and did but imperfectly or mistakenly, was accomplished in what is called the *éclaircissement* of the eighteenth century, or in our own generation; and what really belongs to the revival of the fifteenth century is but the leading instinct, the curiosity, the initiatory idea. It is so with this very question of the reconciliation of the religion of antiquity with the religion of Christ" (*Renaissance*, 33). Of this fifteenth-century Renaissance Prior Saint-Jean was a precursor, but the work taken up so vigorously was not completed, says Pater, until "our own generation." Yet the visions of these earlier children of Apollo pointed the way.

## V   *"Sebastian van Storck"*

Set in Holland sometime between the 1648 Congress of Munster and Spinoza's excommunication in 1656, "Sebastian van Storck" portrays a sensitive adolescent who progressively isolates himself from the busy well-being of Dutch life. Consumptive, and convinced that the world is an illusion, Sebastian is a parody of Pater's diaphanous man—in sickness instead of in health. Sharing Amiel's "metaphysical prejudice for the 'Absolute'" and "constitutional shrinking" (*Essays*, 32 - 33) from the concrete, he very nearly fails to escape from the prison of the self. Vignettes of the world that Sebastian spurns, including his cruel rejection of the girl who loves him, comprise the details of this portrait. Driven finally by depression to the stark alternatives of suicide or sacrifice, Sebastian heroically gives his life to save a child.

A passage in Pater's *Plato* introduces the reader to the antecedents of this Absolutist metaphysics and indicates what sort of a judgment Pater would pass upon it were he called upon to do so. He derisively writes that, as a result of Parmenides' overwhelming emphasis upon the One,

the European mind . . . will never be quite sane again. It has been put on a quest (vain quest it may prove to be) after a kind of knowledge perhaps not properly attainable. Hereafter, in every age, some will be found to start afresh quixotically, through what wastes of words! in search of the true Substance, the One, the Absolute, which to the majority of acute people is after all but zero, and a mere algebraic symbol for nothingness . . . . It is assumed, in the words of Plato, that to be colourless, formless, impalpable is the note of the superior grade of knowledge and existence, evanescing steadily, as one ascends towards that perfect (perhaps not quite attainable) condition of either, which in truth can only be attained by the suppression of all rule and outline of one's own actual experience and thought. (*Plato*, 40 - 41)

This doctrine of the One, which extends from the time of Parmenides to the seventeenth century, found its most current expression "in the hard and ambitious intellectualism of Spinoza; a doctrine of pure repellent substance—substance 'in vacuo,' to be lost in which, however, would be the proper consummation of the transitory individual life. Spinoza's own absolutely colourless existence was a practical comment upon it" (41). In the spirit of this philosophy, Sebastian van Storck molded his life, and he becomes Pater's most striking example (though the Emperor Aurelius in *Marius* is a close second) of the individual who has almost destroyed his life by this not quite sane philosophy of the One. Unlike Pater's other heroes, Sebastian is neither an artist nor, as is quite evident, even a truly creative thinker.

Sebastian's ideal of the *tabula rasa* is symbolized by the sea, the eternal washing of which reduces all the signs of life to a dead level.

The country that Pliny despised "as scarcely dry land at all" (*Imaginary Portraits,* 92) is for this reason a most congenial surrounding for Sebastian: "In his passion for *Schwindsucht*—we haven't the word—he found it pleasant to think of the resistless element which left one hardly a foot-space amidst the yielding sand; of the old beds of lost rivers, surviving now only as deeper channels in the sea; of the remains of a certain ancient town, which within men's memory had lost its few remaining inhabitants, and, with its already empty tombs, dissolved and disappeared in the flood" (93). "From time to time," says Pater, "the mind of Sebastian had been occupied on the subject of monastic life, its quiet, its negation . . . . But what he could not away with in the Catholic religion was its unfailing drift towards the concrete—the positive imageries of a faith, so richly beset with persons, things, historical incidents" (97 - 98). So, instead, Sebastian withdrew by a winding staircase and a long passage to an empty room shut off from the world—a room not unlike Aurelius' chamber without furniture.

In sharp contrast to Sebastian's philosophy of the impalpable is the tremendously active life of the Dutch people that was a successful self-assertion against the Spaniards in the Eighty Years' War, against the sea in a war without beginning or end, and against hostile religious factions in a conflict just then beginning. Concomitant with the material prosperity of the Dutch came the culmination of an artistic development that reflected this life in unexcelled painting, and Sebastian has no choice but to be an unwilling witness to this love of art. At one of Burgomaster van Storck's arts-and-letters gatherings, the names of the guests suggest a walking, talking catalogue of the Rijksmuseum; and they one and all mirror the warm, busy life of Holland, whether they paint exotic flower arrangements (van Aelst) or sunny summer scenes (Cuyp) or everyday household life (de Hooch) or seascapes (van de Velde) or domestic birds and wild game (the Hondecoeters). This charm of the Netherlands is all the more touching because the treacherous sea, so loved by Sebastian, can always break in and destroy it.

Pater portrays Sebastian's rejection of this world by indicating his refusal to be painted. In mid-seventeenth-century Holland, everything is put on canvas—except Sebastian. Only as a boy was he sufficiently indifferent to allow Isaac van Ostade to paint his portrait, though not from life but from a sketch made at a skating party. But some years later, perhaps as a consequence of failing health or maturing philosophy, when Thomas de Keyser saw Sebastian skating and requested permission to paint him, "the young man declined the offer; not graciously, as was thought" (84). The other members of the van Storck family, however, have no aversion to portraiture. Sebastian's father figures in Gérard Terburgh's picture of the Congress of Munster and Gabriel Metsu painted his mother. Even the van Storck residence is painted by Jan van der Heyde, and the friends who visited the home seemed only to need a heavy Baroque frame to be ready for the museum wall: "Grave ministers of religion assembled sometimes, as in the painted scene by Rembrandt, in the Burgomaster's house" (97). But Sebastian is painted only in the burgomaster's ambitious imagination as the admiral-general of Holland; and, on two occasions, he is sketched without his knowledge by Thomas de Keyser and Baruch de Spinoza. That Spinoza does not share Sebastian's aversion indicates that ultimately (the *Ethics* is not composed until 1675) the master does not carry his uncongenial philosophy to such abnormal extremes.

Sebastian's obsessive determination not to be painted reflects a neo-Albigensian distaste of entanglement in the web of the material world—a distaste so great that, when he wrote to anyone, he even left his letters unsigned. Sebastian prided himself on his realization that "this picturesque and sensuous world of Dutch art and Dutch reality all around that would fain have made him the prisoner of its colours, its genial warmth, its struggle for life, its selfish and crafty love, was but a transient perturbation of the one absolute mind" (106). His refusal to take his place even in the family portrait summarizes all his eccentricities and not only suggests his desire to evanesce to a superior grade of existence but foreshadows his climactic rejection of Mademoiselle van Westrheene. If he is unwilling to appear with his own family, Sebastian is most certainly not going to establish a family of his own. He rejects marriage with the girl, withdraws to his lonely tower by the sea, and is never again seen alive by his parents. To make his sterility complete, he slashes to fragments, just before he leaves, "the one portrait of him in existence" (103).

Although Sebastian preferred Spinoza's *amor intellectualis* to human affection, the story of Grotius' escape from the isolation of his prison through the great love of his wife impressed him and perhaps suggested the role that tangible human relationships play. Isolated in his tower by the sea like the solitary prisoner in his "dream of a world," a sudden storm blows up, and Sebastian gives his life to save a child. Appropriately, Pater's discarded 1868 metaphor of "one washed out beyond the bar" is made the literal and ironic means of Sebastian's death. But his last action, reversing that "intellectual pride" that sacrificed "a thousand possible sympathies" (*Marius*, II, 22) gave to Sebastian's contemplative ideal the necessary awareness that it was not some disembodied Absolute that had first claim upon his sympathies but his fellow man, among whom at every moment, touched by the One, "some form grows perfect in hand or face" (*Renaissance*, 236). Paradoxically, the solitary prisoner escapes from his "isolating narrowness" (*Marius*, II, 14) into the larger life of the One only when it has such a humanized form.

## VI  *"Duke Carl of Rosenmold"*

The princely German hero of "Duke Carl of Rosenmold" feels imprisoned in his semi-feudal, eighteenth-century duchy. The indulgent grand duke, incapable of responding to his grandson's artistic aspirations, indirectly provokes Carl to stage and attend his own funeral so that he might escape south to the culture of Italy. As he journeys, Carl discovers the potential of German genius itself; but, at his return, his plans for a Renaissance are betrayed; and he and the girl he is about to marry are trampled to death by an invading army. Like J. J. Winckelmann, Carl was the last fruit of the Italian Renaissance and the first fruit of the German Enlightenment that culminated in the figure of Goethe. Both Carl and Winckelmann long for the spirit of antiquity in the alien German environment of the eighteenth century, and both died tragically before the desired *Aufklarüng* arrived. The purpose of the portrait of Duke Carl and of the earlier essay on Winckelmann is to define the beginnings of the artistic patriotism that Lessing proclaimed and the return to nature of which Goethe was the herald. Revolting against the rococo of the eighteenth century, Carl's successors directed German literature away from its pseudo-Classicism and toward the true antique; and, by their insistence that literature be national and sincere, they also emancipated German art from the French influence.

In the bright light of the topmost room of his castle, Carl discovered Conrad Celtes' *Art of Versification and Song* (1486). Celtes was one of the leading German humanists of his century—poet laureate, librarian of the Imperial University, a friend of Albrecht Dürer—and his home city of Heidelberg, with its imposing castle rising above the jumble of gables and roofs of the town below, may well be Pater's model for the courtly city of the Rosenmolds. This German Renaissance of which Carl was the precursor belonged in special measure to Heidelberg; for here, between the appearance of the *Athenaeum* and the Battle of Leipzig, Romantic vitality brought new life to the old Classicism and also restored the city to the literary prominence it had enjoyed once before in the days of Conrad Celtes. After reading Celtes' "Ode to Apollo," Carl begins to function as the German Apollo of the eighteenth century; he is the bringer of light to northern darkness: "To bring Apollo with his lyre to Germany! It was precisely what he, Carl, desired to do—was, as he might flatter himself, actually doing" (*Imaginary Portraits,* 124). Indeed, Carl's life becomes patterned after the actual incidents found in the Classical and Teutonic myths of the sun god.

The plight of Duke Carl, like so many of Pater's heroes, is that he finds himself in the midst of a frozen culture altogether lacking the rejuvenating Romanticism of "the pleasures of the senses and the imagination" (*Renaissance,* 24). The duchy of Rosenmold, a relic of the Middle Ages, is stiff, dark, and dead; its only minimal activity is "a sleepy ceremonial, to make the hours just noticeable as they slipped away" (*Imaginary Portraits,* 122). In the god Apollo, the young duke catches a glimpse of a new ideal of freedom and happiness and a rebirth of the arts. Carl's vision was of "the hyperborean Apollo, sojourning, in the revolutions of time, in the sluggish north for a season, yet Apollo still, prompting art, music, poetry, and the philosophy which interprets man's life, making a sort of intercalary day amid the natural darkness; not meridian day, of course, but a soft derivative daylight, good enough for us" (132). Even if Pater does laugh a little at the young duke's imitating so enthusiastically the French imitation of true Classicism, his aspirations and his mythic role are genuine. Although initially Carl had been conscious only of performing the same function as Apollo, he is gradually led to conceive of himself as the god indeed: " 'You are the Apollo you tell us of, the northern Apollo,' people were beginning to say to him" (128). Carl accepts this idea and actually fancies "that he must really belong by descent to a southern race, that a physical cause might lie beneath this strange restlessness, like the imperfect reminiscence of something that had passed in earlier life" (133). Carl's musings parallel Pater's description of Winckelmann as one who embodies "the reminiscence of a forgotten culture," the mind "beginning its spiritual progress over

again, but with a certain power of anticipating its stages"
(*Renaissance*, 194).

In order to imitate specific events in the hyperborean myth, Duke
Carl takes to acting. What the court organist had conceived as light
entertainment in the form of a musical satire on the duke
himself—*Balder, an Interlude,* as he titled it—becomes recast, under the prompting of Carl, into a serious musical drama in which
Carl's proposed part is that of Balder himself—the hyperborean
Apollo. Unlike the Classical imitation of Marivaux's play, *Hannibal,*
in which Carl had previously acted the chief role, *Balder* was a
native theme handled by native Germans. At this point in his
development, Carl does not sufficiently recognize the value of
"home-born German genius" (*Imaginary Portraits,* 147); he, like his
contemporary Watteau in the following portrait, must free himself
from the rococo world of Paris. Pater's source for Carl's
mythological theme was possibly Matthew Arnold's poem, "Balder
Dead," which told how the young god of light is killed by Loki;
and, because one aged hag refused to weep for him, he must wait in
hell until the coming of the new golden age when the heavenly city
of Asgard, after destruction, will be reconstituted on a higher
ethical and moral plane. Balder's cycle of death and resurrection,
accompanied by a spiritual rejuvenation of the golden city, must
have appealed immensely to the young duke who undoubtedly in-
corporated the whole scheme in his opera as a not too subtle comment upon the condition of his courtly city, a once-golden Asgard
now covered with a "venerable dark-green mouldiness" (121). This
mouldiness was especially noticeable in the vicinity of the burial
vaults which loom large in the eyes of the sensitive young man. He
presumably envisioned the grand-ducal burial vaults as not unlike
Hela's mouldering realm where Balder lay with the spiritually and
physically dead until he could return victorious.

Having perceived the similarity of function between himself and
the god, having been told he was the god, and having then played
the role in *Balder,* Carl now turns his whole life into an actual re-
enactment of the Apollo-Balder myth. After the manner of his illustrious namesake, Emperor Charles V, he will stage a mock
funeral and then reappear. Between his death and his reappearance
Carl planned to escape the confines of the court and to take his
long-desired pilgrimage to the sources of culture, after which he
would be fit to return as the bringer of a new way of life. Thus his
death is the prelude to cultural renewal, and his empty coffin,

emblazoned with the word *Resurgam* (a popular motto also used in Chapter XIV of *Vanity Fair* and Chapter IX of *Jane Eyre*, meaning "I shall rise again"), remains "as a kind of symbolical 'coronation incident' " (140) that crowns Carl as the initiator of the German Renaissance. Pater writes that, after the episode of the funeral, Carl "would never again be quite so near people's lives as in the past—a fitful, intermittent visitor—almost as if he had been properly dead" (140).

But Carl never travels beyond the extreme limits of the German cultural sphere. Simultaneously with his discovery that Germany itself carries the seeds of its own awakening, the old grand duke dies; and Carl is proclaimed sovereign—an auspicious moment, surely, for the advent of the *Aufklariing*. The new grand duke resolves to take for his bride the peasant girl who had wept for him at his death, she being like Lisa, Cecilia, Artemis, and Ariane a goddess of nature. Carl senses something of the mystic body of the earth about her: she was "like clear sunny weather, with bluebells and the green leaves between rainy days, and seemed to embody *Die Ruh auf dem Gipfel*—all the restful hours he had spent of late in the wood-sides and on the hilltops" (148 - 49).

Carl's former love of the artificial is incompatible with his new love of the peasant girl, and the decision to marry her, by "our lover of artificial roses, who had cared so little hitherto for the like of her," brings him into true contact with the vital source of all art: " 'Go straight to life!' said his new poetic code; and here was the opportunity;—here, also, the real 'adventure,' in comparison of which his previous efforts that way seemed childish theatricalities, fit only to cheat a little the profound *ennui* of actual life" (149). But, on his marriage night, he is betrayed by his old counselors; and the invading army tramples him and his bride into the earth. Carl, although only a half-rococo Apollo, must nonetheless undergo an actual death. It is not Carl who effects the German Renaissance; for Carl, like Balder, is early dead. He revives not in his own person, but in the beautiful skating figure of Goethe fifty years later who, " 'like a son of the gods' " (153), seems the true Apollo at last.

Significantly, neither Carl's nor Gretchen's body is found and placed in the grand-ducal vaults—a sterile place. In the Balder legend, a distinction was made between the cowards, the weak, and the inglorious who are kept in the sterile realm of Hela and those who heroically die on the battlefield. Carl, in a sense, dies on a battlefield, since he is destroyed by the trampling army in his fight to bring light to Germany. He thus merges with the earth, with nature, the source of all vitality. As his name suggests, he is the mold, the seed bed, out of which the "roses" of the German Romantic school will eventually grow. In the opening of the portrait, Pater describes a yew that fell and exposed the remains of two persons. Carl, as the end of his genealogical tree and at the roots of the natural tree, occupies the transitional place, precisely as Marius did, between the burial vaults and the new enfranchisement of passion. In the figure of Goethe, writes Pater, "I seem to see the fulfillment of the *Resurgam* on Carl's empty coffin—the aspiring soul of Carl himself, in freedom and effective, at last" (153).

## VII   "*A Prince of Court Painters*"

"The last century was pre-eminently a classical age . . . . Yet, it is in the heart of this century . . . of Watteau . . . that the modern or French romanticism really originates," Pater writes in the "Postscript" to *Appreciations* (263). Thus the portrait, "A Prince of Court Painters," presented by means of extracts from an old French journal, describes the efforts of Anthony Watteau (as he is called here) to express the Romantic aspirations of his soul in the rococo forms of Parisian life. Marie-Marguerite, the ostensible writer of this imaginary journal, is the older sister of the historical Jean-Baptiste Pater, a protégé of Watteau. Despite the popularity Watteau achieved by painting the trivial graces of Parisian society, his artistic longings remain unfulfilled in his charming but ephemeral work; ironically, he never suspects that Marie-Marguerite, who quietly chronicles in her journal his fevered comings and goings, is also revealing there the sort of love that would satisfy all his ideal aspirations. Pater's *donnée* for this portrait may well have been a brochure written by his friend Frederick Wedmore for an exhibition of French eighteenth-century art in which Watteau's role is stressed and his connection with Jean-Baptiste Pater noted. Although "A Prince of Court Painters" is the only imaginary portrait based completely upon historical incidents and personalities, Pater here practices a deception upon the fabric of history by attributing to Marie-Marguerite a hidden love for Watteau. In *Marius the Epicurean,* the hero was wholly Pater's invention, but the other events and characters were mostly drawn from pre-existing sources. By mingling fact and fancy Pater seemingly desires to reveal the hidden figure in the historical tapestry—the existence of a personality expressive of the era, but never before portrayed.

The fictional pattern in which Pater casts his factual data takes the familiar form of a contrast between the restless, gay, and myriad-minded life of the courtly city of Paris (representing for Watteau what Pisa and Athens had been to Marius and Hippolytus) and the calm, austere, and sleepy atmosphere of the northern provincial capital of Valenciennes (not unlike the courtly city of the Rosenmolds). The heavy and restrictive nature of Watteau's Valenciennes environment finds its expression in images of stone. He is the son of a stonemason who had built and who lives in an all-stone house which, "big and gray and cold" (*Imaginary Portraits*, 6), creates in the young lad a desire for the graceful and the elegant. Marie-Marguerite writes that "the rudeness of his home has turned his feeling for even the simpler graces of life into a physical want, like hunger or thirst, which might come to greed; and methinks he perhaps over-values these things" (7). He turns, dissatisfied, from his native city to Paris. Of central importance in Pater's delineation of Watteau is the problem of expanding experience, of "getting as many pulsations as possible into the given time" (*Renaissance*, 238). On the face of it, Paris might seem the perfect city for the realization of this aim. However, the purpose of the portrait is to demonstrate that for Watteau Parisian life cannot really satisfy the demand for expanded experience—it only gives the illusion of doing so.

But, because Watteau has gained depth of vision from his early environment, he is able to invest the trivial graces of Paris with a nobility far beyond their actual worth. In a passage that recalls the momentarily opened gateway through which Florian glimpsed the red hawthorn, Marie-Marguerite remarks of Watteau's visions of beauty:

He will never overcome his early training; and these light things will possess for him always a kind of representative or borrowed worth, as characterising that impossible or forbidden world which the mason's boy saw through the closed gateways of the enchanted garden. Those trifling and petty graces, the *insignia* to him of that nobler world of aspiration and idea, even now that he is aware, as I conceive, of their true littleness, bring back to him, by the power of association, all the old magical exhilaration of his dream—his dream of a better world than the real one. (*Imaginary Portraits*, 34 - 35)

Although Watteau succeeds in transforming the social graces of the Parisian ladies into art, this world of fragile things in flux is still not adequate to contain his vision; thus, he is never at peace. "Those coquetries, those vain and perishable graces, can be rendered so perfectly, only through an intimate understanding of them," writes Marie-Marguerite; but, she adds, for Watteau "to understand must be to despise them" (27).

Watteau's tragedy is that he cannot wholly escape from the illusion that Paris offers. If courtly life had been able to answer to the longings of his soul, such an environment would have had to possess something of the principle of moral authority, of coherence within the flux, but, because everything about rococo Paris is fragmented, "little," Watteau remains a dreamer, longing for escape from his solitary prison. "People talk of a new era now dawning upon the world," writes Marie-Marguerite; but she adds that it is perhaps an era "of infinite littleness also" (33). Only Jean-Baptiste, whose soul has no urge to expand beyond the rococo littleness of things, fails to find it restrictive. "As for me," says Marie-Marguerite to her journal, "I suffocate this summer afternoon in this pretty *Watteau* chamber of ours, where Jean-Baptiste is at work so contentedly" (30). Unable to synthesize the extremes of Paris and Valenciennes, Watteau reflects the contrast in *Marius* between Flavian, lost in the fragmentation of experience, and Aurelius, imprisoned in pure form. If Marie-Marguerite could only be Watteau's Cecilia, the ideal could be given its concrete embodiment.

Watteau's failure to find a world large enough to contain his ideal creates in him a dissatisfaction with his art. Again and again Marie-Marguerite finds in his pictures the resulting incompleteness: "It is pleasanter to him to sketch and plan than to paint and finish; and he is often out of humour with himself because he cannot project into a picture the life and spirit of his first thought with the *crayon.* He would fain begin where that famous master Gerard Dow left off, and snatch, as it were with a single stroke, what in him was the result of infinite patience . . . . To my thinking there is a kind of greed or grasping in that humour; as if things were not to last very long, and one must snatch opportunity" (35 - 36). And so, in 1714, when Anthony begins his picture of her, she records that "my own portrait remains unfinished at his sudden departure" (24). And, after another visit in 1717, her "own poor likeness, begun so long ago still remains unfinished on the easel, at his departure from Valenciennes . . . . He has commanded Jean-Baptiste to finish it;

and so it must be" (35 - 36). Watteau cannot complete Marie-Marguerite's portrait because, unlike the Leonardo of the Mona Lisa, he finds neither in his environment nor in himself the cohesive quality that would make this possible.

And so not only are Watteau's pictures incomplete, but what is finished is ephemeral. The painting "Four Seasons" replaces the sombre Spanish style with a "fairy arrangement" (22) that lasts, like delicate music, only momentarily. When Marie-Marguerite first sees Watteau's picture, she thinks it "a pity to incorporate so much of his work, of himself, with objects of use, which must perish by use, or disappear, like our own old furniture, with mere changes of fashion" (23). A few years later she writes of his art in general and of the "Four Seasons" and her portrait in particular:

Alas! it is already apparent that the result also loses something of longevity, of durability—the colours fading or changing, from the first, somewhat rapidly, as Jean-Baptiste notes. 'Tis true, a mere trifle alters or produces the expression. But then, on the other hand, in pictures the whole effect of which lies in a kind of harmony, the treachery of a single colour must needs involve the failure of the whole to outlast the fleeting grace of those social conjunctions it is meant to perpetuate. This is what has happened, in part, to that portrait on the easel. (36).

This problem is, of course, that of a perpetual flux without the coherence of the Divine Idea. Watteau is an artist who manages to burn only fitfully with the hard, gem-like flame of the divine fire.

Like Watteau, Marie-Marguerite is a sensitive soul who feels trapped by her environment. The day after he returns from his first visit home to seek again the "freedom" of Parisian life, she writes:

I am just returned from early Mass. I lingered long after the office was ended, watching, pondering how in the world one could help a small bird which had flown into the church but could find no way out again. I suspect it will remain there, fluttering round and round distractedly, far up under the arched roof, till it dies exhausted. I seem to have heard of a writer who likened man's life to a bird passing just once only, on some winter night, from window to window, across a cheerfully-lighted hall. The bird, taken captive by the ill-luck of a moment, re-tracing its issueless circle till it expires within the close vaulting of that great stone church:—human life may be like that bird too! (14 - 15).

The writer of whom she "seems to have heard" is the Venerable Bede in whose *Ecclesiastical History* is found the famous image that she recalls. But the problem facing the worthy thane and his king some thirteen centuries earlier was what came before and after life, not life itself. For Marie-Marguerite, sheer existence presents the problem. Some years later, in 1714, she writes: "With myself, how to get through time becomes the question,—unavoidably; though it strikes me as a thing unspeakably sad in a life so short as ours" (25). Her plight is like that of the bird trapped in the stone church, an image that recalls not only the stone home of Watteau's childhood, but also the old house of Florian Deleal which, like the church, became a trap for the bird-soul.

Marie-Marguerite's love for Anthony provided her what success she has in furnishing her time, but hers remains an unfulfilled love since he is to her, as to everyone else, "distant and preoccupied" (20). As a substitute, she participates vicariously in his career. She follows him through her younger brother, Jean-Baptiste, who goes almost as her spy, she hopes, to study in Paris under the tuition of his idol, Watteau. "I have made him promise to write often to me" she notes in her journal, and adds: "With how small a part of my whole life shall I be really living at Valenciennes!" (18). It is evident that at first Marie-Marguerite had hoped to marry Watteau, and in a poignant passage—it almost seems that Pater himself is speaking—she writes that "there are good things, attractive things, in life, meant for one and not for another—not meant perhaps for me" (28). As with Mademoiselle van Westrheene, she represents a lost possibility for vision, her journal with its dated entries suggesting a potential for structuring the flux of successive moments.

As death approaches, Watteau turns, exhausted, from his Paris friends to Jean-Baptiste and to the pietistic heritage of Valenciennes. Resting on the estate of the Abbé Haranger, Watteau spends his last days in the fashioning of a crucifix. The crucifix, as an image large enough to encompass the soul and its dreams of a world of immortal love, is an art form superior to the rococo triviality of Paris. It also signifies Watteau's discovery of the visible church which he joins by taking Communion, a larger and yet concrete order in which his limited self can find freedom. But, unlike Marius' entrance into the Christian community, Watteau's deathbed conversion is too late to give him more than a glimpse of the beatific vision; and the last sentence of Marie-Marguerite's journal expresses her deepest insight into Watteau's character: "He was," she writes, "always a seeker after something in the world that is there in no satisfying measure, or not at all" (44).

## VIII   *"Emerald Uthwart"*

"Emerald Uthwart" was written soon after Pater's visit in the summer of 1891 to the King's School which reawakened old memories. The work is unquestionably his most autobiographical study since his first portrait, "The Child in the House." The character Emerald, however, enjoys a more distinct fictional life of his own than did Florian Deleal. Unlike Pater, Emerald is good at school sports and goes off gaily to fight Napoleon. In the army, he follows his school friend, James Stokes, in an irregular venture that issues in Stokes' execution and his own reprieve and dishonorable discharge. Spiritually and physically wounded, Emerald returns home and receives on his deathbed a belated vindication. Like so many of Pater's gifted young heroes, he is a descendant of those children in Victorian novels who enter life without a settled identity or vocation. His quest for identity, pursued through school and army, took the form of a need to transcend the uninspired heritage of his childhood which was symbolized by his buried ancestors who were "sleeping all around under the windows, deposited there as quietly as fallen trees on their native soil, and almost unrecorded, as there had been almost nothing to record" (*Miscellaneous Studies*, 200). The Uthwart home life exhibits a complete lack of disciplined purpose, and the "littleness" in its almost vegetative way of living reflects the flow of discrete entities untouched and unstructured by any ennobling ideal—the flux without the gem-like flame. With the appearance of Emerald, however, the gem and flame images find their embodiment, as his given name and gleaming golden hair indicate.

Pater describes Emerald as a flower who is "plucked forth" (203) from the undisciplined existence of the Uthwarts and sent away to a school environment totally different from that of his home:

Centuries of almost "still" life—of birth, death, and the rest, as merely natural processes—had made them and their home what we find them. Centuries of conscious endeavour, on the other hand, had builded, shaped, and coloured the place, a small cell, which Emerald Uthwart was now to occupy, a place such as our most characteristic English education has rightly tended to "find itself a house" in—a place full, for those who came within

its influences, of a will of its own. Here everything, one's very games, have
gone by rule onwards from the dim old monastic days, and the Benedictine
school for novices with the wholesome severities which have descended to
our own time. (203 - 204)

At the school, a cultural tradition is gradually revealed within the
ebb and flow of outward events; and Emerald molds his personality
on its subtle rhythms, finding his true place within that tradition,
small cell though it be. His sense of submissiveness and self-mastery
is at heart an expression of the diaphanous hero's wholeness, a
renunciation of one-sided growth and strident self-assertion in favor
of a balance of gifts and a sympathy with the entire range of human
interests. Studying his pagan classics at the shrine of Chaucer's
pilgrims, Emerald, like Marius, discovers a unity of culture in which
all forms of beauty—pagan and Christian—are reconciled: "The
old heathen's way of looking at things, his melodious expression of
it, blends, or contrasts itself oddly with the everyday detail, with the
very stones, the Gothic stones. . . . The builders . . . had built up
their intellectual edifice more than they were aware of from
fragments of pagan thought, as, quite consciously, they constructed
their churches of old Roman bricks and pillars, or frank imitations of
them" (215).

The discipline or submission that characterizes Emerald has as its
background the Platonistic ideas with which Pater was at this time
working. In particular, the chapter in *Plato* entitled "Lacedaemon,"
which appeared in the summer of 1892 in periodical form, is the
perfect companion piece for the portrait of Emerald published at the
same time. Plato's ideal of public life regimented in a military
manner, war itself occupying an important place in the total pattern,
was perhaps most closely approximated in antiquity by the Spartans.
And just as the Spartan ethos was "half-military, half monastic"
(*Plato*, 218), so the Dorian spirit that reigned at Canterbury expressed
itself as a military monasticism. Although Emerald's school certainly demands a Spartan measure of conformity from its students,
it nevertheless tolerates some variety within the unity. But the army
to which he comes insists on total conformity and lacks, therefore, a
sense of the "privilege of his individual being" (*Miscellaneous
Studies*, 210). Emerald's single act of rebellion against the military's
over-structured and narrow system, a complete antithesis to the
original freedom of his home, represents an assertion of the liberty

of the heart, which, as Pater describes it, is in spirit not unlike the Romanticism of thirteenth-century France.

At school, Emerald and James had been almost like brothers, had been "bracketed together" (224), and had always been "side by side" (225). Pater tells us that James Stokes looked for "the Greek or the Latin model of their antique friendship" but that "none fits exactly" (214). However, subsequent action does create one model that fits, and there could hardly be found anywhere in Pater's writings a more satisfactory example of the star-bright hero who burns with the gem-like flame. Pater notes in his "Lacedaemon" chapter that the Dioscuri, the twin brothers Polydeuces and Castor, had an important cult in Sparta. This myth of the Dioscuri, says Pater, tells of the twin stars called Gemini, "those two half-earthly, half-celestial brothers, one of whom, Polydeuces, was immortal. The other, Castor, the younger, subject to old age and death, had fallen in battle, was found breathing his last. Polydeuces thereupon, at his own prayer, was permitted to die: with undying fraternal affection, had foregone one moiety of his privilege, and lay in the grave for a day in his brother's stead, but shone out again on the morrow; the brothers thus ever coming and going, interchangeably, but both alike gifted now with immortal youth" (*Plato*, 230 - 31). In recounting the tale of Amis and Amile in the first essay of *The Renaissance*, Pater there also called attention to "that curious interest of the Doppelgänger, which begins among the stars with the Dioscuri, being entwined in and out through all the incidents of the story, like an outward token of the inward similitude of their souls" (*Renaissance*, 9). This myth of the Dioscuri is strikingly applicable to Emerald and James; the two are so much like brothers that Emerald, at the execution of James, felt as though "one half of himself had then descended" (*Miscellaneous Studies*, 240) into the grave. The two coffins, one filled and the other empty, represent the merely temporary power of death over this friendship of the two mythical "brothers."

While yet at school, something of their starry apotheosis was perhaps foreshadowed in Emerald's long-remembered cricket hit in which the ball is comically supposed to have become a stellar satellite. Also at school, the substitution of one brother for the other had been foreshadowed by the incident of a prank for which Emerald incurred the blame that Stokes had merited. (Such brotherly substitution also occurs in the tale of Amis and Amile, in Prior

Saint-Jean's acceptance of Apollyon's guilt, in Sebastian's rescue of the child, and in Marius' taking upon himself Cornelius' peril.) After his beating by the headmaster, Emerald had remarked submissively, "And now, sir, that I have taken my punishment, I hope you will forgive my fault" (217). So later, at the end of the story, having taken their punishment, James and Emerald are forgiven their negligence by the sympathetic nation. But prior to this belated vindication, in his grief-stricken wanderings over Flanders' fields, Emerald must endure a chastening that calls to mind not only the figure of Demeter searching for her lost daughter but also the disgraced ghost of Elpenor (Emerald's valedictory address had been Elpenor's speech in Book XI of *The Odyssey*) entreating Odysseus for the burial rites of a soldier honorably dead in battle. This state of death-in-life is dramatized by an exacerbating bullet from an old gunshot wound in the heart muscle, the coldness of death carried at the core of Emerald's being. The belated restoration of his army commission reminds the reader of the arrival, on the day Prior Saint-Jean dies, of the permission to return to the valley of the monks, and it suggests that the sufferer does not himself taste the mature fruits of his success.

Pater closed his portrait of Emerald with a curious question: "What did it matter—the gifts, the good-fortune, its terrible withdrawal, the long agony?" (243). With much the same question directed at some hypothetical Lacedaemonian, Pater had closed his "portrait" of the visitor to Sparta: "Why this strenuous task-work day after day; why this loyalty to a system, so costly to you individually, though it may be thought to have survived its original purpose; this laborious, endless, education, which does not propose to give you anything very useful or enjoyable in itself?" (*Plato*, 232). In *Plato* Pater does not answer the question directly. Echoing his own visit to the King's School, he says only that because the Spartans "puzzle us by a paradoxical idealism" it is good to visit them on occasion "like some of our old English places of education, though we might not care to live always at school there" (234). The question is, however, answered when one considers the opening of "Emerald Uthwart" in which the "unnumbered" days of the young German student's epitaph become "numberless" days by virtue of his having applied himself to the cultural tradition " 'even with much labour' " (*Miscellaneous Studies*, 198), gaining thereby an expanded hold on what Pater elsewhere called "that divine ideal, which above the wear and tear of creeds has been forming itself for ages as the possession of nobler souls" (*Renaissance*, 89).

Both the "Conclusion" to *The Renaissance* and afterwards the essay on Wordsworth scorn action for the sake of its "fruit" (*Renaissance*, 236; *Appreciations*, 61), those morally mistaken or illusory ends; rather, cultural experience for its own sake creates an "intangible perfection" (*Appreciations*, 61) of character through sympathetic participation in the spiritual community. Pater amplified his idea of the relation of the individual to the unseen but real ideal in *Marius:* "Without him there is a venerable system of sentiment and idea, widely extended in time and place, in a kind of impregnable possession of human life—a system, which, like some other great products of the conjoint efforts of human mind through many generations, is rich in the world's experience; so that, in attaching oneself to it, one lets in a great tide of that experience, and makes, as it were with a single step, a great experience of one's own, and with great consequent increase to one's sense of colour, variety, and relief, in the spectacle of men and things" (*Marius*, II, 26). And the way to attach oneself to that experience is by an "impassioned contemplation" (*Marius*, I, 148; *Appreciations*, 62), by fixing one's thoughts, "with appropriate emotions, on the spectacle of those great facts in man's existence . . . . To witness this spectacle with appropriate emotions is the aim of all culture; and of these emotions poetry . . . is a great nourisher and stimulant" (*Appreciations*, 63). Much like Marius' visualizing in the context of the Mass the martyrdom of the Christians, Emerald witnesses with an impassioned attitude the "spectacle" (*spectare*, to behold) of Stokes' martyrdom-execution. Emerald and Stokes, Marius and Cornelius, are Doppelgängers of each other, reflections of the two halves of experience. Like the interchangeable Dioscuri, each partakes of the condition of the other, both alike assimilated into the eternal cycle of generation and destruction represented in *Marius* by Cecilia. If one regards "Cecilia" as the goal of aesthetic vision, the art for art's sake strategy of Pater's "Conclusion" becomes clear; eschewing limited moral ends, aesthetic experience perfects the self by completing it through the avenue of sympathetic participation.

Arthur Symons observed of Pater's Aesthetic heroes in *Imaginary Portraits* that "the story of each, like that of 'Marius,' is a vague tragedy, with some subtlely ironic effect in the accident of its conclusion."[11] Others besides Symons have noted the unexpected or incongruous tragedies spanning the ages from Hippolytus in antiquity to Emerald in Pater's own century and have found the irony more often grim than subtle. Certainly the ceaselessly interacting antinomies between which man runs his course remain the eternal

constant in human experience. But Marius' so very unheroic martyrdom and the deaths of Emerald and all the others do not mock
their spiritual aspirations; rather, as Pater noted in his first published essay, that "struggle" of "sincere and beautiful spirits" in the
face of suffering and death is the "substance" of history itself. In
the final analysis, Pater does not deal in rare, "aesthetic" emotions,
for the secret of his art lies in keeping close to life, in giving to simple, familiar things a full measure of pity and care. Not one of
Pater's young heroes or anything else of human worth—"no
language they have spoken, nor oracle beside which they have
hushed their voices, no dream which has once been entertained by
actual human minds, nothing about which they have ever been
passionate, or expended time and zeal" (*Renaissance*, 49)—is
denied its share of that *pietas* that treasures up the memory of its
existence.

CHAPTER 5

# *The* Prosateur *of the 1890s*

**P**RIOR to his return in July, 1893, from London to Oxford, where he took a house at 64 St. Giles' Street, Pater had been engaged on an extended study of Plato's philosophy. Chapters of this study began to appear in 1892, and the completed work, entitled *Plato and Platonism*, was published the following year. When shortly thereafter a friend inquired of Pater whether he believed *The Renaissance* or *Marius* to be his best book, he replied, "Oh no, neither. If there is anything of mine that has a chance of surviving, I should say it was my *Plato*."[1] Perhaps such confidence reflects the enthusiasm not only of the public but also of the students for whom the lectures were first given. "As long ago as 1890," recalled a reviewer, Pater had "announced a series of lectures on Plato to be given in one of the small lecture-rooms in Brasenose"; but within a week or two of the first address, his "audience had so grown in numbers as to overflow every available seat in the room he had selected; and he was forced—(a rare occurrence in a lecturer's experience)—to transport his hearers to one of the larger public halls of the University."[2]

## I  *Plato, Platonism, and Language*

Ironically, owing to his presumed deficiencies as a tutor, Pater initially had been assigned the task of teaching Plato as a last resort. However, lectures in his rooms at Brasenose proved popular with the more serious students. One such recalled: "We sat where there were sitting-places; at the table, in arm-chairs, on the window-seat. Pater liked to be listened to, and did not like to have his every word noted down. But there were one or two of us who had equal objection to letting his words escape us. We hit upon a compromise. Some few of us would listen, writing nothing, and endeavor to hold the lecturer's eye; the others wrote for dear life, and forewent the

understanding of what they heard till the hour was over. Of course
the ruse was seen through, as many an amused smile showed; but
no rebuke came." Between lectures, Pater assigned for translation
passages from such dialogues as the *Apology* and the *Meno*. "Most
of the translations came of course from cheap cribs, but one was
always from Jowett's translation in order that the learner might discover to his delight the number of mistakes which one man of learning found in the translation of a rival."[3]

As *Marius* has been Pater's most sustained fictional effort to bring
to life a figure out of the past by reconstructing the historical
milieu, *Plato* was his most sustained nonfictional attempt. In one
sense, the appearance of Pater's volume was predictable, for having
produced several studies of Greek mythology, he might be expected
to follow them with an exploration of Greek ethics, aesthetics, and
epistemology. Structually, Pater's last study resembles both *The
Renaissance* and *Marius* in the centrality accorded to the vision of
the human image. By sheer linguistic genius, Plato, like Leonardo
or Marius, objectifies his inner vision in outer human form:

The lover, who is become a lover of the invisible, but still a lover, and
therefore, literally, a seer, of it, carrying an elaborate cultivation of the
bodily senses . . . into the world of intellectual abstractions, . . . filling
that "hollow land" with delightful colour and form, as if now at last the
mind were veritably dealing with . . . living people who play upon us
through the affinities . . . of *persons*: . . . —There, is the formula of
Plato's genius. . . . No one perhaps has with equal power literally sound-
ed the unseen depths of thought, and, with what may be truly called
"substantial" word and phrase, given locality there to the mere adum-
brations, the dim hints and surmise, of the speculative mind. (*Plato*, 139 -
40)

Plato's genius for embodying mental abstractions in personality
finds its most triumphant expression in Socrates, "a figure most am-
biguously compacted of the real Socrates and Plato himself" (75).

The familiar Pisa - White-nights, Athens-Eleusis, Troyes-Sens antithesis of the sensuous flux and visionary dreams is here expressed
in the Ephesus-Elea opposition of Heraclitus and Parmenides—an
antithesis initially reconciled in Pythagoras but culminating in the
Platonic Socrates. Socrates, like Lady Lisa and St. Cecilia, is one of
the icons of history; Plato, like Leonardo and Marius, is one of the
passionate spectators. Just as the church of history is objectified in
Marius' vision of St. Cecilia, so Plato's vision of the cultural

*Zeitgeist* is expressed by Socrates—primarily, as the speaker of *The Dialogues,* by his words, by language. Having objectified his own inwardness in the personality of Socrates, a figure he half creates and half perceives, Plato discovers in the accounts of Socrates' martyrdom the same avenue of sympathetic participation with those "sincere and beautiful spirits" of history which Marius will find later in the Mass and the martyrdom of the Christians. Yet, ultimately, Plato like Aurelius is frustrated in his vision of the City of the Perfect: "he for one would not be surprised if no eyes actually see it" (266). Neither Plato nor Socrates could quite find in language a structure adequate to contain the dreams and passions of the spirit. It is left to others—to Marius, to Leonardo—to achieve what Plato aspired to do; and to some he seems, rather sadly, to be "a mind trying to feed itself on its own emptiness" (143).

Although the instructional intent of *Plato and Platonism* is too prominent for it to qualify as one of Pater's major literary works, the study does advance significantly Pater's understanding of the potential of language for reconciling the Absolute with the actual. In "The Doctrine of Plato," Pater explains that the "dialogue of the mind with itself" (183), that life-long search for the equivalent of the Ideal in sensuous experience, finds its closest verbal expression not in the metaphysics of a formal treatise, such as that of Prior Saint-Jean or Sebastian van Storck, but in the dialectic of the essay—although Edmund Gosse found the "too-perpetually conversational tone" of *Plato* itself a stylistically new and not quite successful innovation. The "final insecurity" (185) of the dialectic method may not please those who want certainty (especially those of Pater's own readers who demand of Marius a theologically reasoned assent), but at the very least it creates an open mind and promotes a receptive attitude towards "the great perhaps" (196). If in this study Pater has not altogether returned full circle to the Neoplatonism of his first essay in which he had hymned the Absolute among the select circle of Old Mortals, nevertheless his preoccupation with the elusive relationship of art to truth represents a clear distancing of himself from any celebration of ecstatic moments isolated within the flux of sensations. The main implication of *Plato* is that beauty has an ethical function that cannot be disavowed—"The close connection between what may be called the aesthetic qualities of the world about us and the formation of moral character, between aesthetics and ethics" (269).

If, on the one hand, the Plato of Pater could never be mistaken

for that of Jowett—as a spokesman for aesthetic values, Pater's Plato
"anticipates the modern notion that art has no end but its own
perfection, 'art for art's sake' " (268)—on the other hand, Pater's
growing concession to the One of Idealist tradition is neatly
epitomized in the softening of his attitude toward the "Dorian influence" (the principle of continuity amid the flux) as seen in
revisions of an 1880 passage from "The Marbles of Aegina" (*Greek
Studies*, 252 - 53) which reappears in the present volume (*Plato*,
103 - 105). Although Plato ultimately fails to reconcile the Absolute
with the sensuous (and only if judged from a later historical
perspective), the resemblance of Plato to Pater is closer than any
previous Aesthetic hero, for both are writer-thinkers, cultural
historians; and common to both is an especial awareness of the
potential of language and literature for relating the individual to
the continuities of history: "we come into the world, each one of us,
'not in nakedness,' but . . . clothed . . . in a vesture of the
past; . . . in the language which is more than half of our thoughts;
in the moral and mental habits, the customs, the literature, the very
houses, which we did not make for ourselves; in the vesture of a
past, which is (so science would assure us) not ours, but of the race,
the species: that *Zeit-geist*, or abstract secular process" (72). Hence
the isolated self and its individual impressions are joined to a
general consciousness; analogously, the formal, "aesthetic"
qualities of any object are vitalized by participation in this common
cultural sphere of meaning. *Plato* is thus important both as an extension of Pater's earlier discussions of style and as the ultimate
statement on his own practices and ambitions as a writer.

## II  *Poetic Prose*

That poetry is greatly inferior to prose for conveying "*les
mouvements de coeur*" was originally, of course, the discovery of
Stendhal and Gustave Flaubert. As a schoolboy, Pater may have
aspired to poetry, but among his Oxford friends he soon revealed his
ambition to be, as he said, a "*prosateur.*"[4] " 'Why do you always
write poetry? Why do you not write prose? Prose is so much more
difficult' " were, later, Pater's Carlylesque words upon meeting Oscar
Wilde.[5] And, again, to the young Arthur Symons, Pater wrote:
"I think the present age an unfavourable one to poets, at least in
England. . . . I should say, make prose your principal *métier*, as a
man of letters" (January 8, 1888). But it was a unique kind of prose

Pater had in mind, if one is to judge from his own work. Symons noted that Pater, like Baudelaire, "has 'rêvé le miracle d'une prose poétique, musicale sans rhythme et sans rime.' An almost oppressive quiet which seems to exhale an atmosphere heavy with the odour of tropical flowers, broods over these pages; a subdued light shadows them. The most felicitous touches come we know not whence, 'a breath, a flame in the doorway, a feather in the wind,' here are the simplest words, but they take colour from each other by the cunning accident of their placing in the sentence, 'the subtle spiritual fire kindling from word to word.' "[6] Paralleling as he does Symbolist technique, it is not conceptual precision that Pater achieves, but the evocation stylistically of emotional associations. Thomas Wright fails to understand the purposiveness of this indistinctness and ridicules a minor instance of it in *Marius the Epicurean:* "On the Campagna 'an animal feeding crept nearer.' We presume it was a cow; and at the Apuleius feast 'a favourite animal purred its way gracefully among the wine-cups.' This probably was not a cow."[7] But like Mallarmé and, especially, Verlaine, Pater loves the fugitive impression, the harmonious murmur of words, and the vague contours of the unfolding image.

Pater's alliterative, impressionistic diction characteristically tends toward abstract nouns ("soul," "truth," "vision," "beauty," "ideal," "grace," "harmony") and idealizing adjectives ("faint," "fresh," "fair," "sacred," "soft," "sweet," "strange," "mystic," "rich," "golden," "delicate," "perfect") and the reader's first response is less to concrete meanings than to a melodious assemblage of words that sing one away from the thought. Since "all art constantly aspired towards the condition of music," the perfection of style, so Pater holds, "often appears to depend, in part, on a certain suppression or vagueness of mere subject, so that the meaning reaches us through ways not distinctly traceable by the understanding" and language "seems to pass for a moment into an actual strain of music" (*Renaissance,* 135 - 38). If on the one hand this harks back to such Wordsworthian examples as the Leech-gatherer, whose voice "was like a stream / Scarce heard; nor word from word could I divide," and the Solitary Reaper, whose song is worded but of indeterminate and universal meaning, on the other hand it anticipates the nondiscursive language of Stéphane Mallarmé and the Symbolists, who conceive of poetry ("there is no such thing as prose: there is the alphabet. . . . So long as there is stylistic effort, there is versification"[8]) as closer to sound with associations than to words with meaning. Such a vision of style both illuminates the perception of Pater's student, G. M. Hopkins, that a poem's sound alone, apart from its meaning, carries a comprehensible "inscape" and points toward T. S. Eliot's statement many years later that "genuine poetry can communicate before it is understood."[9]

By its multiplicity and agreement of sounds as well as by an imaginative catachresis employing a slight dislocation of habitual word associations, Pater's style achieves a dreamlike heightening of feelings and attitudes at times not far removed from states of the surreal. Pater especially admired D. G. Rossetti's "House of Life" because it portrayed just such a dream world in which the barriers between the conscious and the subconscious have been worn thin, and his style came to share with Rossetti's more visionary poetry a rare power of compression, by conscious selection condensing into a few lines or paragraphs a mass of details, hinting with artistic economy at an image rather than working it out fully after the manner of Ruskin. Arthur Symons, commenting on Mallarmé's Symbolist technique, might equally well have been describing Pater's or Rossetti's art: "To evoke, by some elaborate, instantaneous magic of language, without the formality of an after all impossible description; to be, rather than to express: that is what Mallarmé has consistently, and from the first, sought in verse and prose. And he has sought this wandering, illusive, beckoning butterfly, the soul of dreams, over more and more entangled ground."[10] Throughout *Marius*, for example, one senses the "subject" under its musical phrases, and yet the development of the thought from point to point does not obtrude itself on the reader's attention. The story itself, as Symons notes, remains "but a sequence of scenes, woven around a sequence of moods."[11] Although Rossetti's spiritualized biography of Everyman with its personified emotions is more surreal than Pater's novel, both artists have created sound and word patterns designed to flood the conscious mind with the life of the subconscious.

Having forsaken poetry, Pater gradually evolved a rich and concentrated prose, which eddied with many hesitancies and indirections among qualifiers, appositives, synonyms, parentheses, and quotations until at last, flowing out in long, rhythmical periods, it achieved an unbroken harmony of utterance. Such stylistic distinction, for better or worse, was not easily achieved. "I have known writers of every degree," recalled Edmund Gosse, "but never one to whom the act of composition was such a travail and an agony as it was to Pater. In his earlier years the labour of lifting the sentences was so terrific that anyone with less fortitude would have entirely abandoned the effort." Pater's process of composition began with little squares of paper on which he jotted down quotations, references, or phrases—"*memoria technica,*" Gosse calls them—which he

> placed about him, like the pieces of a puzzle; . . . he would [then] begin the labour of actual composition, and so conscious was he of the modifications and additions which would supervene that he always wrote on ruled paper, leaving each alternate line blank. . . . In the first draft the phrase would be a bald one; in the blank alternate line he would at leisure insert fresh descriptive or parenthetical clauses, other adjectives, more exquisitely related adverbs, until the space was filled. It might then be supposed that the MS. was complete. Far from it! Cancelling sheet by sheet, Pater then began to copy out the whole—as before, on alternate lines of copy-book pages; this revise was treated in the same way—corrected, enlarged, interleaved, as it were, with minuter shades of feeling and more elaborate apparatus of parenthesis.[12]

Pater is said to have remarked to a student that he never published anything until he had written it out seven times.[13]

"From his first essay, down to the praise of Dorian discipline in his last book," wrote Lionel Johnson, "Pater loved the travail of the soul in art; his was something of the priest's, the soldier's abiding consciousness of law and limitation in their lives; orderliness, precision, ritual rigour, were dear to him; and to the strictness of artistic duty he gave the obedience of one under the salutary command of a superior." His writings demonstrate, Johnson continued, "a sensitiveness to the value, the precise value, of common words in their precise signification. *Mystery, economy, pagan, gracious, cordial, mortified*—to use such words, with just a hint of their first meanings, is for the scholarly writer and reader a delicate pleasure, heightening the vivid interest of a phrase. Mr. Pater's vocabulary is, for the most part, simple enough; and much of his curious charm comes from such feeling for the associations of ordinary words." At times the almost liturgical rhythm of Pater's language seems to place him before the altar of some religion of beauty, although Johnson preferred to place him in the high conversational tradition of the Oxford common room, observing that the effect of his style is "often that of a courteous, somewhat old-fashioned talker, at once urbane and easy, always leisurely and distinct."[14]

Pater's practice of "sympathetic translation" and his emphasis in the essay on "Style" and in *Plato and Platonism* upon the exercise of self-restraint and economy of means are partially indebted to the *Discourses* (1769 - 90) of Sir Joshua Reynolds. Reynolds insisted that artists must begin by imitating the masters in order that ultimately they may express ideal beauty in " 'the great style' "—a phrase quoted by Pater (*Marius*, I, 101; *Appreciations*, 209). Another of Pater's oft-repeated phrases, "the 'defects of its qualities' " (*Marius*, I, 98, *Appreciations*, 140, 180, 209; *Essays*, 15) was taken from the "Eighth Discourse" in which Reynolds remarks of novelty, variety, and contrast that "those qualities, . . . if they are carried to excess, become defects."[15] Pater's particular defect seems to have been a habit of overloading his sentences. Possibly the steady increase in their length during the first dozen years of his literary career (1866 - 78) reflects not only a refining upon nuances and an experimentation with cadencing, but also in part a desire to tone down vivid images and startling ideas by employing circumlocution. When he came to treat the modern, scientific ideas of the "Conclusion" in the chapter of *Marius* entitled "Animula Vagula," the longer sentences and the remote, antique context seem designed to disguise or mask the core thought. At times the core idea is deeply imbedded within sentence structures such as qualifying clauses, and at other times Pater splinters it by separating nouns and verbs with long phrases and modifying units. Often the central idea is not the concluding, emphasized idea; rather, antithetical clauses that further qualify, define, and control the meaning conclude. Thus the emotional impact of a sentence—even of a sentence with an exclamation point—is intellectually moderated.

Sometimes the idea is simply buried under an avalanche of words. An example from *Marius* (first edition) may serve:

That *Sturm und Drang* of the spirit, as it has been called, those ardent and special apprehensions of half-truths, in the enthusiastic, and as it were prophetic advocacy of which, a devotion to truth, in the case of the young—apprehending but one point at a time in the great circumference—most naturally embodies itself, are levelled down, surely and safely enough, afterwards, as in history so in the individual, by the weakness and mere weariness, as well as by the maturer wisdom, of our nature:—happily! if the enthusiasm which answered to but one phase of intellectual growth really blends, as it loses its decisiveness, in a larger and commoner morality, with wider though perhaps vaguer hopes. (*Marius*, II, 20 - 21)

This does seem to be an indirect way of saying that in time a young man tires of his identity crisis and turns his energies to more socially useful ends. Not surprisingly, Max Beerbohm accused Pater of writing English as if it were Latin (his parody is a classic): "I was angry that he should treat English as a dead language, bored by that sedulous ritual wherewith he laid out every sentence as in a shroud—hanging, like a widower, long over its marmoreal beauty or ever he could lay it, at length, in his book, its sepulchre."[16]

### III  *Le mot juste*

In the laborious process of composition, Pater perhaps took for a model the Parnassians, whose concern for artistic form was best expressed by the lines of Gautier in *Emaux et camées* ("L'Art"):

> Oui, l'oeuvre sort plus belle
> D'une forme au travail
> Rebelle
> Vers, marbre, onyx, émail.

For Pater as for the French Romantics, "literature itself became the most delicate of the arts—like 'goldsmith's work,' says Sainte-Beuve" (*Appreciations*, 255), and accordingly the goldsmiths of antiquity working with precious metal became Pater's exemplars of style (*Marius*, I, 96, 98). In the "Euphuism" chapter of *Marius*, the ancient *Pervigilium Veneris* is described as "a composition shaping itself, little by little, out of a thousand dim perceptions, into singularly definite form (definite and firm as fine-art in metal, thought Marius), . . . a firmness like that of some master of noble metal-work, manipulating tenacious bronze or gold" (I, 104, 115). Earlier, in "An English Poet," Pater had described his ideal style in exactly these terms of the artisan mastering rebellious materials. The verse of the English Poet has, says Pater, "a certain hardness like that of a gem, . . . somehow not altogether unlike that of the metal honeysuckle," the screenwork in his church, which wreathed itself in "metal flowers and flames." The hardness of the gem, taken together with the metal flames, suggests that the Aesthetic style, like the "hard, gemlike flame" of the Aesthetic moment, represents a fusion of palpable form with fluid spirit: "an elastic force in word and phrase, following a tender delicate thought or feeling as the metal followed the curvature of the flower, as seemed to indicate artistic triumph over a material partly resisting, which

yet at last took outline from his thought with the firmness of antique forms of mastery."[17]

In 1889 Pater expanded a review of Flaubert's. *Correspondance*
into the essay "Style," often considered a crystallizing and
rationalizing of his theories and habits as a writer. Certainly
Flaubert's search for *le mot juste*, "the one word for the one thing,
the one thought, amid the multitude of words, terms, that might
just do" (*Appreciations*, 29), typified Pater's own approach to
language. Yet already several years previously Pater had defined his
own style in *Marius*, implicitly paralleling the most prominent Latin
writers of the Antonine Age with the French Decadents and
himself. The attention that he gave in *Marius* to the style of Fronto,
Apuleius, and the author of the *Pervigilium Veneris* (Flavian, fan-
cifully supposed to be its author, echoes Fronto's concern for the
preciousness of words and a revitalized language) is owing to his
belief that in their reaction against the pedantry of the Classicists
they shared with the nineteenth century a common Romantic mode
of expression. Scholars have supported this identification of the
nineteenth-century Romantics with the Frontonian revival: Pater's
Oxford contemporary, G. A. Simcox, compares Fronto's literary
taste with "the French Romanticists of the second generation, few
of whom cared to read any work of the *Grand Siècle; . . .* what
Fronto really likes is a constant stream of far-fetched words coming
in appropriately, which was also what Théophile Gautier
liked—and Fronto knew, like Théophile Gautier, that this could
only be got by reading up old literature."[18] Mallarmé's exquisite
prose-poem, "Autumn Lament" (1864), is the most striking instance of the identification of contemporary Romanticism with
Roman decadence: "I have passed long days alone with . . . one of
the last writers of the Latin decadence; . . . I have loved all that
may be summed up in this word: fall. . . . And . . . the literature
from which my soul demands delight must be the dying poetry of
the last moments of Rome." Thus, together with such miscellaneous
precedents as Sir Thomas Browne and Charles Lamb from the recent past, the verse of Rossetti, the melodies of Swinburne, and the
biblical rhetoric of Ruskin in the present, Pater also had a coherent
"Romantic" prose tradition both of great antiquity and—as exemplified in Mallarmé's exquisite prose-poems—recent vitality.

Throughout his career, Pater continued to learn to write, im-
proving his choice of word forms and idiom and revising to avoid
solecisms and irrelevant details. Edmund Chandler made the in-

teresting observation that "Pater felt he could dismantle *Marius* into its component sentences, and then revise each as an entity in itself—an undertaking rather like cleaning a watch. For though the essay on 'Style' gives little support for such a view, it is clear from the revision that for Pater the art of writing was synonymous with the composition of sentences."[19] Although the second edition of *Marius* (November 1885) differed from the first only in small changes of punctuation and wording—as well as in the suppression of the grotesque scene involving an accidental incineration of a live cat—the third edition (1892) underwent six thousand corrections, many minimal, but several significant. The four versions of *The Renaissance* essays (or five versions if one considers their prior periodical publication) reflect even more sharply Pater's struggle not only with the received morality but also with syntax, diction, and punctuation.[20] Revisions of a description of Titian's coloration are typical of this effort for precision. In the original *Fortnightly* version Pater spoke of "that weaving of imperceptible gold threads of light"; in the third edition it read: "that weaving as of just perceptible gold threads of light"; finally in the fourth edition it became: "that weaving of light, as of just perceptible gold threads" (*Renaissance*, 132). Even such mundane grammatical problems as pronoun reference were only gradually resolved. In speaking of Abelard, the first edition told "how the famous and comely clerk . . . came to live in the house of a canon of the church of Notre Dame, where dwelt a girl Heloïse, believed to be *his* orphan niece, *his* love for whom *he* had testified by giving her an education then unrivalled." In the second edition Pater corrected the most ambiguous pronoun by making the phrase read, "the old priest's orphan niece." Though the meaning was now clear, in the fourth edition Pater both strengthened the parallel structure and, at the expense of a repetition, removed any lingering doubt as to who was Heloise's uncle or who had given her an education by rewriting the final clause to read, "how the old priest had testified his love for her . . ." (4, emphasis added).

Seemingly, only after the second edition did Pater search his text to remove the uneuphonious recurrence of words, many so obvious that it is puzzling how he could have missed them for so long, as, for example: "Perhaps it was a sense of this . . . that made Camilla Rucellai, one of those *prophetesses* whom the preaching of Savonarola had raised up in Florence, *prophesy* . . . that he would depart in the time of lilies." In the third edition he altered the dissonant "prophetesses" to "prophetic women" and "prophesy" to "declare" (44, emphasis added). In another instance, speaking of Michelangelo's incomplete sculpture, Pater only partially succeeded in muting the jarring repetition in the phrase, "if that half-hewn form ever quite emerged from the rough hewn stone," by employing his notorious Paterine *so:* "if that half-hewn form ever quite emerged from the stone, so rough hewn here, so delicately finished there." The problem is resolved only in the third edition by changing "half-hewn" to "half-realised" (68). In yet another instance, as early as the second edition, Pater tried to correct the clash of "sitting in an uneasy sitting attitude" by changing the phrase to "sitting in an uneasy inclined *posture,*" inadvertently—and completely oblivious to it in the third edition—creating a new dissonance with a preceding phrase, "seated in a stooping *posture.*" Not until the final edition did he change the second occurrence of "posture" back to "attitude" (115, emphasis added).

Pater also revised to gain precision of import. For example, the first edition has Michelangelo's broken nose depriving him forever of "the dignity of outward form," but the third, recognizing that dignity should not depend upon the shape of the nose, is emended to "comeliness" (78); and Botticelli, called "a second-rate painter," is in the edition following the first connotatively upgraded to "a secondary painter" (61). Also, in several instances an early exaggerated specificity of image is corrected, indicative of Pater's growing sobriety and restraint of diction. Three examples from the 1877 *Fortnightly* essay on Giorgione are especially illuminating. Pater had originally observed that the perfection of poetry depends on a suppression of subject so that "the definite meaning almost expires, or reaches us through . . . music." In the third edition, Pater eliminated the odd personification, producing instead the simpler: "meaning reaches us through . . . music" (137). A few pages further on in the original essay Pater spoke of paintings that "enrich the air as with a personal aroma," but wisely corrected this to "some choice aroma" (141) in the reprinting. Again, speaking of the "ideal instants" of aesthetic experience, Pater initially had described them as "an extract, or elixir, or consummate fifth part of life," but retreated in the third edition from the awkward literalism to compare those moments to "some consummate extract or quintessence of life" (150). Finally, after the first edition, the cognoscente's liberty with names is made to conform to standard usage, and either English equivalents are substituted for the unexplained foreign words and phrases or else a translation is inserted in apposition.

## IV   *The Expanded Interval*

Pater's care for *le mot juste* was not a mere fussiness over language, but was motivated by his perception that each mind, trapped within the perpetual flux and "keeping as a solitary prisoner its own dream of a world," can transcend isolation and death only by an exact recreation of itself in semiotic systems. "We are all *condemnés*," writes Pater, "we have an interval, and then our place knows us no more"; our one chance "lies in expanding that interval, in getting as many pulsations as possible into the given time" (*Renaissance*, 238). Like the Roman empire or the Roman church, language possesses for the isolated self "the expanding power of a great experience" (*Marius*, II, 26). Through the creation of linguistic structures that mirror his unique configurations of perception and response, Pater-Marius can "expand" his interval, can join collective humanity and establish a permanent form for himself:

Could he but arrest, for others also, certain clauses of experience, as the imaginative memory presented them to himself! In those grand, hot summers, he would have imprisoned the very perfume of the flowers. To create, to live, perhaps, a little while beyond the allotted hours, if it were but in a fragment of perfect expression:—it was thus his longing defined itself for something to hold by amid the "perpetual flux." With men of his vocation, people were apt to say, words were things. Well! with him, words should be indeed things,—the word, the phrase, valuable in exact proportion to the transparency with which it conveyed to others the apprehension, the emotion, the mood, so vividly real within himself. (I, 155)

The deliberate association of "imprisoned" both with "arrest" and with "clauses" (*claudere*, to close up) illustrates perfectly Pater's sensitiveness to the precise signification of words. That imprisonment of which he speaks is not, of course, the self trapped within the flux of sensations, but rather, as with the Symbolists, the fleeting, individual sensations caught in luminous symbols of "the mood," the self freed "to live . . . in a fragment of perfect expression."

It is exactly this relation of one's individual, sensuous impressions to language that emerges as a leading preoccupation of *Plato and Platonism*. Pater's concern in the central chapters is to show that the real difference between, on the one hand, Plato and Socrates and, on the other, the Sophists consisted entirely in their divergent attitudes toward language:

whether it is necessary, or even advantageous, for one . . . to know, and consciously to keep himself in touch with, the truth of his subject as he *knows* or *feels* it; or only with what other people, perhaps quite indolently, *think*, or suppose others to think, about it. . . . That you yourself must have an inward, carefully ascertained, measured, instituted hold over anything you are to convey with any real power to others, is the truth which the Platonic Socrates, in strongly convinced words . . . formulates. . . . It is but a kind of bastard art of mere words . . . that he will have who does not know the *truth* of things, but has tried to hunt out what other people *think* about it. (*Plato*, 116 - 18)

As Pater remarks of Rossetti's "gift of transparency in language," his meaning "was always personal and even recondite; . . . but the term was always, one could see, deliberately chosen from many competitors, as the just transcript of that peculiar phase of soul which he alone knew, precisely as he knew it" (*Appreciations*, 215). Yet such a personal style, although a testament to the artist's individuality, is not proof of solitude, of his entrapment in an isolating dream of a world. Although in the final analysis Socrates had "doubts as to the power of words to convey thoughts" (*Plato*, 88), Pater asserts that artistic expression, although uniquely individual, also participates in a common sphere of meaning.

In Marius' fanciful speculations, as well as according to Realist doctrine, the ontological status of "the word" is assumed "to be not a mere name, *nomen*, as with the nominalists, nor a mere subjective thought as with the conceptualists, but to be *res*, a thing in itself, independent . . . of the particular mind which entertains it." The actual relation of the individual mind to language, however, is defined in Pater's scheme as a compromise between Realist and Conceptualist notions:

there is a general consciousness . . . independent . . . of us, but with which we are . . . in communication . . . [and in which] common or general ideas really reside. And . . . those abstract or common notions come to the individual mind through language, . . . into which one's individual experience, little by little, drop by drop, conveys . . . content; and, by the instrumentality of such terms and notions . . . mediating . . . between our individual experience and the common experience of our kind, we come to understand each other, and to assist each other's thoughts, as in a common mental atmosphere. (151 - 52)

Just as Mona Lisa's experiences created, "little cell by cell," an outward form expressive of "all modes of thought and life"

(*Renaissance*, 125) and just as the *Pervigilium Veneris* shaped itself "little by little, out of a thousand dim perceptions," so also individual experience conveys content, "little by little, drop by drop," into a language expressive of a common mind. This concept of language as a vehicle for multiple meanings coincides so closely with the Symbolist conception of poetry that Pater's 1891 - 92 lectures seem almost verbally to echo Mallarmé's 1891 interview with Jules Huret: "To *name* an object," says Mallarmé, "is to destroy three-fourths of the enjoyment of the poem which comes from deciphering bit by bit. The ideal is to *suggest*. It is the perfect use of this mystery that constitutes symbol: to evoke an object, little by little, in order to show a state of the soul [*évoquer petit à petit un objet pour montrer un état d'âme*] or, conversely, to select an object and extricate a state of soul from it by means of a series of decodings."[21]

Harmonizing like notes in a musical composition, Mallarmé's words evoke through a generalized and multimeaningful symbol a reality beyond the senses. "For what is the magic charm of art, if not this: that, beyond the confines of a handful of dust or of all other reality, beyond the book itself, beyond the very text, it delivers up that volatile scattering which we call the Spirit, Who cares for nothing save universal musicality."[22] Pater, too, finds in the symbolic capacity of language an avenue from the solipsistic predicament. Although the self's experience "is ringed round for each one of us by that thick wall of personality through which no real voice has ever pierced" (235), an indirect, linguistically mediated relation of the individual to the "general consciousness" is possible. And so Pater sought tirelessly for that "pre-existent adaptation, between a relative, somewhere in the world of thought, and its correlative, somewhere in the world of language—both alike, rather, somewhere in the mind of the artist" (*Appreciations*, 30). Through the perfect adaptation of interior sensations and ideas ("the world of thought") to externally existing linguistic possibilities ("the world of language"), the private and inward is re-created in the common and external. By identifying the world of language as that in which its life consists, the self transcends its limited condition and experiences the "dissolving away" or spiritualizing of "that close, impassable prison-wall" (*Marius*, II, 70) of the material world. Analogous to the "clear crystal nature" (*Miscellaneous Studies*, 253) of Pater's ideal hero in "Diaphanéité," this mode of linguistic "transparency" to which Marius aspires is elsewhere described as a state in which "the material and spiritual are fused and blent: if the spiritual attains the definite visibility of a crystal, what is material loses its earthiness and impurity" (*Appreciations*, 212; *Plato*, 135). Mallarmé, too, proposing to spiritualize concrete reality, desires "to give a purer sense to the words of the tribe," as he puts it in his sonnet on Poe's tomb. "The pure work," he says in "Crisis in Poetry," "implies the elocutionary disappearance of the poet who yields the initiative to words set in motion as they meet unequally in collision; they take light from mutual reflection, like an actual train of fire over precious stones, replacing the perceptible breathing in the old lyric afflatus or the passionate, personal control of the phrase."[23] For Pater, as for Mallarmé, the likeliest way to burn with the "hard, gemlike flame" is to create for the evanescent flame of thought or feeling a visible but pure form in the hard, material structures of word or phrase.

It is scarcely necessary to argue a direct influence between Pater and Mallarmé—Pater could not, for example, have known of Hérodiade before writing his passage on Mona Lisa—in order to speak of their profound affinity, for behind each lay powerful common influences: Baudelaire, Gautier, even Swedenborg. Yet, late in their lives they did meet, and that momentous event can only be described as typical of life's ironies, for not one word passed between them. On March 1, 1894, to an audience of two or three dons, a few students, and fifty or sixty ladies, Mallarmé delivered at Oxford his most comprehensive aesthetic statement and greatest prose work, the now-famous lecture on "Music and Literature." The requirement that lectures in the series be delivered in English was circumvented when York Powell, his Oxford host, "made a translation with heroic rapidity one night and read it to a small gathering: the delivery by the author in French before the full audience took place next day." It is altogether likely that Pater was a listener at that February 28 gathering: "An eye-witness describes how Powell invited Walter Pater to his rooms to meet Mallarmé, perhaps his nearest brother-in-arms among the craftsmen of prose. Mallarmé taught English in a *lycée*; Pater was deeply versed in French; but neither would venture on the language of the other master. They regarded each other in silence, and were satisfied, while Powell's voice was heard in alternate tongues."[24] But upon returning to France, Mallarmé composed "Cloîtres," in which, evoking his experiences and discoveries among the Oxford and Cambridge cloisters, he proudly mentioned his acquaintance with the pre-eminent "*prosateur*" of the time, later specifying in his notes that this was "the late illustrious Walter Pater."[25]

That Pater ultimately influenced such younger writers as Yeats, Eliot, and Joyce is in no small measure owing to the fact that he could write English the way Mallarmé and the others wrote French. As early as 1874 critics had divined the "impossible" poetic nature of *The Renaissance.* "This is plain, downright, unmistakable poetry," thundered the critical W. J. Courthope the year after its appearance.[26] Courthope's outrage, sparked by the description of Leonardo's lady Lisa, is an indication of Pater's originality, for whereas on the one hand his "poetic prose" harked back to the Euphuists, Elizabethan or Antonine, on the other hand it was so attuned to contemporary theory that W. B. Yeats' collection of modern verse offered Pater's passage on the Mona Lisa as its first poem:

> She is older than the rocks among which she sits;
> Like the Vampire,
> She has been dead many times,
> And learned the secrets of the grave;
> And has been a diver in deep seas,
> And keeps their fallen day about her;
> And trafficked for strange webs with Eastern merchants;
> And, as Leda,
> Was the mother of Helen of Troy,
> And, as St Anne,
> Was the mother of Mary;
> And all this has been to her but as the sound of lyres and flutes,
> And lives
> Only in the delicacy
> With which it has moulded the changing lineaments,
> And tinged the eyelids and the hands.

Its exotic anaphora seemingly reserved specifically for the climax of Pater's volume, this became the passage, so Yeats testifies, that "dominated a generation"—dominated both by its surreal sound patterns as well as by its eerily corresponding reduction of the whole sweep of human history to the symbol of a single smile.[27]

In general, the strong emotional and sensuous coloring of this early style gradually yields to an increased gravity, simplicity, and restraint. Arthur Symons, who had been among the first to note the stylistic evolution that occurred during the twelve years that separated *The Renaissance* from *Marius,* found the style of the novel to be "less coloured" and "in its more arduous self-repression, has a graver note, and brings with it a severer kind of beauty."[28]

Pater's diction seems more abstract, the sharp images and concrete nouns used literally to enhance the forcefulness of certain 1873 passages are absent in *Marius*; there is no equivalent image to the gem-like flame nor any "purple panels" of the Gioconda kind. Playing down the rarified emotional effects and the exaggerated sensuous aspects of phrase and image, *Marius* is distinguished less by color than by light, although its richness and elaboration is still a far cry from the "archaic and monochromatic purity"[29] of Pater's last volume. This last work, *Plato and Platonism,* is an important consideration of language and of the connection between art and life, but the limitations of the study lie in its genesis as a series of lectures offered to the Brasenose undergraduates. Although highly polished (Israel Zangwell recalled that when he told Pater the book had a pun, Pater "asked anxiously for its precise locality, so that he might remove it"[30]), few critics have been wholly in sympathy with the outcome of Pater's stylistic development. "In his return to an early, and one might think, in a certain sense, immature interest," writes Symons, "it need not surprise us to find a development, which I cannot but consider as technically something of a return to a primitive lengthiness and involution, towards a style which came to lose many of the rarer qualities of its perfect achievement."[31] Symons is possibly thinking here of Pater's first published essay on Coleridge as metaphysician, an essay that espoused the predominantly Positivist philosophy of the *Westminster Review* and that, owing to the abstractions of its subject, was stylistically not far from the arid and complicated prose of Herbert Spencer. Because of its "perfection of style," Edmund Gosse ultimately selected *Marius* as "the work by which, I believe, Pater will pre-eminently be known to posterity."[32] But Kenneth Clark, comparing *The Renaissance* to *Marius*, dismissed Pater's novel as "a prolonged piece of self-justification," which, "in spite of many beautiful passages, is almost unreadable as a whole. The 'gem-like' flame which he recommends in his suppressed Conclusion was discreetly shaded, and *The Renaissance* remains his most vivid and accessible work."[33] Pater himself seems to have favored successively his *Imaginary Portraits* and *Plato and Platonism* though the "legitimate contention," as he perhaps might have maintained, should not be of one book against another, but of all alike "against the stupidity which is dead to the substance, and the vulgarity which is dead to form" (*Appreciations,* 261).

## V *Summit of Career*

By 1894 Pater stood pre-eminent among the living English critics of the day—Matthew Arnold, the great critical voice of the century, had died in 1888 and John Ruskin had long since sunk into despair and insanity. The Pater who scandalized Oxford by challenging all the solemnities of the mid-century was gone, and Edmund Gosse approved. "One of our novelists has been described as always writing at the top of his voice," but Pater, said Gosse, "never writes above a whisper."[34] What was figuratively true of Pater's later prose style could be said literally of his public lectures, which, according to Oscar Wilde, Pater's auditors did not so much hear as overhear.[35] With students in his private quarters at the college, Pater also seemed a reserved and contemplative preceptor. Quoting Sir Arthur Quiller-Couch's recollection of Pater as sitting "upon a hearthrug with his back to the fire, . . . cross-legged, with the light flickering on his baldish cranium, his moustaches pendulous in the shadow: a somewhat Oriental figure," another undergraduate recalled that for him Pater's "characteristic attitude is sitting sideways, head on hand, on the window-seat of his room in Brasenose. But the revealing word is 'Oriental.' Something Oriental there was, perhaps, in the set of the cheek-bones and the eyes; but to a youngster much more in the impression of profound wisdom and manifold experience."[36] Will Rothenstein verbally sketched Pater at this time as

neatly dressed; slightly stooping shoulders: a thick moustache, above rather heavy lips, grey eyes a shade too close together, a little restless, even evasive, under dark eyebrows. He had a habit, disquieting to young people, of assuming ignorance on subjects about which he was perfectly informed. He questioned me closely about Mallarmé and Verlaine, Huysmans and de Goncourt, and the younger French writers. Guarded in his talk, careful of expressing his own opinions, he was adept at inviting indiscretions from his guests. . . . He asked much about Whistler, for whom he had no great admiration. I did try one day to get his opinion of Oscar Wilde, who regarded Pater as his master. "Oh Wilde, yes, he always has a phrase." I told this afterwards to Oscar, who affected to be delighted. "A perfect thing to have said of one," he murmured, "he always has a phrase."

Rothenstein had wanted to include Pater in a lithograph series of Oxford notables, but found him "morbidly self-conscious about his appearance." Pater's closest Oxford friend in these years, F. W. Bussell, fellow and chaplain of Brasenose, sat first for Rothenstein.

Bussell reported that Pater had approved the result and was "no longer averse to sitting." But, Rothenstein recalls, when the proofs came, Pater was upset at his portrait. "He had taken the print into Bussell's room, lying it on the table without comment. They then went together for their usual walk; but not a word was spoken. On their return, as Pater left Bussell at his door, he broke silence. 'Bussell, do I look like a Barbary ape?' "[37]

Although Pater felt academic honor might most fittingly have come from his own university of Oxford, he traveled to Glasgow in April of 1894 to receive the first and only honorary degree of his career. Writing busily now, he anticipated many more years of fruitful labor. Not only was there *Gaston de Latour* to finish, but he had also gotten well along with two shorter imaginary portraits, "Tibalt the Albigense" and "Gaudioso, the Second." Then there were numerous essays on topics ranging from evil in Greek art to the relation of art to religion, not to mention studies of Thomas Hobbes, Samuel Johnson, Sappho, John Henry Newman, and Blaise Pascal. Pater was occupied with the Pascal in early June when he suffered an attack of rheumatic fever. In Paris, on her way to England, Violet Paget heard that he was ill and remarked to her mother in a letter of June 9 that the Paters could not have her at their home. After an apparent quiescence of the disease during which he resumed work on the Pascal lecture, Pater developed pleurisy in consequence of writing too close to an open window. Under the care of his sisters, he rallied sufficiently to suppose mistakenly that it was medically safe to leave his room. But the following morning, July 30, 1894, on again going downstairs he suffered a heart attack and died in the arms of his sister. Pater had been so oblivious to the necessity of extensive bed-rest that apparently during his first convalescence he had contemplated a rural holiday. Bussell afterwards recalled that "his death took place on the very day for which he had planned a visit to an old farmhouse of mine in Devon; with infinite forethought and care mapped out for the pleasure of his sisters, and by me expected with keen anticipation of walks and drives together."[38] Pater was buried at Holywell Cemetery, Oxford, and, according to his request, the words of the Psalmist were inscribed on a large marble cross that marks his grave: *"In te, Domine, speravi"* ("In you, Lord, I have hoped"). For Pater, if not for the poet of sacred song, the text chosen hinted for the last time at the mental atmosphere of the skeptical probabilist, free of dogmatic certainty yet with "a duly receptive attitude towards such possible truth, discovery, or revelation, as may one day . . . shed itself on the purified air" (*Plato*, 188). Bussell, who according to Pater had preached some remarkable sermons in Saint Mary's pulpit, delivered the memorial tribute for his friend in the college chapel the following October.

CHAPTER 6

# *Pater and the Modern Temper*

IN *The Romantic '90s*, Richard Le Gallienne pays tribute to the centrality of Pater among the literati of the *fin de siècle:* "Among the men . . . who were rapidly putting on immortality under our very eyes, perhaps the most important of all, as in certain directions the most influential, was . . . Walter Pater. Mr. George Moore has put himself on record more than once to the effect that Pater's 'Marius the Epicurean' is the most beautiful book in the English tongue. This was the opinion also of many young men in the '90s."[1] In his *Confessions of a Young Man,* Moore had praised Pater's novel as "the book to which I owe the last temple of my soul," declaring that he shared with the novel "the same incurable belief that the beauty of material things is sufficient for all the needs of life."[2] When Moore sent Pater a copy of the *Confessions,* the master acknowledged his enjoyment of the book, but commented on its hedonistic philosophy (March 4, 1888): " 'Thou com'st in such a questionable shape!'—I feel inclined to say, on finishing your book: 'shape'—morally, I mean; not in reference to style. . . . I wonder how much you may be losing, both for yourself and for your writings, by what, in spite of its gaiety and good-nature and genuine sense of the beauty of many things, I must still call a cynical, and therefore exclusive, way of looking at the world. You call it only 'realistic'. Still—!' "

## I   *The Rhymers' Club*

In the 1870s, certainly, it was easy to misread Pater; and if he had failed to publish successive "correctives" in the 1880s and 1890s, one could justly accuse him of being culpably vague about Aesthetic ideals. Even so, for the young man of the 1890s, no mere "corrective" succeeded in altering Pater's message, and in aftertimes one of their number blamed the "attitude of mind" expressed in *Marius*, rather than in the "Conclusion," for putting them on the "tight-rope" of intensity: "Three or four years ago I reread *Marius the Epicurean*, expecting to find I cared for it no longer," wrote W. B. Yeats in his *Autobiography* in 1922, "but it still seemed to me, as I think it seemed to us all, the only great prose in modern English, and yet I begin to wonder if it, or the attitude of mind of which it was the noblest expression, had not caused the disaster of my friends. It taught us to walk upon a rope, tightly stretched through serene air, and we were left to keep our feet upon a swaying rope in a storm."[3]

The "friends" to whom Yeats is here specifically making reference were members of the Rhymers' Club, fellow walkers on the tightrope of ecstasy, precariously alienated from their audience and isolated from each other. Obsessed with innocence and evil in a society that cared merely for respectability, they led lives that were at best "untidy," and, as one critic observed, most died as soon as their constitutions would decently permit. In Pater's novel, the Rhymers saw only the solitary figure of Marius, isolated from life as if on some high-wire, balancing between birth and death a whole dreamworld of ideally exquisite passions. They loved those choice moments of revelation or near revelation extracted from among common events; their spirits soared in awe at the suggestion of a vision lurking just behind the veil of gross reality. John Davidson might aestheticize telegraph wires and factory chimneys; Symons might find inspiration in the theater, the dance hall, the café; and Le Gallienne might allude to the "iron lilies of the Strand" (the gaslights); but in general the Rhymers tended to avoid as far as possible any contamination by quotidian life. They learned from the writings of Pater the paradoxical lesson that beauty was both the supreme manifestation of culture and yet radically independent of that culture. They looked to an inner vision, not out toward the world around them, and drifted ever deeper into their private world of rarefied emotions.

Among the Rhymers, Yeats, Johnson, Dowson, Symons, Herbert Horne, and Wilde (who was an occasional visitor to the club when it met in private houses) could be numbered as the chief disciples of Pater. In 1894, the Rhymers were associated together in John Lane's quarterly, *The Yellow Book*; and Pater was listed in its "Prospectus" as a forthcoming contributor, but he died three months after the issue of the first number. Although these young men barely articulated an artistic philosophy of their own, Pater's "Conclusion" focused much of what they believed. It more than any other document sums up his influence on his disciples, and such passages in *Marius* as the "Animula Vagula" chapter, which Yeats later cites in his *Memoirs* as influential, were simply viewed as giving an antique setting to the modern Aesthetic doctrines of *The Renaissance*. Pater may have wished the "Conclusion" to be read as merely a prologue to his broader concern with cultural heritage, but just as his writings had extended the premises of Arnold's, Rossetti's, and Ruskin's views of art, so among the Rhymers there occurred a certain drawing out of attitudes that pertained almost exclusively to the "Conclusion." During the three or four years of its existence, the club carried the banner of art for art's sake and celebrated Pater's writings as the ultimate expression of that slogan.

In his "Introduction" to *The Oxford Book of Modern Verse*, Yeats wrote:

The revolt against Victorianism meant to the young poet a revolt against irrelevant descriptions of nature, the scientific and moral discursiveness of *In Memoriam*, . . . the political eloquence of Swinburne, the psychological curiosity of Browning, and the poetical diction of everybody. . . . Poetry was a tradition like religion and liable to corruption, and it seemed that [poets] could best restore it by writing lyrics technically perfect, their emotion pitched high, and as Pater offered instead of moral earnestness life lived as "a pure gem-like flame" all accepted him for master.[4]

Then, as an example of pure poetry detaching itself from the flux in a moment of ecstasy, Yeats began his anthology by printing in *vers libre* Pater's purple passage on the Mona Lisa. In his *Autobiography*, Yeats explained something of the tragedy in the lives of two of the most promising Rhymers, Ernest Dowson and Lionel Johnson, precisely in terms of this obsession with a "pure" beauty "separated from all the general purposes of life." They made in their writing, said Yeats, "what Arnold has called that 'morbid effort,' that search for 'perfection of thought and feeling, and to unite this to perfection of form,' sought this new, pure beauty, and suffered in their lives because of it."[5]

In later years Yeats acknowledged that whereas Rossetti's work had held an emotional, subconscious attraction for him, the Paterian celebration of pure, intense experience provided him with his conscious aesthetic program. Stylistically the early Yeats out-

Paters Pater, attempting in the sensuous languor and rich, per-fumed, verbal voluptuousness of his poetry and prose to attain to ideal forms of purified, hieratic passion. Particularly notable is Yeats' fantasy, "Rosa Alchemica" (1896), modeled on Pater's prose rhythms and presenting an 1890s-style Marius as its hero: "I gathered about me all gods because I believed in none, and ex-perienced every pleasure because I gave myself to none, but held myself apart, individual, indissoluble, a mirror of polished steel."[6] As Yeats evolved toward a poetic style with a new, astringent beau-ty, he sloughed off the stock Romantic pathos and derivative diction of the 1890s. In "The Phases of the Moon" (1919), Yeats had his puppet figure Robartes complain, "He wrote of me in that ex-travagant style / He had learnt from Pater." But as a *prosateur*, Yeats never repudiated Pater's polyphonic richness and subtle con-sonance. From such earlier visionary prose-poems as "The Moods" (1895) and "The Autumn of the Body" (1898) to later works such as *Per Amica Silentia Lunae* (1917), the *Autobiography* (1914, 1922), and "Dove or Swan" in *A Vision* (1925), Yeats displayed a diction and cadence worthy of the most ardent of Pater's stylistic disciples.

But more sinister than any stylistic indulgence was Yeats' pursuit of that intensity that Pater had suggested as the chief end of man. Art, Pater had affirmed, should convey the most intense moments of life, refining experience until, nearing the purity and elevation of religious ritual, passion yields up knowledge and vision. For the Rhymers this Paterian "ecstasy" connoted the perfect absence of ideology or value judgments. In a broadcast entitled "Modern Poetry," Yeats recalled that the Rhymers "wished to express life at its intense moments, those moments that are brief because of their intensity, and at those moments alone."[7] This poetry of ecstasy looked to the flux of immediate impressions for its nourishment, and Yeats noted that when he began to write he avowed for his models those poets of "the aesthetic school" who "intermixed into their poetry no elements from the general thought, but wrote out of the impression made by the world upon their delicate senses."[8] He is undoubtedly recalling here the antecedent Keatsian celebration of beauty mediated so impressively through Rossetti; however, it was Pater who explicitly proclaimed these subjective impressions of beauty as the only knowable reality. The first step of critic and artist alike is "to know one's own impression as it really is" (*Renaissance*, viii).[9] Pater used the word *impression* a half dozen times in the sec-ond paragraph alone of the "Preface" to *The Renaissance*, and in the "Conclusion" he exhorted the young man of Oxford "to be for ever curiously testing new opinions and courting new impressions" (237). But Yeats lived long enough eventually to be troubled by the exclusion of so much from this poetry of intense moments, for it left him, as he says, "alone amid the obscure impressions of the senses."[10]

Because of difference of opinion and the clash of personalities, the Rhymers gradually separated in 1894 or 1895. But Yeats never abandoned his belief in Paterian intensity; rather, as his contemplative passions became active he quit the ivory tower and descended into the marketplace. His discovery that the gem-like flame burned not only as emblem of the isolated dream but also, Janus-faced, as emblem of the larger vision of cultural history led him to reconsider his strictures on the isolation of the aesthetic moment. In his elegy for the active, social Robert Gregory, Yeats created after the fashion of Pater a portrait of the urbane yet impassioned aesthete dead in his prime. Like an aristocratic Irish version of Pater's Duke Carl, Gregory burned with the Paterian "intensity" of a true Renaissance polymath: "Our Sidney and our perfect man." Yeats put the Mona Lisa passage on page one of his Oxford anthology precisely because he came to realize that Gregory's flame and Lisa's smile foreshadowed alike a modern poetry in which human experience is "no longer shut into brief lives, cut off into this place and that place."[11] Yeats ultimately seems to have found Pater's female goddess not the fatally isolating mistress of Rhymers, but an emblem of domestic and societal renascence. In "A Prayer for my Daughter" (1919), he sought the custom and ceremony of Cecilia's holy house for his child Anne, who, he prayed, might also be learned in "courtesy" and mistress of a house where innocence and beauty are born "in custom and ceremony." Anne's "radical innocence" of soul and her ritualistic bridegroom are Yeats' elaboration of the Psyche-Cecilia ideal as Pater had portrayed it. No longer is Pater's aesthetics an isolating tightrope in a storm; the gale may come howling, but Anne quietly sleeps, guarded by what Pater would call her bond with all worthy men, living and dead.

## II    *Three Paterides*

Although Pater never met Yeats, the three Rhymers who knew Pater well—Arthur Symons, Lionel Johnson, and Oscar Wilde— were the avenue through which most of his ideas reached Yeats. Arthur Symons was only seventeen when he discovered Pater's work. "It was from reading Pater's 'Studies in the History of the Renaissance,' in its first edition on ribbed paper (I have the feel of it still in my fingers), that I realized that prose also could be a fine art," he recalled. "That book opened a new world to me, or, rather, gave me the key or secret of the world in which I was living."[12] Symons was delighted when Pater wrote a favorable review of his study of Browning, and some two years later, after exchanging occasional letters, they met in 1888. They became more intimately acquainted a few months later on the occasion of their second meeting after Pater's reserve and Symons' veneration had moderated: "I spent some hours very pleasantly with Pater at Oxford," Symons reported to a friend of this visit, "lunched in his rooms, and . . . went with him all about the place. You would never imagine what a cicerone—almost bustling—he can be! I like him much better than I did in the first meeting—we met more as friends, naturally, and I was less awed, so much less, indeed, as to discover in him an unsuspected and most charming *simplicity*."[13]

About three or four years later some slackening in the friendship occurred, possibly because certain decadent and erotic overtones emerging in Symons' poetry and life caused Pater to reassess his young admirer. Symons used the art for art's sake theories of the "Conclusion" to justify his attempt to capture the sensate possibilities in every passing instant. In "Credo" he wrote: "For of our time we lose so large a part / In serious trifles, and so oft let slip / The wine of every moment, at the lip / Its moment, the moment of the heart." And in a passage which seems almost a verbal echo of the "Conclusion" (with the definite exception of the last image), Symons wrote: "If ever there was a religion of the eyes . . . I practised that religion . . . always the same eager hope of seeing some beautiful or interesting person, some gracious movement, or delicate expression, which would be gone if I did not catch it. . . . Life ran past me continually, and I tried to make all its bubbles my own."[14] Symons carried this philosophy with him when he became literary editor of *The Savoy* (1896), that magazine so typical of the temper of the 1890s. An incessant traveler, Symons was forever snatching at one impression after another, and he never really could sustain a general argument for longer than the length of an essay.

Ernest Dowson, who sang of remote, ideal love and the vanity of life, produced in his "Non Sum Qualis Eram Bonae Sub Regno Cynarae" (1896) the definitive expression of alienation: "I have

forgot much, Cynara! gone with the wind, / Flung roses, roses
riotously with the throng, / Dancing, to put thy pale, lost lilies out
of mind. . . ." The distance from the "Conclusion" to this expression of the brevity of life and its despair was shorter than Pater had
realized. *Marius*, too, with its almost mystical love of religious ritual
and its beatific vision of the saintly Cecilia and the Christian community was easily assimilated into Dowson's despairing
Catholicism. There are specific echoes, even, such as the one in
Dowson's "Extreme Unction" in which the phrase "all the passages
of sense" is taken from Pater's description of the last sacrament
(*Marius*, II, 224). Pater's fatal Lady Lisa shadowed not only Dowson's profane loves but also his sacred ideal, Cynara, who as
Adelaide Foltinowitz was his twelve-year-old epitome of innocence.
Failing to capture this beatific vision of purity, Dowson stumbled
toward death, memorably portrayed by Symons as having the face
of a "demoralized Keats." Or perhaps he was more like a Pater who
had visited the France of Verlaine, Baudelaire, and Gautier and on
whose return the sea-change was apparent, the taint of mortality
was upon him. And so in his "Villanelle" Dowson cries: "Unto us
they belong / Us the bitter and gay, / Wine and women and song."
He was dead of tuberculosis and drink at thirty-two.

Lionel Johnson in his self-imposed isolation was another casualty.
While he was yet a schoolboy, Lionel Johnson was echoing in his
letters the Aestheticism of the early Pater:

I do not love sensuality; I do not hate it; I do not love purity; I do not hate
it, I regard both as artistic aspects of life. . . . I will not call anything "sin"; I
deal neither in "poison nor pap"; I am an "impressionist" in
life. . . . "Aestheticism" . . . so far as it means the gospel of emotion waking an artistic morality . . . is a high hope for mankind. . . . A man's life
is not his acts of profession; drills, sermons, death beds, stone breaking, are
not the Life; but the accidents of life; the life is the sunsets we worship, the
books we read, the faces we love.

But Johnson's mature work repudiates much of this. "I heartily hate
the cant of 'art for art's sake,' " he wrote, "I have spent years in trying to understand what is meant by that imbecile phrase."[15]
Perhaps the circumstance that Johnson happened to have read
*Marius* before reading *The Renaissance* explains why the Pater of
the 1870s was less an influence on him than the Pater of the 1880s
and 1890s. Thomas Wright claims that after Pater honored his
young friend with a presentation copy of *Plato*, Johnson wrote an

essay on him that he submitted to the master "who praised both its style and the scholarship it displayed."[16] This does suggest that Johnson's interpretation has a special authority, and it is safe to say that his tribute in the *Fortnightly* is the best evaluation of Pater's work by any of his contemporaries.

Somehow the friendship between the two flourished despite Johnson's self-imposed isolation. He rose at six in the evening, spent his waking hours in his library in the company of whisky, and went to bed at dawn. Like Sebastian van Storck, he hated his image, and after the age of twenty-one would not allow himself to be photographed or drawn. But Pater was worth the effort of a visit, and Johnson reported after one such excursion that the master had "talked theology and praised Anglicanism for its 'reverent doubt and sober mysticism.' "[17] Sharing religious mysticism and a tendency to distill the intellectual aspects of religion into gracious sentiment, the two also shared a style sensitive to the precise value of words, a style that often pressed words back into their Latinate meanings. Twice Johnson wrote of Pater in his poetry. "A Friend" (1894) begins: "His are the whitenesses of soul, / That Virgil had. . . ." And in the 1902 elegy Johnson praised Pater as the "Hierarch of the spirit" and "Scholarship's constant saint," extolling him at the conclusion as "that unforgettably most gracious friend." But the Paterian contrast between the ideal whiteness of soul and the life of the senses becomes in Johnson's religious poetry a tragic conflict exacerbated by the introspective melancholia of his spiritual isolation. Although he understood Pater's humanism and his call for an aesthetic in harmony with cultural norms, Johnson almost despite himself felt the sinister undertow of a shadow self, the "Dark Angel": "Through thee, the gracious Muses turn / To Furies, O mine Enemy! / And all the things of beauty burn / With flames of evil ecstasy." Pater, too, had spoken of the "ecstasy" of burning, but his enthusiastic desire in the seventies to explore the possibilities of aesthetic life had, with the Rhymers, entered into a new and terrifying phase which, tragically, Johnson could not escape. He became "one of those who fall,"[18] morally and physically, until, trying to sit on one pub stool too many, he fell off, fractured his skull and died. He was thirty-five.

Without doubt the aesthetic flame was most dangerously fanned to conflagration by Oscar Wilde who, in 1877 during his last year at Oxford, met and became a frequent visitor of Pater, continuing to see him from time to time for the next dozen years. Although Wilde was himself only a peripheral Rhymer, his literary influence in the last decade of the century (*Dorian Gray* had been published in 1890) may very well have been partially responsible for the misdirected aesthetic enthusiasm of the younger Rhymers. In his *Autobiography*, Yeats recalled first meeting Wilde one evening when he was verbally demolishing a witless interlocutor:

> That . . . night he praised Walter Pater's *Studies in the History of the Renaissance*: "It is my golden book; I never travel anywhere without it; but it is the very flower of decadence: the last trumpet should have sounded the moment it was written." "But," said the dull man, "would you not have given us time to read it?" "Oh no," was the retort, "there would have been plenty of time afterwards—in either world." I think he seemed to us, baffled as we were by youth, or by infirmity, a triumphant figure, and to some of us a figure from another age, an audacious Italian fifteenth-century figure.[19]

Insofar as Wilde responded to the later works of Pater, he simply interpreted them in the light of the misunderstood Aestheticism of *The Renaissance*. The essence of Lord Henry's gospel of "new Hedonism," the aim of which "was to be experience itself, and not the fruits of experience, sweet or bitter as they may be,"[20] found its antecedent in Pater's "Conclusion": "Not the fruit of experience, but experience itself, is the end" (*Renaissance*, 236). Although Aubrey Beardsley's fragmentary *Story of Venus and Tannhauser* may be the quintessential text of Aesthetic decadence, Wilde's *Picture of Dorian Gray*, a fictionalized adaptation of the "Conclusion," definitely had the greater impact on the literary world.

A Greek pagan, as his name suggests, Dorian wanders like one of Pater's gods in exile in a grey Victorian morality. In effect, Wilde's hero becomes a remastering of the Mona Lisa image (the most elaborate of Pater's gods-in-exile figures) in terms of the supposedly hedonistic "Conclusion": "There were times when it appeared to Dorian Gray that the whole of history was merely the record of his own life. . . . He felt that he had known them all, those strange terrible figures that had passed across the stage of the world and made sin so marvellous and evil so full of subtlety. It seemed to him that in some mysterious way their lives had been his own." Later, Lord Henry tells Dorian, "You have drunk deeply of everything . . . and it has been to you no more than the sound of music. . . . Life is a question of nerves, and fibres, and slowly built-up cells in which thought hides itself and passion has its dreams."[21] Just as

Mona Lisa's picture is a tainted version of "one of those white Greek goddesses . . . into which the soul with all its maladies has passed" (125), so Dorian too is a corruption of Greek innocence, and his picture likewise is expressive of the maladies of the soul.

In a letter to an admirer of *Dorian Gray*, Wilde wrote: "I am so glad you like that strange many coloured book of mine: it contains much of me in it. Basil Hallward is what I think I am: Lord Henry, what the world thinks me: Dorian what I would like to be—in other ages, perhaps."[22] There is a similarity and contrast with Pater in this. Pater's novel, like Wilde's, also contains much of its author; and Pater might have written that Marius was what he thought he was; Flavian, what the world took him to be; and Cornelius, what he would like to be. But whereas Pater-Marius resolves the conflict between innocence and corruption, the author of *Dorian Gray*, finding no way to reconcile their conflicting claims, proceeded to portray the suicidal disavowal of the moral world, making sensuous beauty the only absolute. The book may have had a moral, Pater realized, but it certainly was not a moral book since its author clearly had a partiality for the atmosphere of exotic depravity in which his characters moved. Basil's love of Dorian, as a decadent reflection of Marius' love of Flavian, may have forcefully brought that home to Pater.

Wilde testified at his trials that he had corresponded with Pater concerning his novel before its publication and been persuaded to modify one morally questionable passage. Possibly Wilde may have wished also to cite *The Renaissance* as Dorian's corrupting "golden book" (Apuleius' book had transformed Pater's hero in just such a sensuous direction), but chose instead J. K. Huysmans' novel, *A Rebours*, so as not to compromise Pater. In an unenthusiastic review, however, Pater wrote that: "A true Epicureanism aims at a complete though harmonious development of man's entire organism. To lose the moral sense, therefore, for instance, the sense of sin and righteousness, as Mr. Wilde's heroes are bent on doing as speedily, as completely as they can, is to lose, or lower organisation, to become less complex, to pass from a higher to a lower degree of development."[23] Given Pater's belief in progress toward the diaphanous condition of the cultural ideal, this criticism of *Dorian Gray* implies that it is through "the moral sense," which recognizes the claims of humanity upon one, and not through affirming one's superiority to it, that the humanistic goal is won. The Rhymers, tragically, sought to substitute for the injustice and sickness of public life a private vision. Living alone amid the impressions of the senses, they lost the outer world—lost its moral presence if not the moral sense—and paid Dorian's price for that mistake. Beardsley alone surpassed Wilde's decadence by imitating perfectly the climate of ancient Greek and Roman erotica in which "the sense of sin and righteousness" was not simply disavowed, but unknown.

The temper of the 1890s perhaps dictated that the Rhymers' pursuit of beauty should lack Pater's stress on the artist's participation in the moral side of culture. The major poets of mid-century— Tennyson, Browning, Arnold—were spokesmen for their times, artists with social obligations to the Victorian public. In his *Autobiography* and elsewhere, Yeats never tired of noting that these poets "had filled their work with what I called 'impurities,' curiosities about politics, about science, about history, about religion; and that we [the artists of the 1890s] must create once more the pure work."[24] Thus Yeats' generation moved from an emphasis on deeds or ideas to a preoccupation with either private fantasies or sheer technical ingenuity—"idle singers of an empty day." It was a shift, one may say, from a concern with the needs of the audience for reassurance to a stress on the private vision of the artist and may be regarded as a late recrudescence of the Keatsian belief that the artist is superior to society by virtue of his special insight. Elements in Pater's thought doubtless promoted this tendency, but only in part. Other and quite different artistic creeds also helped to shape the temper of the 1890s, such as those of the Symbolists, Parnassians, Realists, and Naturalists.

### III    *Mr. Rose and Father Hopkins*

Although G. M. Hopkins died several years before Pater and was, chronologically, as much a Victorian as he, the belated publication of Hopkins' poetry in 1918 caused him to be welcomed as a contemporary by the young poets who came to maturity in the decade following World War I. Entering the cultural mainstream at this late date, Hopkins may with some justification be treated as the first of the major Modernists to exhibit Pater's influence. The earliest record of his awareness of Pater was in 1864 when Hopkins related to Canon Liddon Pater's denial in an Old Mortality paper of a future life, and the first recorded meeting of the two was in 1866 when Hopkins began coaching that term with him. Long before the 1873 publication of Pater's *Renaissance* and the public outcry against its apparent neohedonism, Hopkins had ample opportunity to gauge his tutor's sentiments on the score of religious belief. The curious fact remains that their friendship was uninterrupted by Hopkins' conversion to Catholicism (1866) and continued even after his ordination as a priest (1877). In the first year of their acquaintance Hopkins quotes with relish a typically Paterian sentiment to the effect that "the Sussex downs are seductive as Pater says, if there is a church"; the following year he writes to another friend that in August "Pater is going to ask me down to Sidmouth." Humphry Ward seems to have taken Hopkins' place that year and the anticipated invitation never came, but in 1878 and 1879, when Hopkins was attached to St. Aloysius' Church in North Oxford, Pater became "one of the men I saw most of," he later told a friend.[25] Even before his return to Oxford, Hopkins was delighted to learn of Pater's regard for him. He wrote to Robert Bridges: "It was pleasing and flattering to hear that Mr. Pater remembers and takes an interest in me."[26]

Apparently Mallock's notorious caricature of Pater as Mr. Rose was less a detterent than the prelude to a brief but sincerely renewed friendship. This relation between the moral iconoclast and the priest who sacrificed so much for the sake of his religious scruples would be puzzling were it not for certain common metaphysical preoccupations that united them. Behind the Aesthetic façade Hopkins discerned both an intelligent seriousness of character and a stimulating approach to contemporary philosophical problems. In particular, Hopkins' interest in the distinctive "design" or "pattern" of selfhood, which he called "inscape," seems unavoidably linked to Pater's metaphysics of the self. Though Hopkins' inscapes and Pater's selves are conceived to be windows opening on a divine and permanent reality, both men recognized that neither inscape nor self is impervious to destruction. "I wished to die and not see the inscapes of the world destroyed any more,"[27] cried Hopkins at the felling of a favourite ash tree (a similar poetic lament occurs in "Binsey Poplars"), and in "Spelt from Sibyl's Leaves" when this destruction actually befalls the inscape of man himself, the poet is brought to the pitch of real terror as he envisions how "self ín self" is "steepèd and páshed." Pater, too, experiences an overwhelming sense of loss at man's physical death and the destruction of all his beauties with him; such thoughts are "desolate," in which "all the bitterness of life seems concentrated."[28]

Another consequence of the finitude of inscapes and selves is their potential isolation from the rest of creation. Both Hopkins and Pater had struggled to describe in what precise way the solipsistic prison of the self could be opened to the higher life, and in confronting this problem the two writers are most typically alike. "My selfbeing," says Hopkins, "my consciousness and feeling of myself, that taste of myself, of *I* and *me* above and in all things . . . is more distinctive than the taste of ale or alum, more distinctive than the smell of walnut leaf or camphor, and is incommunicable by any means to another man." Consequently, continues Hopkins, "when I compare myself, my being-myself, with anything else whatever, all things alike, all in the same degree, rebuff me with blank unlikeness."[29] In his so-called "Terrible Sonnets," Hopkins laments this isolation, this paralyzing and inescapable taste of self and nothing but self: "I am gall, I am heartburn. God's most deep decree / Bitter would have me taste: my taste was me," cries Hopkins in "I Wake." For Pater also the self is "ringed round for each one of us by that thick wall of personality through which no real voice has ever pierced"; all selves are thus isolated within the dizzying flux of their subjective impressions, "each mind keeping as a solitary prisoner its own dream of a world" (*Renaissance*, 235).

The starting point for this sense of personal isolation and spiritual vertigo was the new science; namely, the modern spirit of relativism, of flux. A year before Pater first published his "Conclusion," Hopkins, in an undergraduate essay on "The Probable Future of Metaphysics" (1867), professes himself dissatisfied with "the prevalent philosophy of continuity or flux." He says that for the proponents of a flux in which there are no absolutely fixed types or species, no "*saltus* or breaks" in the developmental chain, "nature is a string all the differences in which are really chromatic but certain places in it have become accidentally fixed and the series of fixed points becomes an arbitrary scale."[30] He rejects this evolutionary chromatism (a sliding series of semitones with a shifting key center) and prefers in its stead the diatonic music of the Platonists (a fixed scale in a certain key) in which the inscapes of, for example, Indian cones and *fleurs-de-lis*, deriving from a sort of Christianized realm of Ideas, correspond to a predetermined pattern of organization. In contrast to Pater's paradigm of process in which there is no enduring circle of self, Hopkins claims for himself a fixed inscape: "If the centre of reference [i.e., the self] has concentric circles round it, one of these, the inmost, say, is its own, is óf it, the rest are to it only. Within a certain bounding line all will be self, outside of it nothing: with it self begins from side and ends from the other."[31]

Hopkins' paradigm might profitably be contrasted not only with the "Conclusion," but also with the opening paragraph of "The Child in the House" in which Pater speaks of "the gradual expansion of the soul" by means of which the child's physical dwelling place "had actually become a part" of its very selfhood, "inward and outward being woven through and through each other into one inextricable texture—half, tint and trace and accident of homely colour and form, from the wood and the bricks; half, mere soul-stuff, floated thither from who knows how far" (*Miscellaneous Studies*, 173). This Paterian "expansion" of the circle of self into the "belonging field" is again described in a previously noted passage in which Pater describes one's house as " 'only an expansion of the body; as the body . . . is but a process, an expansion of the soul. For such an orderly soul, as life proceeds, all sorts of delicate affinities establish themselves between herself and . . . her outward dwelling-place, until she may seem incorporate with it—until at last . . . there is for her . . . between outward and inward, no longer any distinction at all' " (*Marius*, II, 92 - 93). The final expression of this gradual expansion of the circle of self is the "clear crystal nature" (*Miscellaneous Studies*, 253) of the diaphanous hero in which "the material and spiritual are fused and blent" (*Appreciations*, 212).

Although their chosen paradigms of selfhood differ, Pater insists that an intrinsic ordering of selves produces as meaningful a pattern as Hopkins' extrinsic power of organization. Almost as if taking his cue from Hopkins' chromatic analogy, Pater writes: "In this 'perpetual flux' of things and souls, there was, as Heraclitus conceived, a continuance, if not of their material or spiritual elements, yet of orderly intelligible relationships, like the harmony of musical notes, wrought out in and through the series of their mutations—ordinances of the divine reason, maintained through the changes of the phenomenal world" (*Marius*, I, 131). And in *Plato*, using the same musical analogy, Pater writes that Heraclitus sought for "the notation, if there be such, of an antiphonal rhythm, or logic, which, proceeding uniformly from movement to movement, as in some intricate musical theme, might link together in one those contending, infinitely diverse impulses" (*Plato*, 17 - 18). Thus if the "things and souls" in Pater's flux undergo chromatic "mutations," their existence, although defined as less a product than a process, is not considered by Pater to be the result of some disjointed and meaningless transformation as feared by Hopkins. There exists, says Pater in an unfinished essay, a "collective humanity" that "assists and rounds . . . our transient, individual intelligence." All perishing selves, by participating no matter howsoever humbly in the cultural community, have gained thereby a durable existence in the greater Self. Even the humblest individual can share in that light by placing himself in the "great order" of collective humanity, "by conceiving his isolated *aperçus* under the terms of that, by admitting their just complement, by passing out of himself with them into an external world, which as he conveys into it something of personal and peculiar [understanding] so affects him in turn by its support."[32]

Pater's real Self is an unseen core of cultural relationships, and the visible person is simply the shell of an infinite companionship of like-oriented selves that pervade and shape the personality. The shifting "key centers" of the chromatic flux are those diaphanous heroes of each age who advance the cultural Ideal on its way to perfect realization: "they give utterance to that great consensus, though they also partly lead it."[33] Expression of that "consensus" constitutes the ultimate outward expansion of the circle of the self so that there is, finally, no external world left—inner and outer are one Self. Of this Marius also was aware: "The human body in its beauty, as the highest potency of the beauty of material objects, seemed to him just then to be matter no longer, but, having taken celestial fire, to assert itself as indeed the true, though visible, soul or spirit in things" (*Marius*, I, 92 - 93). Similarly, in his 1887 sonnet, "Harry Ploughman," Hopkins described the human form as mirroring the perfection of God and thereby glorifying Him. But whereas Pater's heroes participate in a progressively self-realizing "collective humanity" by a gradual "self-surrender to the suggestions of an abstract reason or ideality in things" (*Appreciations*, 79), Hopkins' inscapes participate in the multiple enrichment of creation only by anticipating their final sudden redemption into the inscape of Christ: "In a flash . . . I am all at once what Christ is, . . . immortal diamond." (Both Pater's gem-like flame and the star-spark-diamond imagery of this "Heraclitean Fire" sonnet possibly echo Heraclitus' metaphor of the soul as a spark of starry essence.) In the final analysis, however, individual "crystal" or "diamond" is not reduced to a totally superpersonal reality; both are lost in the light, yet they contain and give a shape to it. But, typically, for Hopkins, escape from solipsistic selfhood is not an expansion into Self, but rather an intuition of the counterpointing and rhyming of all selves in God, as in his sonnets "Pied Beauty" (1877) and "As Kingfishers" (1881).

Neither Pater nor Hopkins was a philosophical purist in either temperament or method. Both were always more eager to assimilate current findings and to render artistically the implications of "inscape" and "self" than to scrutinize the elements of their thought for inconsistencies. Their conversations must often have touched on other interests also, such as Pater's growing respect for the writings of Hopkins' mentor, Cardinal Newman. Pater's fellow victims satirized by Mallock and other Oxford personalities, perhaps too obscure to rate such notoriety, would also have led them finally to a discussion of beauty, mortal beauty that perishes and ideal beauty purified and spiritualized by the divine fire. They may even have gotten around to confessing how each had burnt his youthful poems. But sad as it may seem, Hopkins may only have quoted a few lines to Pater from his recent unpublished masterpieces, *The Wreck of the Deutschland* and the nature sonnets of 1877. Nor is it known whether in later years Hopkins read Pater's *Marius the Epicurean* or his *Imaginary Portraits*. Perhaps it was a certain isola- tion of spirit each intuitively sensed in the other that allowed them to accept as final the inevitable parting of ways. Basic to both their temperaments was a celibate strain, a love of the rich solitudes of the soul which let others "go by . . . till death or distance buys them quite."[34] Then, too, Pater hated to write letters, and Hopkins had his Liverpool slums and the debility and despair of his Dublin years to endure.


## IV   *Influence on Poetry*

Much as T. S. Eliot attempted to do fifty years later, Hopkins re- established the religious significance of the Paterian "moment." Despite Eliot's dismissals, the influence on modern literature of Pater's moments of aesthetic ecstasy has been extensive, though not yet fully documented.[35] In addition to Yeats and Hopkins, poets as diverse as Ezra Pound, Wallace Stevens, W. H. Auden, Louis MacNeice, and even Eliot, and novelists such as Henry James, Joseph Conrad, Virginia Woolf, James Joyce, D. H. Lawrence, and Marcel Proust have exhibited Pater's influence. Among artists,

aestheticians, and historians of art, George Santayana's and Bernard
Berenson's experience of being dazzled as undergraduates at Harvard by Pater's *Renaissance* seems not unusual. Although Pater missed
the chance in 1888 to admit the future historian of Italian art to
his lectures, in after years Berenson testified that Pater's mythic and
imaginary portraits "revealed to me what from childhood I had
been instinctively tending toward. . . . It is for that I have loved
him since youth and shall be grateful to him even to the House of
Hades where, in the words of Nausicaa to Odysseus, I shall hail him
as god. It was he who encouraged me to extract from the chaotic
succession of events in the common day what was wholesome and
sweet, what fed and sustained the spirit."[36]

Seemingly for Berenson and for many in the twentieth century,
the ideal of the gem-like flame suggested only moments of aesthetic
ecstasy isolated within the flux of sensations. Pater's significance for
most major Modernists lay almost entirely in the misrepresentation
by the Rhymers of this moment of "ecstasy" as a revolt against
"rhetoric" (the climate of nineteenth-century philosophy and
morals) and as a celebration of pure sensation and form—a
"de-idealizing" of a type of experience that went all the way back to
Wordsworth's "spots of time." Just why the Moderns could so
lightheartedly dismiss Pater's Goethe-and-Gautier Aestheticism, as
it was called, may in part be explained by the fact that these
younger writers no longer wished to admit their debt to *any* Victorian. To protect his image as a revolutionary modern, Yeats' close
friend, Ezra Pound, covered up his embarrassment at Pater's early
influence with the patronizing confession that he "is not dull in the
least. He is adolescent reading, and very excellent bait."[37] Yet in
three of his early essays, "Vortex," "Vorticism," and "Vor-
tographs," Pound, who would have been a thirty-one-year-old
"adolescent" when he wrote the last of these essays, credits "the
immediate ancestry" of his school to Pater's dictum that "All art
constantly aspires towards the condition of music."[38] Pound quotes
Whistler as ancestor also, but Pater's insight is accorded priority,
doubtless owing to Pound's experimentation with the "rhythm-
phrase."

Just as surely as the poets of the nineties, isolated amidst the flux,
owed their despair to Pater, the poets in the first decades of the
following century who proclaimed the kinetic gospel of vital forces
were also his heirs—the Paterian flame, "point" of "purest energy"
(*Renaissance*, 236), became the Poundian vortex, "point of maxi-

mum energy."[39] Small wonder Yeats was led to inquire a shade apprehensively: "Did Pater foreshadow a poetry, a philosophy, where the individual is nothing, the flux of *The Cantos* of Ezra Pound?"[40] Pound seized upon Pater's argument in *The Renaissance* (130 - 38) that the arts are "a matter of pure perception," and "the sensuous material of each art brings with it a special phase or quality of beauty, untranslatable into the forms of any other." Pater's assertion that "In its primary aspect, a great picture has no more definite message for us than an accidental play of . . . fallen light, caught as the colours are in an Eastern carpet" epitomizes Pound's argument in "Vorticism" that patterns of form and color seen and felt directly are superior to symbols used merely "to back up some creed or some system of ethics or economics."[41] Not only does Pound's phrasing here echo Pater's "Conclusion" in particular ("theory or idea or system" [237]), but when Pound defines the poetic image as "a radiant node or cluster, . . . a VORTEX, from which, and through which, and into which, ideas are constantly rushing,"[42] he both adapts Pater's metaphor of the gem-like flame and reaffirms the Paterian perception of consciousness as a "whirlpool" (for this image Yeats also had uses). The theoretical passages from "The School of Giorgione" and the "Conclusion" doubtless explain Pound's inclusion of Pater among "the great critics" in his 1909 introductory lecture at the Regent Street Polytechnic.[43]

Pound's fellow countryman Wallace Stevens was equally indebted to what, afterwards, he called the "dreadful goings-on of Walter Pater," adding that "it would be impossible nowadays, I suppose, to concede anything at all in that direction."[44] Certainly the Paterian sensibility informs Stevens' richly sensuous first volume, *Harmonium* (1923), especially "Tea at the Palaz of Hoon," which may be cited as echoing the aesthetic self-sufficiency of Pater's "supreme, artistic view of life" (229). Pater is again present in "Two or Three Ideas" and in *The Necessary Angel's* "morality of the right sensation," as well as in "the impossible possible philosophers' man" of "Asides on the Oboe," and above all in "Notes Toward a Supreme Fiction" which tentatively sanctions Pound's "magic moments" and Pater's "ideal instants": "Perhaps there are times of inherent excellence, / . . . . / Perhaps there are moments of awakening, / Extreme, fortutious, personal, in which / We more than awaken." Pater's influence on Stevens may be traced at least in part to his Harvard mentor, George Santayana, friend of Berenson and of Pater's ardent disciple, Lionel Johnson. A charm-

ing stylist and aesthete whose "sense of beauty" shaped itself in
the intellectual milieu of Ruskin and Pater, Santayana began as a
poet of fragile sonnets not unworthy of Edmund Gosse. During
Stevens' Harvard years, Santayana's *Sense of Beauty* (1896) and
*Interpretations of Poetry and Religion* (1900) unveiled a Pateresque
"materialistic Platonism" that blended neopagan naturalism with
the metaphysics of the flux and elevated poetry to the seat of
religion—all of which left a lasting impression on Stevens'
aesthetics. In one of his best late poems, "To an Old Philosopher in
Rome," Stevens pays tribute to Santayana and depicts the moods
and sensations of death in terms similar to Pater's description of
Marius' last illness. Such lines as "The threshold, Rome, and that
more merciful Rome / Beyond, the two alike in the make of the
mind" forcefully recall Pater's description of the earthly city and
the Rome on high.

## V  *Influence on Fiction*

When Pound set out "to bring poetry up to the level of prose,"[45]
he was, of course, thinking not only of the French prose masters but
of Pater as well, and it may be that Pater's influence was greater on
the novelists of the twentieth century than on its poets. Possibly
Henry James best expressed the paradoxical response of the emerging twentieth-century novelist when in an 1894 letter to Gosse after
Pater's death he parodied the image of the gem-like flame and yet
concluded with a line of absolutely genuine praise: "Faint, pale,
embarrassed, exquisite Pater! He reminds me, in the disturbed midnight of our actual literature, of one of those lucent matchboxes
which you place, on going to bed, near the candle, to show you, in
the darkness, where you can strike a light: he shines in the uneasy
gloom—vaguely, and has a phosphorescence, not a flame. But I
agree with you that he is not of the little day—but of the longer
time."[46] Certainly one such reason for Pater's durability lay in the
distinguishing technical characteristic of his prose romances, their
emphasis not on action, but on attitudes. He does not render immediate gesture and utterance, but their temperamental equivalents; that is, finely discriminated "sensations and ideas." Although
his "imaginary portraits" lie outside the generic categories of Victorian literature, they may be considered because of their dimin-
ished plot emphasis as forerunners of one of the major developments
of twentieth-century literature, the "psychological novel" with its

stress on the rendering of impressions, on character and point of view. Writers such as Henry James, Joseph Conrad, Ford Madox Ford, and Virginia Woolf translated into fictional technique the concepts of self and time explored by William James and Henri Bergson, but they were anticipated in Pater's preoccupations by nearly a quarter of a century.

Soon after James first "took possession" of London, he met Pater and found him "far from being as beautiful as his own prose."[47] In the 1880s the two men often had the opportunity of conversing at "literary tea-drinkings" and dinner parties; at one such gathering for J. S. Sargent, Violet Paget observed "Pater limping with gout and Henry James wrinkling his forehead as usual for tight boots, and a lot of artists buzzing about."[48] As early as 1873 James had wanted to review Pater's *Renaissance*, but found "it treats of several things I know nothing about."[49] Yet by 1879 he is citing Pater in his fiction ("A Bundle of Letters") as the exponent of the life-is-an-art doctrine; and by 1881 the Paterian exhortation for a "quickened sense of life" and a "quickened, multiplied consciousness" (*Renaissance*, 238) is echoing in his description of Isabel Archer's "quickened consciousness" and "multiplied life."[50] James, sharing with Pater a celibate dedication to art, was likewise an aesthetic observer, a spectator of life, recording in an "architectural" style rich in preciosity of phrase—albeit mixed with un-Paterian touches of the colloquial—the multiplicity and intensity of his impressions. A few years later Pater's influence becomes equally evident in Joseph Conrad's 1897 "Preface" to *The Nigger of the "Narcissus."* It begins: "A work that aspires, however, humbly, to the condition of art should carry its justification in every line." With this brash conflation of dicta from the "Giorgione" and "Style" essays, Conrad introduces his famous symbolist manifesto saturated with verbal echoes from Pater's work. In its final paragraph (to leap to the end), Conrad assimilates two of Pater's most striking sentences describing Giorgione's "ideal instants." The verbs "arrest" and "pause" and the phrases "a sigh, a smile" and "all the truth of life"[51] echo their Paterian original: "a look, a smile" and "all the fulness . . . of life" (150). In a letter of November 6, 1896, Conrad, as he was finishing *The Nigger*, slyly described to Edward Garnett a Cambridge don who admired his work: "He—I fancy—is not made in the image of God like other men but is fashioned after the pattern of Walter Pater which, you cannot but admit, is a much greater distinction."[52]

Virginia Woolf's absorption in the "moment of being" likewise betrays an indebtedness to Pater. The "tiny bead of pure life" in her "Death of the Moth" precisely illustrates Pater's notion of the confluence of forces momentarily crossing to create the gem-like flame, and her vocabulary is full of Paterian words: "net," "fibre," "thread," "energy," "force." In "Modern Fiction" she portrays in true Paterian fashion the mind itself as receiving "a myriad impressions—trivial, fantastic, evanescent, or engraved with the sharpness of steel"—and in "The Moment: Summer Night" she describes "the terror, the exultation" as the walls of the moment open and the self is freed (at the close of *Mrs. Dalloway*, Woolf substitutes the even more Paterian "ecstasy" for the second noun in this pair).[53] Clarissa Dalloway herself might serve as an excellent fictional equivalent to Pater's awareness that "not to discriminate every moment some passionate attitude in those about us, and in the very brilliancy of their gifts some tragic dividing of forces on their ways, is, on this short day of frost and sun, to sleep before evening" (237). Even more typical of Pater's metaphysics of multipersonal selfhood and its gem-like confluence is Woolf's delineation of a series of Clarissa-selves which attempt to consolidate, as she describes it in a Paterian passage, into "one centre, one diamond."[54] Elsewhere, she develops other aspects of the multiplicity of self, utilizing the mythic theme of the double much as Pater had done in *Marius*.

At the age of eighteen, Woolf began to study Greek with Pater's sister Clara. She wrote to a friend remarking that Hester was ill and continued: "Tomorrow I am going to have my first class with Miss [Clara] Pater, she looks very white and shrivelled, poor Love—Dont you think those two old ladies most pathetic, growing old together, and one of them will drop off, and the other will be left. They seem so desolate with no young friends or relations." And several years later she anticipates a Bloomsbury "house warming" to which Clara is expected to come "in a new Empire gown of scarlet plush, with amber beads, and a little old Lace."[55] Woolf explicitly acknowledged her debt to Walter Pater in the "Preface" to *Orlando* in which she thanked the friends who had helped in the writing of the book, beginning with those dead "and so illustrious that I scarcely dare name them, yet no one can read or write without being perpetually in the[ir] debt."[56] Pater's name rounds out her brief list; and for good reason, since *Orlando* not only displays a very Paterian interest in the relation of the present moment to the changing flux of time and experience, but the hero-heroine is a symbolic figure of multiple selfhood who, like Pater's Mona Lisa, spans the centuries and epitomizes history in a culminating vision of the present moment. In "The Modern Essay," Woolf praised Pater's "vision" of Leonardo da Vinci—"a vision, such as we get in a good novel where everything contributes to bring the writer's conception as a whole before us. Only here, in the essay, where the bounds are so strict and the facts have to be used in their nakedness, the true writer like Walter Pater makes these limitations yield their own quality." Though Woolf felt compelled to note that "nowadays"—Stevens used this identical adverbial disclaimer—"nobody would have the courage to embark on the once-famous description of Leonardo's lady," she cannot resist either quoting Pater's purple panel or berating Max Beerbohm for failing to write like Pater. But Woolf admitted that polysyllables and purple were "nowadays" passé, and she confessed that "the only living Englishman who ever looks into these volumes is, of course, a gentleman of Polish extraction."[57]

Sensing the uniqueness of individual experience as basic to fiction, Pater nevertheless failed to explore the possibilities inherent in the first-person narrator; and, had it not been for that omission, Pater's imaginary portraits might have provided the "new form" for the novel that Conrad and others desired to find. Notwithstanding, on the Continent in the works of a gentleman of French lineage, also much admired by Woolf, this failed Paterian "spectator persona" was triumphantly translated into the first person and so redeemed. Some years before Marcel Proust began publishing on John Ruskin, he met Oscar Wilde, then at the height of his vogue. Proust would have been intrigued by his contacts with Ruskin, but Wilde and his friend Montesquiou could hardly have failed to praise that rival Oxonian apostle of beauty, Pater. It cannot be determined when Proust first read Pater, but Pater's friend, Douglas Ainslie, who had originally been introduced to Pater by Wilde, wrote of his conversations with Proust in 1897: "We fairly often began discussions on the respective value of Ruskin and Walter Pater. . . . He did not want anyone glorying in Pater rather than Ruskin, and when I told him that Pater had said to me one day: 'I can't believe Ruskin has been able to discover in St. Mark's more things than I,' he shrugged his shoulders and said: 'As you wish, we shall never agree about English literature.' "[58] Probably Proust effectively discovered Pater only after he began, painfully but successfully, to read him in the original; on one occasion he exclaimed: "What an interesting collection one could make with the landscapes of France seen through English eyes: the French rivers of Turner, the Versailles of Bonnington; the Auxerre or Valenciences, the Vezelay or Amiens of Walter Pater; the Fontainebleau of Stevenson, and many others!"[59]

On a profounder level, the impressionistic Ruskinian-Paterian tradition of perception—that insistence less upon the Arnoldian seeing of the *object* as it really is than upon knowing one's *impression*, the moment as it lives in the memory—sets the stage for Proust's exploration of interior, psychic reality. In particular, the opening chapters of *Swann's Way* evoke the veiled autobiography of Pater's "Child in the House" by their nostalgic recollection of childhood and mother love (evoking *Marius* here also) from the vantage of middle age, by their sequence of moods woven from sharply etched memories and conveyed through idealizing adjectives and intricately balanced syntax, and by the central vision of the pink hawthorn in the garden near Combray. Proust's vision contains nearly the same components as Pater's: a fenced and forbidden park; the perfume in the wind and the thickness of the blossoms on the aged stock; the boy's loitering along the pathway with the massed flowers at his feet; authorial comparisons to tapestry and painting; the initial unexpectedness and subsequent mysterious longing; and the blossoms gathered for decoration, as seen earlier in the white hawthorns on the altar. Perhaps Proust even noticed those moments when Pater stumbled by technical error toward the twentieth century (by saying "the child of whom *I* am writing" instead of "the child of whom *Florian* was thinking") as his third-person mask slipped halfway into first-person narration.

## VI   *Pater as Praeter-Source*

As the Modernists read him, Pater alone among the major Victorian prose-prophets seemed to reject the Victorian conception of art as quasi-ethics and to urge in its stead the morality of pure sight and sensation. Pater alone conceived of the revelation of personality (Marius' and Lisa's) in terms of mythic archetypes. But because these insights have become so widely assimilated and hidden within the modern sensibility, the literal minded might question the propriety or maybe the sobriety of claiming that this impotent Oxford don (pater of no little feat) fathered the future. Yet circumstances suggest that when Proust groped among his memories

of Albertine and found the ego to be "composed of the superimposi-
tion of our successive states," each "fresh memory" bringing a
"different Albertine,"[60] he was aware of how Mona Lisa had embodied the antinomies of the flux, perhaps aware too of how Marius
had gathered successive visions of Cecilia and her equivalents or an-
titheses. Or again, as the ultimate source of Woolf's multipersonal
self, of her sense of the divisibility of time in contrast to the "moment of being," of her emphasis upon the androgyne and upon
the intensity-death equation (all but embodied in Clarissa Dalloway
and exemplified in herself), and of her Ezra-Poundian interest in
the primary significance of rhythm and syntax, Pater stands as the
*Ur*-modern. But he is a modern whose greatest contributions often
lie beyond the range or compass of sources either peripheral or
direct; rather, he exists as a "praeter-source" in unacknowledged,
subliminal associations that have combined with other influences
and emphases not exclusively his own. Considered in this light,
countless twentieth-century threads lead back to him, as for example D. H. Lawrence's "Poetry of the Present" which describes a
supercharged Paterian intuition of "the immediate, instant self":
"The quivering nimble hour of the present, this is the quick of
Time. This is the immanence. The quick of the universe is the
*pulsating, carnal self*, mysterious and palpable."[61] To imagine Pater
murmuring this to a friend would be (one hopes) more parody than
truth; yet Pater did suggest something not unlike it.

James Joyce, entangled by the critics in Aquinas, Vico, and
whatever, might also be described as the beneficiary, pre-eminently
so, of Pater as praeter-source. Whereas Joyce's extended parody of
Pater's style in the "Oxen of the Sun" episode in *Ulysses* is truly
comic, the postcard Joyce sent his brother, a "photograph" of Pater
he claimed, was more heartless, picturing as it did the distorted face
and swollen brass nose of the Brasenose College gate knocker (in
*Finnegans Wake* Pater's college is parodied as "Bruisenose" and
"Brazenaze"). Yet Joyce's 1902 "portrait" of James Clarence
Mangan is Pateresque both in its rhythms and in its lyric love of
beauty; and not only does Joyce, in comparing Mangan's brooding
lady to the Mona Lisa (*Renaissance*, 124 - 26), utilize Pater's in-
tuitions (a figure of "many lives"), words ("presence," "delicacy,"
"lust," "weariness"), and phrases (*Joyce:* "distant terrors and
riotous dreams, and that strange stillness," *Pater:* "strange
thoughts and fantastic reveries and exquisite passions"; *Joyce:* "embodiment of that idea," *Pater:* "embodiment of the . . . idea"), but

he also explicitly describes the Irish poet himself as a questing Paterian hero: "he seems to seek in the world . . . . 'what is there in no satisfying measure or not at all.' "[62] In the concluding paragraphs of this essay, Joyce borrows Pater's myth of the exiled pagan gods reborn in Pico della Mirandola (passionately alive though unreadable) to describe Mangan (unread yet imaginatively vital), verbally echoing the eloquent culminating affirmation of Pater's study. Joyce's unconscious caricature of the heroic Pico in the feeble-bodied Mangan with his confused learning, pitiful loves, baggy pants, and early death, may possibly anticipate such later parodies as Finnegan's comic death and rebirth, in which case the Paterian motif of the gods reborn takes its place alongside theosophical schemes and Viconian cycles as an influence on this most experimental novel of the century.

T. S. Eliot was closer to the truth than he probably had a right to be when in a discussion of *Ulysses* with Virginia Woolf he called Joyce "a purely literary writer . . . founded upon Walter Pater with a dash of Newman."[63] Significant Paterian motifs in the Mangan essay migrate to *Stephen Hero* and afterwards are found in Joyce's Pateresquely entitled *Portrait* as well as in *Ulysses* and *Finnegan*—not only a sentence from "Pico" parodied in *Ulysses* or the lines on Mona Lisa burlesqued in *Ulysses* and *Finnegan*, significant as these may be, but the entire idea of the "epiphany" itself. That moment of revelation that Joyce described in "Mangan" and the *Portrait* as "less than the pulsation of an artery, [but] equal in its period and value to six thousand years," derives from Blake's *Milton* via Pater's "pulses"-"pulsations" imagery in the "Conclusion." These epiphanies which occur throughout Joyce's work are very much like the expanded interval of the gem-like flame or such other indelible Paterian moments as Florian's discovery of the hawthorn (in Joycean terms Pater's "Child in the House" is a study in the epiphanies of an artist's childhood) or Marius' vision in the Sabine Hills or Giorgione's "ideal instants."[64] As illustrative of the manner in which Pater as praeter-source functions, it could be shown how completely Joyce dramatizes Pater's "Conclusion" in Stephen Dedalus' climactic epiphany on the beach at the end of the fourth chapter of the *Portrait*. The spirit liberated or reborn through its passion for art is the subject of both passages, and the general Paterian celebration of new impressions as well as the basic vocabulary of "ecstasy" and "flame" is everywhere applied to Stephen.

Pertinent to Joyce's description of Stephen's epiphany is Pater's definition of aesthetic passion as the only escape from the prison of one's experience of time and history; the mind, isolated like "a solitary prisoner," is seemingly "ringed round for each one of us by that thick wall of personality through which no real voice has ever pierced on its way to us, or from us to that which we can only conjecture to be without" (*Renaissance*, 235). For Stephen, this "incertitude that had ringed him round" tinged with unreality the calls of his bathing friends until the mythic overtones in their banter struck him like a "voice from beyond the world," a note "piercing" his isolation, and he conceived an aching "desire to cry aloud, the cry of a hawk or eagle on high, to cry piercingly of his deliverance."[65] As is frequently noted, the bird imagery in this passage defines Joyce's central Daedalus-Icarus archetype of the artist, and this on the praeter-source hypothesis, now appears to hark back to Pater's prison image and his stress on the power of art to "set the spirit free." Nor could Joyce have missed Pater's description of Rousseau's desired liberation from death in aesthetic passion as "the awakening in him of the literary sense." Not only is Stephen's apprenticeship as an artist initiated by his sense of "cerements shaken from the body of death," but it also coincides with a repudiation of the priesthood in harmony with Pater's assertion that any facile orthodoxy "which requires of us the sacrifice of any part of [aesthetic] experience, in consideration of some interest into which we cannot enter, . . . has no real claim upon us" (237 - 38). Finally, Leonardo's ambiguous Mona Lisa, the "presence that rose thus so strangely beside the waters" (124), may well have served as the prototype for Stephen's culminating vision of the bird-girl, his avowedly sensual "angel of mortal youth and beauty." As we see him later, writing a villanelle to his "temptress," Stephen is little more than a budding Decadent. He was lucky to have escaped.

Unlike Joyce and the other major Modernists, Pater is not now and probably never will become popular again with any number of readers outside the walls of academia. But T. S. Eliot himself has given the lie to his own assertion that Pater failed to influence any first-rate mind: "No! Shakespeare's kings are not, nor are meant to be, great men" writes Pater (*Appreciations*, 199); "No! I am not Prince Hamlet, nor was meant to be" comes the Prufrockian echo of the young Eliot. And on the more elusive level of unacknowledged associations, the mature Eliot in the second of his moving "Four Quartets" proves he has not forgotten either Pater's "Conclusion" or the pilgrimage of Marius:

Home is where one starts from. As we grow older
The world becomes stranger, the pattern more complicated
Of dead and living. Not the intense moment
Isolated, with no before and after,
But a lifetime burning in every moment
And not the lifetime of one man only
But of old stones that cannot be deciphered.[66]

If one looks, one can find in Pater's ideal of the gem-like flame many such fugitive threads from which our present literature is woven.

# Notes and References

*Preface*

1. T. S. Eliot, "Arnold and Pater," in *Selected Essays: New Edition* (New York, 1960), pp. 382 - 93. First published in 1930.

2. Oscar Wilde, *De Profundis,* in *The Works of Oscar Wilde,* ed. G. F. Maine (New York, 1954), p. 867.

3. Wilhelm Dilthey, *Pattern and Meaning in History,* ed. H. P. Rickman (New York, 1961), p. 79; A. Fleishman, *The English Historical Novel* (Baltimore, 1971), pp. 11 - 13.

4. Walter Pater, "Coleridge's Writings," *The Westminster Review,* NS 29 (1866), 129.

5. Dilthey, p. 167.

6. Henry James, *The Letters of Henry James,* ed. Percy Lubbock (New York, 1920), I, 222.

*Chapter One*

1. Arthur Symons, "Introduction," *The Renaissance* (New York, n.d.), p. xxi.

2. Thomas Wright, *The Life of Walter Pater* (London, 1907), I, 86.

3. Quoted by Kenneth Clark, "Introduction," *The Renaissance* (New York, 1961), p. 11.

4. Wright, I, 216.

5. *Ibid.,* I, 110.

6. Richard Aldington, "Introduction," *Walter Pater: Selected Works* (London, 1948), p. 3. From his sickbed, Pater begged that the offender not be expelled. This indeed may have been the magnanimous act of Christian forbearance the head master supposed it to be; but later, when one considers the outcry Pater caused by his "Conclusion" to *The Renaissance,* one is reminded of the observation (I forget whose) made apropos of Samuel Beckett's Murphy: the kick that the physical Murphy received, the mental Murphy gave—the same kick, but corrected as to direction.

7. William Sharp, *Papers Critical and Reminiscent* (London, 1912), pp. 203 - 204.

8. J. W. Mackail, *The Life of William Morris* (London, 1899), I, 29.

9. G. M. Hopkins, "Duns Scotus's Oxford," in *The Poems of G. M. Hopkins,* ed. W. H. Gardner and N. H. Mackenzie (London, 1967), p. 79.

10. Wright, I, 188.

11. "Coleridge's Writings," pp. 126 - 27.

12. Wright, I, 196 - 97.

13. *Letters of Walter Pater,* ed. Lawrence Evans (Oxford, 1970), p. 154.

14. William W. Jackson, *Ingram Bywater, the Memoir of an Oxford Scholar* (Oxford, 1917), pp. 196 - 97.

15. Edmund Gosse, "Pater," *The Dictionary of National Biography,* 15 (London, 1917), 459; William Knight, *Memoir of John Nichol* (Glasgow, 1896), p. 150.

16. Jackson, p. 79.

17. A. C. Benson, *Walter Pater* (London, 1906), pp. 193 - 94.

18. *Ibid.,* p. 22.

19. *Ibid.,* p. 210.

20. M. J. C. McCausland, "Walter Pater," *Times Literary Supplement,* 2 April 1971, pp. 369 - 97.

21. Quoted by Gerald Monsman, "Old Mortality at Oxford," *Studies in Philology,* 67 (1970), 371.

22. *Ibid.,* p. 380.

23. G. M. Hopkins, *The Journals and Papers of Gerard Manley Hopkins,* ed. Humphry House and Graham Storey (London, 1959), p. 353.

24. Quoted by Gerald Monsman, "Pater, Hopkins, and Fichte's Ideal Student," *The South Atlantic Quarterly,* 70 (1971), 367.

25. *Ibid.,* p. 368.

26. J. O. Johnson, *Life and Letters of Henry Parry Liddon* (London, 1904), pp. 90 - 92.

27. Hopkins, *Journals,* pp. 133, 138.

28. J. G. Fichte, *The Popular Works of Johann Gottlieb Fichte,* tr. William Smith (London, 1889), I, 210 - 11, 284 - 85.

29. Samuel Wright, *A Bibliography of the Writings of Walter H. Pater* (New York, 1975), p. 188; see also Edward Thomas, *Walter Pater* (London, 1913), p. 32.

30. Quoted in Aldington, p. 11, and T. Wright, II, 277, 119.

31. Quoted in Benson, p. 18.

32. Sharp, pp. 200 - 201.

33. S. Wright, p. 188.

34. D. S. MacColl, "A Batch of Memories. XII—Walter Pater," *The Weekend Review,* 12 December 1931, p. 760.

35. S. Wright, pp. 189 - 90.

36. Louise Creighton, *Life and Letters of Mandell Creighton* (London, 1906), II, 112; see also H. Pearson, *Life of Wilde* (London, 1946), pp. 30 - 31.

37. Edmund Gosse, "Walter Pater," in *Critical Kit-Kats* (New York, 1896), pp. 268 - 69; see also T. Wright, II, 51 - 52.

38. T. Wright, I, 239.

39. Lewis R. Farnell, *An Oxonian Looks Back* (London, 1934), pp. 76 - 77.

40. Gerald Monsman and Samuel Wright, "Walter Pater: Style and Text," *The South Atlantic Quarterly*, 71 (1972), 111.

41. Benson, p. 25; Humphry Ward, "The Nineteenth Century," in *Brasenose College Quatercentenary Monographs* (Oxford, 1909), II, Monog. XIV, 75.

42. Ward, p. 24.

43. Creighton, II, 112.

44. Gosse, "Walter Pater," pp. 269 - 70.

45. Mrs. Humphry Ward, *A Writer's Recollections* (London, 1918), pp. 123 - 24.

46. *Letters*, pp. xxxii - xxxiii.

47. Janet E. Courtney, *An Oxford Portrait Gallery* (London, 1931), p. 228.

48. Benson, p. 191.

49. William Rothenstein, *Men and Memories* (New York, 1931), I, 232.

50. Violet Paget, *Vernon Lee's Letters,* ed. Irene Cooper Willis (Privately printed, 1937), pp. 78, 109 - 10.

51. Gosse, "Walter Pater," p. 255.

52. Benson, p. 190; Gosse, "Walter Pater," p. 268; T. Wright, I, 253; II, 118 - 19.

53. [Ian Fletcher and Donald Gordon], "The Art of the High Wire: Pater in Letters," review of *Letters*, ed. Evans, *Times Literary Supplement*, 26 February 1971, p. 230.

54. Richmond Crinkley, *Walter Pater: Humanist* (Lexington, Ky., 1970), p. 155.

55. Frederick Wedmore, *Memories* (London, 1912), pp. 163 - 64.

56. Rothenstein, I, 139.

57. Quoted in *Letters*, p. xxxiv.

58. Oliver Elton, *Frederick York Powell, A Life* (Oxford, 1906), I, 158 - 59.

59. Gordon McKenzie, *The Literary Character of Walter Pater* (Berkeley, 1967), p. 37.

60. Edmund Chandler, "Pater on Style," *Anglistica*, XI (1958), 78.

61. Brian Reade, *Sexual Heretics* (London, 1970), p. 22.

62. Samuel Wright, "Richard Charles Jackson," *The Antigonish Review*, I (1971), 87.

63. *Ibid.*, p. 86.

64. Symons, p. xiii.

### Chapter Two

1. Symons, p. xxiii.

2. *Letters*, p. 41 and n. 2; John Ruskin, *Complete Works of John Ruskin*, ed. E. T. Cook and Alexander Wedderburn, XXII (London, 1903), xxxvii, n. 4.

3. John Ruskin, *The Seven Lamps of Architecture*, in *Works*, ed. Cook and Wedderburn, VIII, 98.

4. Quoted in *Letters*, p. xxiii.

5. Walter Pater, "Poems by William Morris," *The Westminster Review*, NS 34 (1868), 311.

6. *Ibid.*, p. 309.

7. T. H. Huxley, "On the Physical Basis of Life," *The Fortnightly Review*, NS 5 (1868), 311.

8. Anthony Ward, *Walter Pater: The Idea in Nature* (London, 1966), p. 64; see also the unpublished manuscript material in the Houghton Library, Harvard University.

9. Dilthey, p. 87.

10. Mrs. Mark Pattison, "Art," rev. of several volumes, including *The Renaissance*, *The Westminster Review*, NS 43 (1873), 639 - 40.

11. A. C. Swinburne, *The Swinburne Letters*, ed. Cecil Y. Lang, II (London, 1959), 240 - 41.

12. John Morley, "Mr. Pater's Essays," *The Fortnightly Review*, NS 13 (1873), p. 476.

13. J. A. Symonds, Review of *The Renaissance*, *The Academy*, 4 (1873), 104; *The Letters of John Addington Symonds*, ed. Herbert M. Schueller and Robert L. Peters, II (Detroit, 1968), 273; John Addington Symonds, *Letters and Papers*, ed. Horatio F. Brown (London, 1923), p. 231.

14. Margaret Oliphant, *Blackwood's Edinburgh Magazine*, 114 (1873), 604 - 609.

15. George Eliot, *The George Eliot Letters*, ed. Gordon S. Haight, V (New Haven, 1955), 455.

16. John Fielder Mackarness, *A Charge Delivered to the Clergy of the Diocese of Oxford at his Second Visitation in the Cathedral Church of Christ, April 20, 1875* (Oxford and London, 1875), n. p.

17. William Sharp, "Some Personal Reminiscences of Walter Pater," *Atlantic Monthly*, 74 (1894), 811.

18. W. J. Courthope, "Wordsworth and Gray," *The Quarterly Review*, 141 (1876), 132, 136.

19. W. H. Mallock, *The New Republic or Culture, Faith, and Philosophy in an English Country House*, ed. J. Max Patrick (Gainesville, Florida, 1950), pp. 177, 21. Mallock's choice of the name *Rose* suggests the influence of Rossetti on Pater's Aestheticism.

20. *Ibid.*, pp. 125 - 26. Hood's poem is "The Bridge of Sighs."

21. Gosse, "Walter Pater," p. 258.

22. Simon Nowell-Smith, *Letters to Macmillan* (London, 1967), pp. 143 - 44.

## *Chapter Three*

1. Gosse, "Mr. Walter Pater on Platonism," *The New Review*, 8 (1893), 421.

2. Quoted in Germain d'Hangest, *Walter Pater: l'homme et l'oeuvre* (Paris, 1961), II, 45.

3. D. G. Rossetti, *The Works of Dante Gabriel Rossetti*, ed. W. M. Rossetti (London, 1911), p. 555.

4. "Poems by William Morris," p. 309.

5. Symons, p. xxii.

6. *Ibid.*

7. *Letters*, p. xxix.

8. Henry Sidgwick, "Arthur Hugh Clough," *Miscellaneous Essays and Addresses* (London, 1904), p. 60.

9. John Tyndall, "An Address to Students," *Fragments of Science* (New York, 1897), II, 98 - 99.

10. William Sharp, Review of *Gaston de Latour*, ed. C. L. Shadwell, *The Athenaeum*, 17 October 1896, p. 518; Sharp, "Reminiscences," p. 809.

11. Walter Pater, "Introduction," *The "Purgatory" of Dante Alighieri*, trans. Charles Shadwell (London, 1892), p. xx.

12. Walter Pater, "A Novel by Mr. Oscar Wilde," *Uncollected Essays*, ed. T. B. Mosher (Portland, Maine, 1903), p. 128.

13. William Wordsworth, *The Prelude*, Book XII. In "The Convention of Cintra" (1809) Wordsworth reaffirmed the concept of "a spiritual community binding together the living and the dead," a concept of religious-cultural unity which Pater also may have encountered in Newman's "social commonwealth" described in the *Idea of a University* ("Christianity and Letters").

14. Creighton, II, 111 - 12.

15. Curtis Dahl, "Pater's *Marius* and Historical Novels on Early Christian Times," *Nineteenth-Century Fiction*, 28 (1973), 1 - 24; Roland G. Frean, "Walter Pater's *Marius the Epicurean:* Notes and Commentary Preliminary to a Critical Edition" (Dissertation, University of Toronto, 1961).

16. Ward, *Recollections*, pp. 121 - 22.

17. Letter of D. Convers to R. W. Woodward (14 December 1898) quoted in D. A. Downes, *The Temper of Victorian Belief* (New York, 1972), p. 2; the first extended recognition of Pater's indebtedness to Newman and the only study to date citing relevant passages from Pater's unpublished essay on Newman is G. Monsman, "Pater's Portrait" (Dissertation, Johns Hopkins, 1965), pp. 233 - 48; see also D. J. DeLaura, *Hebrew and Hellene in Victorian England* (Austin, 1969).

## Chapter Four

1. Paget, pp. 223 - 24.

2. Frank Harris, "Walter Pater," *Contemporary Portraits*, Second Series (New York, 1919), pp. 205 - 207.

3. Anon., "Q and Pater," *Times Literary Supplement*, 16 December 1944, p. 611.

4. *Letters*, p. xxxi.

5. George Moore, *Avowals* (New York, 1919), pp. 212 - 13.

6. Arthur Symons, "Walter Pater," in *Studies in Prose and Verse* (London, 1904), p. 76.

7. Symons, "Introduction" to *The Renaissance*, pp. xxi - xxii.

8. "Poems by William Morris," p. 307.

9. Pater, *Essays*, pp. 8 - 9.

10. Heinrich Heine, *The Works of Heinrich Heine*, trans. Charles G. Leland, XII (London, 1893), 306.

11. Symons, "Walter Pater," p. 68.

## Chapter Five

1. Benson, p. 162.

2. Arthur Waugh, "London Letter," *The Critic* (New York), 25 March 1893, p. 187; *Letters*, p. 116 n. 2.

3. E. B. Titchener, "Walter Horatio Pater," *Book Reviews*, October 1894, p. 202; G. B. Grundy, *Fifty-Five Years at Oxford* (London, 1945), p. 81.

4. Anon., Review of *Miscellaneous Studies*, ed. C. L. Shadwell, *The Athenaeum*, 7 December 1895, p. 783, col. 2.

5. Oscar Wilde, "Mr. Pater's Last Volume," *Reviews* (London, 1908), p. 538.

6. Symons, "Walter Pater," p. 65; see also d'Hangest, II, 175, 183, 191.

7. T. Wright, II, 86.

8. William Wordsworth, "Resolution and Independence," *Wordsworth: Poetical Works*, ed. T. Hutchinson and E. de Selincourt (London, 1936), p. 156; Stéphane Mallarmé, "Des Enquêtes," *Oeuvres complètes de Stéphane Mallarmé*, ed. Henri Mondor and G. Jean-Aubry (Paris, 1945), p. 867. Mallarmé's statements in the opening paragraphs of "Crisis in Poetry" and in the 1891 interview with Jules Huret can be compared with Pater: "let us understand by poetry all literary production which attains the power of giving pleasure by its form, as distinct from its matter" (*Renaissance*, 230).

9. T. S. Eliot, "Dante," *Selected Essays: New Edition* (New York, 1950), p. 200.

10. Arthur Symons, *The Symbolist Movement in Literature* (New York, 1958), p. 71.

11. Symons, "Walter Pater," p. 66.

12. Gosse, "Walter Pater," pp. 262 - 64; see also Titchener, p. 202.

13. Monsman and Wright, p. 111.

14. Lionel Johnson, "Notes on Walter Pater," *Post Liminium: Essays and Critical Papers by Lionel Johnson*, ed. Thomas Whittemore (London, 1911), pp. 23, 31.

15. See Frean, pp. 129 - 31.

16. Max Beerbohm, "Diminuendo," *The Works of Max Beerbohm* (London, 1922), p. 129.

17. Walter Pater, "An English Poet," *Imaginary Portraits by Walter Pater*, ed. Eugene Brzenk (New York, 1964), pp. 46, 39.

18. George Augustus Simcox, *A History of Latin Literature* (London, 1883), II, 235 - 36. See also M. Dorothy Brock, *Studies in Fronto and His Age* (Cambridge, 1911), pp. 105, n. 1; 109, n. 6; 113ʳ- 14; Désiré Nisard, *Études sur les pöetes latins* (Paris, 1877), II, 381 - 94; and both Gautier's 1868 preface for *Les Fleurs du mal* in Baudelaire, *Oeuvres poétique complètes* (Brussels: Editions Minerve, n.d.), p. 12, and Symons' Introduction to *The Symbolist Movement*, p. 4.

19. Chandler, p. 82.

20. A useful variorum edition of Pater's first volume has been prepared by Bruce E. Vardon, "Variant Readings in Walter Pater's *Studies in the History of the Renaissance*" (Dissertation, University of Chicago, 1950).

21. Stéphane Mallarmé, "Sur l'évolution littéraire," *Oeuvres*, ed. Henri Mondor and G. Jean-Aubry (Paris, 1945), p. 869.

22. Stéphane Mallarmé, "La musique et les lettres," *Oeuvres*, p. 645.

23. Stéphane Mallarmé, "Crise de vers," p. 366.

24. Oliver Elton, *Frederick York Powell: A Life* (Oxford, 1906), I, 158.

25. Mallarmé, "La musique et les lettres," pp. 636, 1576.

26. W. J. Courthope, "Modern Culture," *The Quarterly Review*, 137 (1874), 411.

27. *The Oxford Book of Modern Verse 1892 - 1935*, ed. W. B. Yeats (Oxford, 1936), p. viii.

28. Symons, "Walter Pater," p. 65.

29. Gosse, "Pater on Platonism," p. 421.

30. Israel Zangwell, *Without Prejudice* (New York, 1896), p. 208.

31. Symons, "Walter Pater," pp. 75 - 76.

32. Gosse, "Walter Pater," p. 258.

33. Clark, "Introduction," p. 12.

34. Gosse, "Pater on Platonism," pp. 420 - 21.

35. Michael Field, *Works and Days: From the Journal of Michael Field*, ed. T. and D. C. Sturge Moore (London, 1933), pp. 120 - 21; Robert Ross, *Masques and Phases* (London, 1909), p. 131.

36. "Q and Pater," p. 611.

37. Rothenstein, I, 138-39, 155.

38. S. Wright, p. 190.

### Chapter Six

1. Richard Le Gallienne, *The Romantic '90s* (New York, 1925), p. 97.

2. John Pick, "Divergent Disciples of Walter Pater," *Thought*, 23 (1948), 123.

3. W. B. Yeats, *Autobiography of W. B. Yeats* (New York, 1953), p. 181; Yeats, *Letters to the New Island* (Cambridge, Mass., 1934), pp. 137 - 38.

4. *Oxford Book of Modern Verse*, ed. Yeats, p. ix.

5. Yeats, *Autobiography*, p. 188.

6. W. B. Yeats, *The Secret Rose* (London, 1897), pp. 223 - 24.

7. W. B. Yeats, *Essays and Introductions* (London, 1961), p. 494.

8. *Ibid.*, p. 347.

9. In effect, Pater is using Ruskin's critical impressionism to undercut Matthew Arnold's famous dictum that the aim of criticism is "to see the object as in itself it really is." See "The Function of Criticism at the Present Time," in *The Complete Prose Works of Matthew Arnold*, ed. R. H. Super, III (Ann Arbor, Mich., 1962), 258.

10. Yeats, *Essays,* p. 349.

11. *Oxford Book of Modern Verse*, ed. Yeats, p. xxx.

12. Pick, p. 124.

13. *Letters*, p. xl.

14. Pick, p. 124.

15. *Ibid.*, pp. 125 - 26.

16. T. Wright, II, 207.

17. *Letters*, p. xxiv.

18. Lionel Johnson, "Mystic and Cavalier," *The Complete Poems of Lionel Johnson*, ed. Ian Fletcher (London, 1953), p. 29; alluded to in Yeats' elegy for Robert Gregory and quoted in the *Autobiography* as emblematic of Johnson and his tragically "fallen" generation.

19. Yeats, *Autobiography*, p. 80.

20. Oscar Wilde, *The Picture of Dorian Gray*, in *Works*, p. 104 (ch. XI).

21. *Ibid.*, pp. 113, 162 (chs. XI, XIX).

22. Oscar Wilde, *The Letters of Oscar Wilde*, ed. Rupert Hart-Davis (New York, 1962), p. 352.

23. Walter Pater, "A Novel by Mr. Oscar Wilde," *Sketches and Reviews* (New York, 1919), p. 132.

24. Yeats, *Autobiography*, p. 102.

25. G. M. Hopkins, *Further Letters of Gerard Manley Hopkins*, ed. C. C. Abbott, 2nd ed. (London, 1956), pp. 20, 38, 246.

26. G. M. Hopkins, *The Letters of Gerard Manley Hopkins to Robert Bridges*, ed. C. C. Abbott (London, 1956), p. 48.

27. Hopkins, *Journals*, p. 120.

28. "Poems by William Morris," p. 311.

29. G. M. Hopkins, *The Sermons and Devotional Writings of Gerard Manley Hopkins*, ed. Christopher Devlin (London, 1959), p. 123.

30. Hopkins, *Journals*, p. 120.

31. Hopkins, *Sermons*, p. 127.

32. Quoted in A. Ward, pp. 64, 66.

33. *Ibid.*, p. 66.

34. G. M. Hopkins, "The Lantern out of Doors," in *Poems*, p. 71.

35. Studies of influence are cited by Lawrence Evans in *Victorian Prose:*

*A Guide to Research,* ed. David DeLaura (New York, 1973), pp. 355 - 56. Added to Evans' list should be the work of Harold Bloom, "Late Victorian Poetry and Pater," in *Yeats* (New York, 1970) and "Introduction," *Selected Writings of Walter Pater* (New York, 1974).

36. Bernard Berenson, Sketch for a Self-Portrait (New York, 1949), p. 163. See also Berenson, *Sunset and Twilight: From the Diaries of 1947 - 1958* (New York, 1963), pp. 343, 526; *Letters,* p. 172; Sylvia Sprigge, *Berenson: A Biography* (Boston, 1960), p. 42 and *passim;* and George Santayana, *The Letters of George Santayana,* ed. Daniel Cory (New York, 1955), pp. 238 - 39.

37. Ezra Pound, *Guide to Kulchur* (New York, 1952), p. 160.

38. Ezra Pound, "Vortex," *Blast,* No. 1 (June, 1914), 153 - 54; see also Pound's "Vorticism" in *The Fortnightly Review,* NS 96 (1914), 461.

39. Pound, "Vortex," p. 153.

40. *Oxford Book of Modern Verse,* ed. Yeats, p. xxx.

41. Pound, "Vorticism," p. 464.

42. *Ibid.,* p. 469.

43. Charles Norman, *Ezra Pound* (London, 1969), p. 31.

44. Wallace Stevens, *Letters,* ed. Holly Stevens (New York, 1966), p. 606.

45. Pound, "Vorticism," p. 462.

46. James, *Letters,* ed. Lubbock, I, 222.

47. Henry James, *Henry James Letters,* ed. Leon Edel, II (Cambridge, Mass., 1975), 212.

48. Quoted in Leon Edel, *Henry James: The Middle Years* (New York, 1962), p. 116.

49. James, *Letters,* ed. Edel, I, 391.

50. Henry James, *The Portrait of a Lady,* ed. Leon Edel (Boston, 1963), pp. 65, 349 (chs. VII, XLII). In *The Tragic Muse* (1892), the so-called "Montesquiou-Whistler-Wilde aestheticism" of Gabriel Nash (who is partially a persona for James himself) has its closest Victorian analogue in Pater's writings; and in *The Wings of a Dove* (1902), Susan Stringham's imagination has been fed on Pater as well as Maeterlinck.

51. Joseph Conrad, *The Nigger of the "Narcissus"* (New York, 1914), pp. xi, xvi.

52. Joseph Conrad, *Letters from Conrad,* ed. Edward Garnett (London, 1928), p. 56.

53. Virginia Woolf, *Death of the Moth and Other Essays* (New York, 1942), pp. 3 - 6; Woolf, *Collected Essays* (New York, 1967), II, 106, 296; Woolf, *Mrs. Dalloway* (New York, 1925), p. 296.

54. Woolf, *Mrs. Dalloway,* p. 55.

55. Virginia Woolf, *The Letters of Virginia Woolf,* ed. Nigel Nicolson, I (London, 1975), 39 - 40, 180.

56. Virginia Woolf, *Orlando: A Biography* (New York, 1928), p. vii.

57. Woolf, *Essays*, II, 43 - 44, 46.

58. Douglas Ainslie, "Hommage à Marcel Proust," *La Nouvelle Revue Française*, XX (1923), 258 - 59.

59. Quoted by E. de Clermont-Tonnerre in *Robert de Montesquiou et Marcel Proust* (Paris, 1925), p. 97.

60. Marcel Proust, *Remembrance of Things Past*, trans. C. K. Scott Moncrieff (New York, 1934), II, 764.

61. D. H. Lawrence, *The Complete Poems of D. H. Lawrence*, ed. V. Pinto and W. Roberts, I (New York, 1964), 185, 183.

62. James Joyce, *The Critical Writings of James Joyce*, ed. E. Mason and R. Ellmann (New York, 1959), pp. 73 - 83. Joyce's quotation of Pater is from "A Prince of Court Painters" (*Imaginary Portraits*, 44). In Joyce's essay, the opening discussion of Classic and Romantic as constant states of mind may possibly derive from Pater's "Postscript" to *Appreciations*.

63. Quoted in Virginia Woolf, *A Writer's Diary*, ed. Leonard Woolf (London, 1959), p. 50.

64. Joyce defined the epiphany as "a sudden spiritual manifestation, whether in the vulgarity of speech or of gesture or in a memorable phase of the mind itself, . . . the most delicate and evanescent of moments." *Stephen Hero*, ed. J. J. Slocum and H. Cahoon (Norfolk, Conn., 1963), p. 211.

65. James Joyce, *A Portrait of the Artist as a Young Man* (New York, 1964), pp. 167 - 73.

66. T. S. Eliot, *The Complete Poems and Plays, 1909 - 1950* (New York, 1952), pp. 7, 129. See also Eliot's use of the metaphor of prison to portray the closed circle of the self in lines 414 - 15 of *The Waste Land*, in *Poems*, p. 49, a figure mediated through F. H. Bradley's *Appearance and Reality* but possibly derived ultimately from the portrayal in the "Conclusion" of those experiences "ringed round" (*Renaissance*, 235) by the shifting but imprisoning wall of personality.

# Selected Bibliography

PRIMARY SOURCES

The standard (though incomplete) edition of Pater's work is the *New Library Edition of the Works of Walter Pater* (London: Macmillan, 1910), consisting of the following (with dates of original publication):

*The Renaissance: Studies in Art and Poetry.* (1873)
*Marius the Epicurean: His Sensations and Ideas.* 2 vols. (1885)
*Imaginary Portraits.* (1887)
*Appreciations: With an Essay on Style.* (1889)
*Plato and Platonism: A Series of Lectures.* (1893)
*Greek Studies: A Series of Essays.* (1895)
*Miscellaneous Studies: A Series of Essays.* (1895)
*Gaston de Latour: An Unfinished Romance.* (1896)
*Essays from "The Guardian."* (1896)

The first six volumes were published during Pater's lifetime, and the following four volumes were posthumously published (the first three imperfectly edited by Charles Shadwell and the last by Edmund Gosse). Important unpublished fragments are in Harvard's Houghton Library and in the private possession of the warden of All Souls College, Oxford.

Writings not included in the Library Edition are gathered in the following:

*Uncollected Essays.* Ed. T. B. Mosher. Portland, Maine: T. B. Mosher, 1903.

*Sketches and Reviews.* New York: Boni and Liveright, 1919.

*Letters of Walter Pater.* Ed. Lawrence Evans. Oxford: Clarendon Press, 1970. Since fewer than three hundred letters (most are just brief notes) seem to have survived, the collection as it stands "is unrepresentative of the probable shape of Pater's total correspondence." But Evans' Introduction and critical apparatus provide the most useful new source of information in many years about Pater.

SECONDARY SOURCES

1. Bibliographical

D'HANGEST, GERMAIN. *Walter Pater: l'homme et l'oeuvre.* 2 vols. Paris: Didier, 1961. The second volume contains an appendix, pages 313 -

197

49, that is an accurate and readily available bibliography for both primary and secondary sources.

EVANS, LAWRENCE. "Walter Pater." In *Victorian Prose: A Guide to Research*. Ed. David J. DeLaura. New York: Modern Language Association, 1973. Evans summarizes and criticizes modern studies of Pater and suggests neglected aspects worthy of attention.

STONEHILL, C. A. AND H. W. *Bibliographies of Modern Authors*. Second Series. London: John Castle, 1925. Pages 127 - 40 contain a descriptive bibliography of the first English editions, but do not include uncollected writings.

UEKI, RENNOSUKE. "A Revaluation of Walter Pater." *Kwansei Gakuin University Annual Studies*, XIV (November 1964), 33 - 48. Lists forty-five books and articles on Pater (the majority between 1945 and date of publication) by Japanese critics.

WATSON, GEORGE. *The New Cambridge Bibliography of English Literature*. Cambridge: Cambridge University Press, 1969. Volume three contains a list compiled by John Sparrow of Pater's collected writings and secondary studies on him up to 1965.

WRIGHT, SAMUEL. *A Bibliography of the Writings of Walter H. Pater*. New York: Garland Publishing, 1975. A chronological record of all Pater's periodical and book publications together with a bibliographical description of the books.

2. Biographical and Critical

ALDINGTON, RICHARD. "Introduction." *Walter Pater: Selected Works*. London: Heinemann, 1948. Provides intelligent, succinct biographical sketch and critical appreciation.

BENSON, ARTHUR C. *Walter Pater*. London: Macmillan, 1906. Enjoying the cooperation of Pater's sisters and literary friends, Benson might have produced a more revealing study had he not been so intent upon idealizing his subject.

BLOOM, HAROLD. "Late Victorian Poetry and Pater." In *Yeats*. New York: Oxford University Press, 1970. A stimulating study of the place of Pater among the poets of the 1890s.

————. "Introduction." In *Selected Writings of Walter Pater*. New York: New American Library, 1974. Bloom sees Pater as one of the central figures in the continuity between Romanticism and Modernism.

BRZENK, EUGENE J. "Introduction." *Imaginary Portraits by Walter Pater*. New York: Harper and Row, 1964. Gives a succinct presentation of data pertinent to Pater's technique of imaginary portraiture.

————. "The Unique Fictional World of Walter Pater." *Nineteenth Century Fiction*, XIII (December 1958), 217 - 26. One of the first attempts to define the specifically fictional coherence of Pater's work.

CHANDLER, EDMUND. "Pater on Style." *Anglistica*, XI (1958), 1 - 100. The only intensive study of style and textual history to date, but it is limited to *Marius*.

CHARLESWORTH, BARBARA. *Dark Passages: The Decadent Consciousness in Victorian Literature*. Madison: University of Wisconsin Press, 1965. Primarily focusing on the figures of the *fin-de-siècle*, this study connects Pater's Aestheticism with the subsequent phase of Decadence.

CHILD, RUTH. *The Aesthetic of Walter Pater*. New York: Macmillan, 1940. Written during a period when Pater was a neglected figure, this study argued convincingly for the significance of Pater's theories of the character of beauty.

DELAURA, DAVID J. *Hebrew and Hellene in Victorian England: Newman, Arnold, and Pater*. Austin: University of Texas Press, 1969. DeLaura takes his direction from T. S. Eliot's famous essay and presents a convincing study of the religious problems common to Arnold, Pater, and Newman.

D'HANGEST, GERMAIN. *Walter Pater: l'homme et l'oeuvre*. 2 vols. Paris: Didier, 1961. Although diffuse and written in French, this book is the only full biography of Pater in the last fifty years.

DOWNES, DAVID ANTHONY. *Victorian Portraits: Hopkins and Pater*. New York: Bookman Associates, 1965. Less a study of influences than affinities, this volume makes a strong case for Pater's religious values.

ELIOT, T. S. "Arnold and Pater." In *Selected Essays: New Edition*. New York: Harcourt Brace, 1960. Eliot attempted to show that Pater, by extending Arnold's view of culture, undermined the religious value structure of the nineteenth century.

FLETCHER, IAN. *Walter Pater*. London: Longmans, 1959. (Second edition, 1971.) In this monograph-length overview of Pater's life and works, Fletcher describes the near solipsism of Pater's isolated sensibility lost amidst the impressions of the flux.

GOSSE, EDMUND. "Walter Pater." In *Critical Kit-Kats*. London, Heinemann, 1896. Though brief, Gosse's biographical outline based on personal knowledge is one of the few primary sources readily available to the student.

HAFLEY, JAMES. "Walter Pater's 'Marius' and the Technique of Modern Fiction." *Modern Fiction Studies*, III (Summer 1957), 99 - 109. Hafley demonstrates that the Cupid-Psyche myth is organic to the narrative and to Pater's quest motif.

HARRISON, JOHN SMITH. "Pater, Heine, and the Old Gods of Greece." *Publications of the Modern Language Association*, XXXIX (September 1924), 655 - 86. Harrison describes Pater's borrowings of the gods-in-exile theme from Heinrich Heine; however, the meaning and the relevance of the mythic pattern are barely suggested.

HOUGH, GRAHAM. *The Last Romantics*. London: Duckworth, 1949. Traces ideas about the arts and their relations to religion and society from Ruskin through Pater to Yeats.

JOHNSON, LIONEL. "Notes on Walter Pater." In *Post Liminium: Essays and Critical Papers*. Ed. Thomas Whittemore. London: Elkin Matthews, 1911. Collected from several journals, these "notes" are the best evaluations of Pater's work by any of his contemporaries.

KNOEPFLMACHER, U. C. *Religious Humanism and the Victorian Novel*. Princeton: Princeton University Press, 1965. Together with Samuel Butler and George Eliot, Pater is seen as presenting in *Marius* a substitution of human values for religious revelation.

MCKENZIE, GORDON. *The Literary Character of Walter Pater*. Berkeley: University of California Press, 1967. Concerned with pattern and symbol, McKenzie brings considerable psychological acumen to his subject but handling of Pater's idealism seems weak.

MONSMAN, GERALD. *Pater's Portraits: Mythic Pattern in the Fiction of Walter Pater*. Baltimore: Johns Hopkins Press, 1967. First full length treatment of Pater's fiction; shifts the critical focus from the stereotype of Pater as permissive father-figure of the 1890s to Pater as modern mythmaker.

PICK, JOHN. "Divergent Disciples of Walter Pater." *Thought*, XXIII (March 1948), 114 - 28. Pick argues that all of Pater's younger contemporaries with the exception of Johnson failed to see that Pater's early ideas were not the same as his later ideas.

SHARP, WILLIAM. "Some Personal Reminiscences of Walter Pater." In *Papers Critical and Reminiscent*. London: Heinemann, 1912. Like Gosse's portrait of Pater, this too is a primary biographical tool; gives the reader a sense of the excitement Sharp felt in observing and conversing with Pater.

STAUB, FRIEDRICH. *Das Imaginäre Porträt Walter Paters*. Zürich: Leemann, 1926. This treatment of Pater's volume *Imaginary Portraits* discusses the portraits' dialectical structure and provides data on Pater's sources.

SYMONS, ARTHUR. "Walter Pater." In *Studies in Prose and Verse*. London: Dent, 1904. Symon's evaluation is a sympathetic portrait of Pater based on personal knowledge; makes some acute observations on Pater's style in passing.

————. "Introduction." *The Renaissance*. New York: Modern Library, n. d. A 1919 evaluation of Pater and likewise a primary source of biographical information.

WARD, ANTHONY. *Walter Pater: The Idea in Nature*. London: MacGibbon and Kee, 1966. Not written with the undergraduate reader in mind, Ward examines the epistemological grounds of Pater's thought and concludes that Pater's "involuntary responses tell you more than his conscious aestheticism."

WRIGHT, THOMAS. *The Life of Walter Pater*. 2 vols. London: Everett, 1907. Thick with gossip and trivia, fraught with misinformation; but this unsympathetic biography is, nonetheless, almost the only source of information on the early years of Pater's life.

# Index

(The works of Pater are listed under his name)

Abelard, Peter, 149
*Academy, The,* 63
Achilles, 89
Adam, 66, 117
Addis, William, 31
Adlington, William, 88
Adonis, 119
*Aelii Aristidis Opera Omnia* (Jebb), 101
Aelst, Willem van, 122
Aesculapius (*or* Asclepius), 87, 88, 91, 96, 101, 120
*Aesthetics* (Hegel), 52
Ainslie, Douglas, 181
Albertine, fictitious character of Proust, 183
Aldington, Richard, 21, 101
Alessandro, Saint, 90
*Alice's Adventures in Wonderland* (Carroll), 41, 79
Amiel, Henri-Frédéric, 97 - 98, 121
Amile, 67, 135
Amis, 67, 135
Amoretti, Carlo, 51, 62
Anne, Saint, 53, 155
*Annual Register, or A View of the History and Politics of the Year 1853, The,* 19
Antiope, 107, 108
Aphrodite, 108. *See also* Venus
Apollo, 116 - 20, 125 - 27
Apollyon, fictitious character of Pater, 116 - 19, 136
*Apologeticum* (Tertullian), 99
*Apology of Socrates, The* (Plato), 140
Apuleius, Lucius, 74, 88 - 89, 94, 100, 143, 148, 169
*Apuleius* (Adlington). *See Golden Asse of Apuleius, The*
Aquinas, Saint Thomas, 183.

*A Rebours* (Huysmans), 169
Ariadne, 114
Ariane, fictitious character of Pater, 114 - 15, 127
*Aristeides* (Jebb). *See Aelii Aristidis*
Aristotle, 21, 38
Arnold, Matthew, 22, 33, 51, 52, 54, 64, 72, 92, 126, 157, 162, 170, 182, 194n9
Arnold, Thomas, 46
Artemis, 107 - 10, 127
*Art of Versification and Song* (Celtes), 124
"Asides on the Oboe" (Stevens), 177
["As Kingfishers Catch Fire"] (Hopkins), 175
Athena (*or* Athene), 109
*Athenaeum, The,* 83, 106, 125
Aucassin, 46, 50, 53, 67
*Aucassin et Nicolette* (Fauriel), 69
Auden, Wystan Hugh, 175
Aunt Eugenia, fictitious character of Pater, 43
Aunt Fancy, fictitious character of Pater, 43
Aunt Tart, fictitious character of Pater, 43
Aurelius, Marcus. *See* Marcus Aurelius
*Aurora Leigh* (Browning), 79
*Autobiography of William Butler Yeats, The* (Yeats), 161, 162, 163, 168, 170, 194n18
"Autumn Lament" (Mallarmé), 148
"Autumn of the Body, The" (Yeats), 163

Bacchus, 53. *See also* Dionysus
Bacon, Francis, 28
Balder, 126 - 27
*Balder, an Interlude,* an imaginary work, 126

203

DATE DUE

| | | | |
|---|---|---|---|
| | | | |
| | | | |
| | | | |
| | | | |
| | | | |
| | | | |
| | | | |
| | | | |
| | | | |
| | | | |
| | | | |
| | | | |
| | | | |
| | | | |
| | | | |